We hope you enjoy this book. Please return or renew it by the due date. You can renew it at **www.norfolk.gov.uk/libraries** or by using our free library app. Otherwise you can phone **0344 800 8020** - please have your library card and PIN ready. You can sign up for email reminders too.

SmackDown

20 YEARS AND COUNTING

Written by
Jake Black, Jon Hill, and Dean Miller

CONTENTS

March 11, 2011: Rey Mysterio's acrobatic assault is too much for his much larger and heavier opponent, Drew McIntyre.

FOREWORD

On April 27, 1999, my creatures of the night witnessed Triple H and I battle Stone Cold Steve Austin and The Rock in the first main event of *SmackDown*. The match descended into chaos, but on that night an eternal flame was ignited that can't be extinguished.

For nearly two decades, I have loomed over *SmackDown* like a shadow. Digging holes and taking souls, I gave every WWE Superstar something to fear. Those who challenged my reign of darkness quickly learned to never summon the dead.

My eyes have seen it all.

These pages collect every match, every moment and every Superstar who has dared to make history on their journey to immortality.

REST IN PEACE...

Undertaker.

April 6, 2007: WWE World Heavyweight Champion Undertaker looks to continue his unprecedented winning streak against Booker T.

1999

SMACKDOWN ARRIVED on television screens in April 1999. A few months later, WWE's latest flagship show joined *RAW* to form a two-pronged attack in WWE's ongoing rivalry with WCW. Broadcast on Thursday nights, in direct competition with WCW's *Thunder,* *SmackDown* was an instant success. With a new set and its own distinct feel, *SmackDown* had all the star-power, unpredictability, and entertainment values of its Monday counterpart, *RAW.* The Attitude Era was in full swing and Superstars such as Stone Cold Steve Austin, The Rock, Mankind, and Undertaker were at the height of their powers. Moreover, the emergence of Triple H, and many crucial moments of the subsequent McMahon-Helmsley era, would also play out on *SmackDown.*

Elsewhere in WWE

March 30: The annual *SummerSlam* spectacular saw Mankind defeat Stone Cold Steve Austin and Triple H in the main event, which featured Jesse Ventura as the special guest referee. Test also defeated Shane McMahon in an entertaining Greenwich Street Fight.

A successful pilot

April 27: While the official launch of *SmackDown* would not take place until the summer, the pilot episode whetted fans' appetites. The show featured a battle of the giants in which Big Show and Test, plus X-Pac and Kane, retained their WWE World Tag Team Championships over the New Age Outlaws (Billy Gunn and Road Dogg). The main event saw Stone Cold Steve Austin and The Rock take on and defeat Triple H and Undertaker in a captivating match.

Immediate controversy

August 26: *SmackDown*'s launch episode was main-evented by Triple H defending his WWE Championship against The Rock. To make sure the match ran smoothly, WWE Commissioner Shawn Michaels was appointed the special guest referee. The Rock appeared to have Triple H beaten with the prone WWE Champion about to receive a People's Elbow; however, before The Rock could deliver his signature move, Michaels attacked The Rock and hit him with his Sweet Chin Music move, gifting Michaels' former D-Generation X ally the match.

April 27: Stone Cold Steve Austin pounds Undertaker, before claiming victory in their tag team encounter in the main event of the *SmackDown* pilot.

September 16: Stone Cold Steve Austin attacks Triple H, costing him the WWE Championship.

Rock 'n' Sock keep their titles

September 2: This show featured several notable moments, including a Tuxedo Match between ring announcers Howard Finkel and Tony Chimel (who won by stripping off Finkel's tux) and an entertaining match between X-Pac and a recent arrival to WWE, Chris Jericho, which ended in a no contest. The excellent main event saw the Rock 'n' Sock Connection—the unlikely duo of The Rock and Mankind—take on WWE Champion Triple H and Shane McMahon and retain their World Tag Team Championships.

Buried alive by an unholy alliance

September 9: The World Tag Team Championship pitted The Rock and Mankind against Undertaker and Big Show. The climax of this brutal, No Disqualification Match featured a shocking twist when Triple H intervened, attacked Mankind from behind, threw him into an empty grave, and buried him alive! The title thus went to the "unholy alliance" of Undertaker and Big Show.

September 9: Mankind tries to hold off Big Show with his sock puppet Mr. Socko.

"Triple H... as long as I am walking... I will hunt you down like the jackass that you are!"

Stone Cold Steve Austin (September 16, 1999)

Stone Cold intervenes

September 16: Rejecting Stone Cold Steve Austin's challenge for a title opportunity, Triple H picked WWE Chairman Mr. McMahon to face him for the WWE Championship. Both he and the WWE Universe were expecting an easy win, but Triple H did not take into account the Chairman's fighting spirit, to say nothing of a certain Stone Cold Steve Austin. As part of their ongoing rivalry, Austin rushed to the ring and hit Triple H with a Stone Cold Stunner, making Mr. McMahon the most unlikely of champions.

1999

September 23: Kane and Triple H grapple amid the flames during their Inferno Match, part of the Gauntlet Challenge set for "The Game" by Mr. McMahon.

Triple H beats the odds, the Outlaws triumph

September 23: Mr. McMahon was out for revenge on Triple H for threatening his family. He pitted Triple H against all of his opponents in the upcoming Six-Pack Challenge Match at *Unforgiven* on the same night. To make Triple H's task tougher, he had to take each of them on in their specialist matches. At least Triple H was spared a Casket Match, when Undertaker refused to participate. Triple H lost to Big Show in a Chokeslam Challenge, but he beat Kane in an Inferno Match (with Undertaker's interference), as well as Mankind in a Boiler Room Brawl, before facing The Rock in a Brahma Bullrope Match. Guest referee The British Bulldog attacked The Rock, helping Triple H to win.

The unlikely tag team of The Rock and Mankind looked on in shock as Road Dogg presented his new tag team partner, Billy Gunn, reuniting three-time champions the New Age Outlaws. The Rock 'n' Sock Connection were no match for the New Age Outlaws, who won this hotly contested match when Gunn hit Mankind with his Fameasser move. The New Age Outlaws were Tag Team Champions for the fourth time.

Terri's invitation, and a shock for "The Game"

September 30: Few teams have been associated with as many legendary matches as Edge and Christian and the Hardy Boyz. Their rivalry began with a Terri Runnels Invitational Tag Team Match on this *SmackDown* edition, with both teams competing for $100,000 and the chance to be managed by Terri. Although this match was won by Edge and Christian, the best-of-five tournament would culminate with the Hardy Boyz winning Terri's managerial services, following an epic match at *No Mercy* in October.

The Rock was supposed to be acting as special guest referee in Triple H's main event match against The British Bulldog. Instead The Rock battered both Superstars. Triple H finally made it back to the locker room, expecting to see his manager, Chyna. Instead, he was ambushed by Stone Cold Steve Austin, who launched a brutal attack on him as a foretaste for their upcoming championship match at *No Mercy*.

October 7: The Rock takes exception to Mankind's blundering, if well meant, interference, which nearly cost The Rock victory against Val Venis.

"Hey, hey, my, my, Rock 'n' Sock will never die!"

Mankind (October 14, 1999)

One more time for Rock 'n' Sock and Big Boss Man

October 14: It was billed as The Rock 'n' Sock Connection's last hurrah. WWE's hugely popular tag team set aside their differences to defeat the New Age Outlaws and become WWE World Tag Team Champions for the third time. They were helped when both Hardcore and Crash Holly interfered to attack Billy Gunn, allowing Mankind to make a simple pinfall. Mankind was deliriously happy with his title, but The Rock was irate that their improbable partnership looked set to continue. (A row over The Rock allegedly throwing Mankind's autobiography in the trash would soon lead to Rock 'n' Sock breaking up and losing their titles on *RAW*.)

Also in this edition, Big Boss Man claimed an impressive victory, defeating both Big Show and reigning WWE Hardcore Champion Al Snow in a Triple Threat Match. This was the fourth time the Big Boss Man had won the championship. He would hold the title until January 2000, losing to Test on *RAW*.

October 14: Big Boss Man claims the WWE Hardcore Title, after coming out on top against Big Show and Al Snow.

Big Show busts out; The Rock lucks in

October 7: Big Show was in control in his match with Big Boss Man until his opponent began using his nightstick. Big Boss Man then attempted to handcuff Big Show to the ropes in order to apply further punishment. The sheer size of Big Show's wrists meant that the handcuffs wouldn't fit, allowing Big Show, in an impressive feat of strength, to chokeslam Big Boss Man for the win.

Val Venis showed he was no pushover in the ring following an entertaining and competitive main event against The Rock. The multiple-time Intercontinental Champion took The Rock to the limit and nearly won, following a botched interference from The Rock's tag team partner Mankind, who accidentally smacked his buddy with a steel chair. The Rock gave both of them a Rock Bottom to win, and the show ended with The Rock 'n' Sock Connection arguing furiously in the center of the ring.

1999

Mankind and Al Snow's titles

November 4: In a packed show, which saw a main event featuring D-Generation X against Shane McMahon, Kane, The Rock, and Stone Cold Steve Austin, the feel-good moment came when long-time friends Mankind and Al Snow captured the World Tag Team Championships. The duo defeated The Holly Cousins to a huge ovation, but their reign would be short-lived: They lost their titles to the New Age Outlaws on *RAW* the following Monday.

Arnold Schwarzenegger makes his presence felt

November 11: The *SmackDown* crowd gave a gigantic ovation to Arnold Schwarzenegger as he was introduced by Mr. McMahon and awarded the title of "Box Office Champion of the World." This did not impress Triple H and the rest of D-Generation X, and they would cross paths in the main event, an Elimination

October 21: Stone Cold Steve Austin hits Val Venis with a Lou Thesz Press on his way to victory.

Double main event decider

October 21: This edition saw two number one contender matches to define who should face Triple H in a Triple-Threat main event at the upcoming *Survivor Series*. The Rock defeated Mankind via a disqualification following an attack from Val Venis to earn his spot. Venis was then defeated by Stone Cold Steve Austin, allowing "The Texas Rattlesnake" to seal his spot in the *Survivor Series* main event. (Stone Cold would not go on to compete in that match after being hit by a car at the pay-per-view itself).

Richards upsets Jericho

October 28: In one of the most bizarre moments of *SmackDown* in 1999, Stevie Richards, dressed as Chyna, defeated Chris Jericho with help from Chyna herself. With Jericho well in control, it appeared as if he would make short work of Richards; however, Chyna struck Jericho with her Intercontinental Championship to allow Richards to score the pinfall.

Match. This culminated with Schwarzenegger abandoning his post as guest commentator to hand match enforcer, Steve Austin, a steel chair. Austin used it to level Triple H, causing him to be pinned by Test. Triple H confronted Schwarzenegger, only to receive several meaty blows from the Terminator.

"Arnold Schwarzenegger has terminated Triple H!"

Commentator Michael Cole (November 11, 1999)

November 11: Stone Cold Steve Austin and Arnold Schwarzenegger celebrate after playing their part in embarrassing Triple H in his loss against Test.

Elsewhere in WWE

November 14: Stone Cold was ambushed by a mystery attacker (who ran him over in a car) at the *Survivor Series* pay-per-view, meaning he could not take part in the main event. This caused Austin to be out of action for nine months and became a huge story line the following year, as Austin searched for his attacker.

November 18: Mr. McMahon looks concerned after he, his stooges, and his family are targeted by Triple H.

Triple H leaves a trail of destruction
November 18: The McMahon family were rushed to a locker room, where they discovered bloody and bruised backstage officials Pat Patterson and Gerald Brisco a.k.a."The Stooges." Triple H had beaten up these members of Mr. McMahon's inner circle to send a message to the McMahons. Triple H was not finished, however; he proceeded to close the show by challenging Mr. McMahon to a match at the upcoming *Armageddon* pay-per-view.

1999

INTRODUCING...

Kurt Angle
November 18: After making his in-ring debut at *Survivor Series* 1999 a few days prior, Hall of Famer, Kurt Angle made his *SmackDown* debut with a quick victory over Gangrel. Kurt Angle would go on to have one of the greatest careers in WWE history, capturing the WWE Championship on four occasions alongside a host of other titles, as well as starring in some of the greatest moments in *SmackDown* history.

The only Olympic gold medallist in WWE history, Angle is also famed for his sharp wit.

November 25: Matt Hardy prevents the New Age Outlaws' Road Dogg from escaping the cage, with the WWE World Tag Team Titles still in the balance.

All-time greats in a cage
November 25: Two of the greatest tag teams of all time, the New Age Outlaws and The Hardy Boyz, took part in a brutal Steel Cage match for the World Tag Team Championships on this episode of *SmackDown*. Despite Jeff Hardy escaping the cage while the match official was incapacitated, an interference from X-Pac aided existing Champions the New Age Outlaws and enabled them to retain their titles. At least The Hardy Boyz could lay claim to a moral victory, winning over the WWE Universe with a series of typically spectacular moves.

Stephanie's vow
December 2: Stephanie McMahon opened the show, clearly upset following the gate-crashing of her wedding to Test by Triple H on *RAW* that week. With the extremely grudging assent of her father, Mr. McMahon, and brother Shane, Stephanie vowed to get her own back on Triple H for abducting her and tricking her into marrying him instead. Stephanie left the WWE Universe wondering how she was going to get revenge on Triple H.

December 2: Stephanie McMahon promises to fight her own battles against Triple H.

Triple H throws Shane McMahon
December 9: Triple H used the contract signing for his upcoming match at *Armageddon* with Chairman Mr. McMahon to send a powerful message. As Shane McMahon delivered the contract to Triple H at the top of the ramp of the *SmackDown* set, he was ambushed by D-Generation X. Triple H then threw Shane off the set, through a wooden table, and onto the floor below—to the horror of the crowd and Mr. McMahon, who was looking on.

December 9: The McMahon family gather in the ring prior to the contract signing for Mr. McMahon's match with Triple H at *Armageddon*.

"This is no longer the McMahon-Helmsley era. This is the McMahon era!"

Stephanie McMahon (December 23, 1999)

McMahon-Helmsley rule

December 16: This show opened with Triple H and Stephanie McMahon promising the WWE roster that everyone would be treated fairly from now on. Their words would soon ring hollow: The main event, a Lumberjack Match between The Rock and Big Show, turned out to be merely an excuse to attack both Superstars. As The Rock and Big Show were being clobbered by a posse of Lumberjacks, Triple H and Stephanie's fun was spoiled by the arrival of Mankind who, armed with a trash can and steel chairs, helped The Rock and Big Show to lay waste to the Lumberjacks.

Mankind is double-crossed

December 23: To convince doubters that she wasn't aligned with Triple H, Stephanie McMahon set up a WWE Championship Match between Big Show and Mankind and, to stop Triple H from interfering, had him suspended above the ring inside a steel cage. However, Stephanie was just fooling—she eventually freed Triple H and then hit Mankind with a low blow. Triple H, accompanied by D-Generation X, then continued the onslaught. The show ended with Triple H and Stephanie locked in a passionate embrace.

December 23: WWE Champion Big Show looks on as Triple H is put in a cage before being suspended high above the ring.

2000

THIS YEAR WAS one of the most incident-packed in *SmackDown* history. It was dominated by two major story lines. The first was the ongoing dominance of the McMahon-Helmsley era, when Stephanie McMahon and her new husband, Triple H, bossed WWE. The second was the return to action of Stone Cold Steve Austin. The year also saw multiple title changes, the debuts of Tazz, Lita, and Trish Stratus, as well as the further development of stars such as Kurt Angle, Chris Jericho, and the tag team Edge and Christian. They joined the established stable of Superstars to make the WWE roster one of the most exciting ever assembled.

February 3: Road Dogg hits Perry Saturn with a crossbody on the way to defeating The Radicalz, alongside his New Age Outlaws partner, Billy Gunn.

Cactus Jack returns

January 13: Triple H had mercilessly mocked Mankind over several weeks. On this occasion, Mankind interrupted Triple H as he was taunting a Mankind lookalike in the ring and proclaimed that he, Mankind, did not have enough to take on Triple H in their upcoming Street Fight at *Royal Rumble*. Mankind said he would have to find a substitute, and, as he walked toward the ring, he tore off his mask and shirt to reveal himself as the menacing Cactus Jack—much to the horror of "The Game" and the joy of the crowd.

Over the top

January 20: Triple H and Stephanie McMahon were up to their tricks again. To weaken some of the main challengers for January 23's *Royal Rumble*, they set up an Over the Top Rope Lumberjack Match (a first for *SmackDown*) between The Rock, Kane, and Big Show. The winner would be the one left in the ring after the other two had been thrown out over the top rope. To ensure maximum carnage when any of the three main participants was thus ejected, the Lumberjacks were made up of all the other entrants to *Royal Rumble*. Kane won the match, but he was then attacked by Big Boss Man—whereupon a mass brawl broke out among the rest of the Lumberjacks.

INTRODUCING...

Tazz
January 27: After making an impactful debut by ending Kurt Angle's winning streak at the *Royal Rumble*, Tazz would make his *SmackDown* debut by defeating the Mean Street Posse in a Handicap Match. The "Human Suplex Machine" would go on to have a successful WWE career on *SmackDown* in particular. He also served as an entertaining co-commentator on the show from 2001-2006.

Tazz celebrates his against-the-odds victory over the Mean Street Posse.

The Radicalz make an impact

February 3: Following their jump from WCW, The Radicalz—Chris Benoit, Eddie Guerrero, Perry Saturn, and Dean Malenko—debuted on *Monday Night RAW* and were desperate for a deal with WWE. Triple H gave them a shot on *SmackDown*, saying that they would earn contracts, providing they could win two of their three matches against the D-Generation X stable. Dean Malenko would take on X-Pac; Saturn and Guerrero would battle the New Age Outlaws; and Chris Benoit would tackle Triple H himself. By various nefarious means, DX went on to a clean sweep of wins. However, The Radicalz ultimately received their WWE contracts.

Kurt Angle adds another title

February 10: Hall of Famer Kurt Angle is one of the few Grand Slam winners in WWE history, having won every major championship available to him. He won his first and only WWE European Championship on this episode, after defeating Val Venis by slamming him to the canvas and hooking his leg for the pin. Angle would hold the championship until *WrestleMania*, before losing it to Chris Jericho.

> # "Not a lot of people here know where Europe actually is!"
>
> ### Kurt Angle (February 10, 2000)

X-Pac sets Kane on fire

February 24: Tori, who had been Kane's girlfriend before aligning herself with X-Pac, interrupted Kane's match with Chris Benoit and lured him up the ramp. At the top, Kane was faced by X-Pac who emerged with a flamethrower and shot a blast of fire into Kane's face. The incident shocked the WWE Universe, who were becoming disgusted by the actions of the members of D-Generation X.

March 9: Bubba Ray Dudley's chair shot stops The Rock hitting his partner D-Von with a Rock Bottom.

The Dudley Boyz turn up the heat

March 9: The deck was stacked against The Rock by Triple H and Stephanie McMahon, who arranged for him to take on The Radicalz and The Dudley Boyz on the same night. "The Great One" was able to defeat The Radicalz but then had to face the World Tag Team Champions in a Handicap Tables Match, their specialty. This proved a contest too far for The Rock, who was defeated by a chair shot and a devastating 3-D move through a table.

Mr. McMahon takes charge

March 16: Shane and Stephanie McMahon were squabbling in the ring after announcing that they would be in the corners of Big Show and Triple H respectively at *WrestleMania*. They were interrupted by their father, WWE Chairman Mr. McMahon, who compared their bickering to a bad soap opera. He announced not only that he was returning to take control of WWE, but also that he would be in the The Rock's corner at *WrestleMania*.

February 24: After an assist from Tori, X-Pac shoots a jet of flame toward Kane's face.

2000

INTRODUCING...

Lita

March 23: Lita made her in-ring debut on *SmackDown* against WWE Women's Champion Jacqueline. Although Lita narrowly lost on this occasion, she would go on to win the WWE Women's Championship four times and also took part in several spectacular matches, both as a solo performer and alongside The Hardy Boyz.

High-flying Lita was inducted into the WWE Hall of Fame in 2014.

Elsewhere in WWE

April 2: The marquee show of the year, *WrestleMania*, saw Triple H capture the WWE Championship in a Fatal Four-Way Match against The Rock, Mankind, and Big Show. In addition, Edge and Christian defeated The Dudley Boyz and The Hardy Boyz in a Ladder Match to win the World Tag Team Championships.

Stephanie McMahon—champion!

March 30: When Mr. McMahon set up Stephanie's first competitive match, he expected that the current WWE Women's Champion, Jacqueline, would teach his daughter a harsh lesson. What the Chairman did not take into account was interference by Triple H, Tori, and others of the D-Generation X faction. While they distracted the match official, Tori hit Jacqueline with a DDT, giving Stephanie an easy pinfall to claim the title. Then virtually every WWE Superstar charged into the ring for a super-brawl!

March 30: Triple H, Stephanie, and Tori jump for joy as Stephanie celebrates winning the WWE Women's Championship.

Chyna and Eddie are an item

April 6: After turning against her boyfriend Chris Jericho on Monday's *RAW*, Chyna announced that she was aligning with Eddie Guerrero because she couldn't resist his "Latino heat." The relationship between Guerrero and his *mamacita*, Chyna, would become a hugely entertaining part of WWE programming. This night did not result in a happy ending, however, with the spurned Jericho rushing the ring to attack the happy couple.

April 6: Eddie Guerrero shows his gratitude to "ninth wonder of the world" Chyna for helping him defeat Chris Jericho for the European Championship.

Tazz takes on Triple H

April 20: After making an unexpected return to ECW and defeating Mike Awesome for the ECW Heavyweight Title, Tazz triumphantly returned to *SmackDown* to take on the WWE Champion, Triple H. Their hugely competitive match ended when ECW's Tommy Dreamer interfered and accidentally hit Tazz with a steel chair meant for Triple H, who thus emerged the winner.

Austin blows up the DX Express

April 27: Having returned to WWE, Stone Cold Steve Austin wasted no time making an impact. D-Generation X and Mr. McMahon were waiting in the ring for "The Texas Rattlesnake," when they were interrupted by The Rock, who introduced Steve Austin on the big screen. In the parking lot, Austin took the controls of a giant crane and proceeded to drop a concrete slab onto the DX Express bus, causing the luxury vehicle to explode.

April 27: Triple H is distraught as the DX Express goes up in flames, thanks to Stone Cold Steve Austin.

Jericho takes his chance

May 4: Chris Jericho achieved the third of his nine WWE Intercontinental Championships by defeating Chris Benoit. A rematch of their confrontation at *Backlash* (won by Benoit), both Superstars hit each other with all they had. "Y2J" capitalized on Benoit shoving the match official and leveled the champion with his own title, before hitting him with his spectacular signature Lionsault move for the win.

Crash Holly, Hardcore Champion

May 11: The British Bulldog had just made a triumphant return to WWE at *Insurrection* in London, England, to defeat Crash Holly for the WWE Hardcore Championship. The Bulldog's reign would last a mere five days, following his defeat to Crash on *SmackDown*. The Bulldog was actually in the midst of taking on Crash's cousin, Bob "Hardcore" Holly, but, owing to the 24/7 rule (whereby the title was always on the line), Crash was able to sneak in for the win.

You snooze, you lose!

May 18: While Gerald Brisco is unquestionably one of the all-time greats of the ring, few expected the veteran Superstar to be challenging for WWE gold in the year 2000. With Crash Holly fast asleep in the offices of the Acolyte Protection Agency, however, the crafty Brisco took full advantage of the 24/7 rule, silently pinning him with one finger as he slept. Brisco thus claimed his first Hardcore Championship.

Counterattack win

June 22: Fan favorite Rikishi defeated Chris Benoit in a back-and-forth match to claim the WWE Intercontinental Championship in an unexpected victory. Despite his huge size, Rikishi also showed off his in-ring skills by countering a Benoit move, allowing him to hit a belly to belly suplex, followed by a splash from the top rope for the championship.

Trish Stratus

June 22: For her in-ring debut on *SmackDown*, Trish Stratus teamed with Test and Albert and defeated The Hardy Boyz and Lita. Trish would go on to become one of the most decorated Superstars in WWE history, winning the WWE Women's Championship on a record seven occasions. She was inducted into the WWE Hall of Fame in 2013.

Stratus has won the WWE Hardcore Championship once and the WWE Women's Championship seven times.

Kane to the rescue

June 29: Undertaker made short work of Edge in their bout; however, after the bell, Christian interfered and began to double-team Undertaker with his brother Edge. Things were looking bleak for Undertaker until his brother, Kane, came down to ringside to even up the score. Eventually "The Brothers of Destruction" laid Christian and Edge low with a synchronized chokeslam and Last Ride respectively.

Grudge match

July 6: Rikishi and Val Venis, abetted by Trish Stratus, had been on bad terms over the past weeks. Their rivalry came to a head on this episode. Rikishi looked to have the match won, until Tazz interfered, hitting Rikishi with a ringside camera. With Rikishi out cold, Venis made an easy pin to claim the Intercontinental Championship for a second time.

June 6: Val Venis hits Rikishi with his Money Shot finisher to take the WWE Intercontinental Championship.

June 22: Rikishi's all-around grappling skills prove too much for Chris Benoit.

An unfortunate misunderstanding

July 27: Triple H was attempting to show newcomer to WWE Trish Stratus the best way to counter a hammerlock when Stephanie McMahon walked in on them. To Stephanie, it clearly appeared that her husband, Triple H, and Trish Stratus were locked in something considerably more intimate than a wrestling hold. Stephanie was spectacularly upset and stormed off, leaving an apologetic Triple H trailing in her wake.

Love triangle

August 3: Commissioner Foley stoked the escalating romantic tension between Stephanie McMahon and Kurt Angle by booking them, alongside Triple H, to take on Lita and the Dudley Boyz in the main event. While Triple H brawled outside of the ring with D-Von Dudley, Bubba Ray was about to powerbomb Stephanie through a table when Kurt Angle came to her rescue. Stephanie then pinned Lita, and Triple H looked on in fury as Angle and Stephanie embraced and celebrated their victory in the center of the ring.

August 3: Stephanie McMahon seems to favor Kurt Angle over husband Triple H.

August 24: Undertaker hits X-Pac with a chokeslam on the way to victory against X-Pac and his tag team partner Road Dogg.

Undertaker beats the odds

August 24: Despite being one of the most formidable Superstars in WWE history, Undertaker still faced an almighty challenge taking on Road Dogg and X-Pac. The outnumbered "Deadman" nevertheless dominated the match and eventually pinned X-Pac after the Road Dogg abandoned his partner and headed for the safety of the backstage area.

Snow claims gold

August 31: Al Snow claimed his first and only WWE European Championship in this episode after defeating Perry Saturn, accompanied by Terri. Both men competed in a technical match with back and forth offense, before Snow countered a Rings of Saturn move with a Dragon Sleeper to claim a submission victory. Snow would hold the title for 46 days.

Stone Cold vows revenge

September 7: Forced out of action for nine months after being hit by a car driven by a mystery assailant at *Survivor Series* in 1999, Stone Cold Steve Austin was back to address the WWE Universe on *SmackDown*. Austin gave his mystery attacker an ultimatum: If he did not turn himself in during the upcoming *Unforgiven* pay-per-view, Stone Cold would interrogate the entire WWE roster himself and take matters into his own hands.

November 2: The WWE Universe celebrates with the new Women's Champion—Ivory.

Commissioner Foley investigates

September 21: The show opened with the entire WWE roster at ringside as Commissioner Foley launched an investigation to discover Stone Cold's mystery assailant. Foley accused The Rock, who denied the allegations, and Triple H, who was also strenuous in his denial. The Commissioner then accused Kurt Angle and X-Pac, who blamed Chris Jericho. Eventually, Stephanie McMahon became involved and accused Undertaker. The investigation was seemingly getting nowhere.

Stone Cold Steve Austin is suspended

October 5: After being hit with a Stone Cold Stunner on Monday's *RAW*, Mick Foley decided to use his authority to suspend Steve Austin until his attacker was found. Predictably, this decision did not meet with the approval of "The Texas Rattlesnake," who proceeded to hit Commissioner Foley with yet another Stunner. Austin was then led away by the police as a dazed Foley looked on.

October 5: Stone Cold Steve Austin hits Commissioner Foley with his second Stunner in a week, earning himself a suspension in the process.

Austin is struck again

October 26: The October 9 episode of *RAW* finally revealed Rikishi as the Superstar who ran over Stone Cold Steve Austin. Now "The Texas Rattlesnake" was out for revenge. Rikishi, who was in the ring, called out Stone Cold, who was in the backstage area. As Stone Cold went to meet Rikishi, he was struck from behind with a wrench by a mystery foe. Dazed, Austin still made it to ringside to attack Rikishi—who left Austin lying in the ring as the show closed.

Ivory becomes WWE Women's Champion

November 2: In a first for *SmackDown*, four future WWE Hall of Fame inductees—Lita, Jacqueline, Ivory, and Trish Stratus—competed in a Four Corners Match for the WWE Women's Championship. Ivory won, following an interference from Edge and Christian, who attacked the defending champion, Lita. With Lita unconscious, Ivory won her third championship.

Triple H is unrepentant

November 9: On the November 6 episode of *RAW*, Triple H was revealed as the mastermind behind Rikishi running over Stone Cold Steve Austin. The WWE Universe wanted some answers, and Triple H proceeded to explain his reasons. Instead of apologizing, he chided fans for not suspecting him before, given that he had gained so much in Stone Cold's absence—becoming WWE Champion, marrying Stephanie McMahon, and taking control of WWE.

November 9: Triple H and Rikishi taunt fans following their sneak attack on Stone Cold Steve Austin.

Elsewhere in WWE

November 19: Kurt Angle retained his championship against Undertaker at *Survivor Series*. However, the event's most memorable moment was the ending, when Stone Cold Steve Austin used a forklift truck to pick up and drop a limousine, with Triple H inside it, upside down onto the parking lot tarmac. Stone Cold thus gained his revenge for Triple H ordering him to be run over at the previous year's event.

Gunn on target

November 23: This show opened with the WWE Intercontinental Champion, Eddie Guerrero, confidently explaining how he would defeat his upcoming opponent, Billy Gunn. However, Gunn was up to the task, pinning Guerrero with a Cobra Clutch Slam in the center of the ring to win his first and only WWE Intercontinental Championship. Gunn would hold the title for 17 days, before losing it to Chris Benoit at *Armageddon*.

"Dad, I'm here to try to save your marriage!"

Stephanie McMahon (December 14, 2000)

Stephanie in pieces

December 14: Stephanie pleaded with her father, Mr. McMahon, to reconsider his threat to divorce his wife, Linda. However, Mr. McMahon was in an unforgiving mood this festive season. Instead of consoling Stephanie, Mr. McMahon proceeded to venomously insult his wife and then his daughter, telling them to "get out of my life and stay out," and promising that there would soon be a new Mrs. McMahon. The row left Stephanie distraught, and she retired to the backstage area in floods of tears.

December 14: In a scathing verbal attack, Mr. McMahon reduces his daughter Stephanie to tears.

December 21: Despite hitting Edge with his Last Ride finishing move, Undertaker and his partner, The Rock, were unable to defend their WWE World Tag Team Championships against Edge and Christian.

Edge and Christian strike gold

December 21: Edge and Christian defeated the formidable team of The Rock and Undertaker to claim the WWE World Tag Team Championships with the help of their ally, Kurt Angle. The match was set up by Mr. McMahon, and suspicions of skulduggery were aroused when Kurt Angle came to the ring dressed as a match official. Despite the deck being stacked against them, The Rock and Undertaker were in control, until Angle hit The Rock with an Angle Slam, allowing Edge to make the pinfall.

March 7, 2000: Another WWE table is trashed as The Rock takes on Bubba Ray of The Dudley Boyz.

2001

IN MARCH, WWE announced the purchase of WCW, ending the Monday night ratings war between the two companies. However, this rivalry was soon replaced by another: The WCW/ECW Alliance, with Shane McMahon helming WCW and his sister Stephanie in charge of ECW, was determined to challenge their father, WWE Chairman Mr. McMahon. The Alliance's invasion of WWE provided a compelling narrative and introduced several new stars to WWE. *SmackDown* hosted some of this invasion's most unforgettable moments and matches, as well as seeing WCW Championships won and lost for the first time on WWE programming.

A terrifying ride
January 4: In this episode of *SmackDown*, William Regal was searching for Stone Cold Steve Austin on behalf of Stephanie McMahon. Regal didn't find him until he was ambushed by "The Texas Rattlesnake" who gave him several blows, leaving Regal lying unconscious on the hood of a limousine. Austin then drove the limousine away at top speed, catapulting Regal into a pile of trash.

Epic *SmackDown* headliners
January 18: Sparks were bound to fly when The Rock, Stone Cold Steve Austin, and Undertaker faced off against Kurt Angle, Kane, and Rikishi—particularly with Triple H as special guest referee. The match did not disappoint, culminating in an epic confrontation, which eventually ended with The Rock pinning Angle after hitting him with his Rock Bottom signature move. Following the match, Stone Cold hit Triple H with an iconic Stunner, before the show ended with Austin and The Rock staring each other down.

January 18: Stone Cold Steve Austin and The Rock face off before their main event at *WrestleMania X-Seven*.

Xtreme *SmackDown*
February 1: A special edition of *SmackDown* saw the show go Xtreme for the night with a series of brutal stipulation matches. Highlights included a Tables Match between The Hardy Boyz and The Dudley Boyz, as well as a First Blood Match with Kane and Undertaker taking on Rikishi and Haku. Kurt Angle retained his WWE Championship against The Rock and Triple H, after an interference from Stone Cold Steve Austin. He forced the hand of an unconscious referee to make the three count while Angle pinned Triple H.

Champion—or not!
February 8: This episode saw the 24/7 rule for defending the WWE Hardcore Championship in full effect. Hardcore Holly had just defeated Raven for the title—despite interference from a female accomplice, the masked ninja. The ninja then attacked Hardcore's cousin, Molly Holly, outside of the ring, before Hardcore came to her aid. Using this to his advantage, Raven attacked Hardcore, and his masked accomplice then hit the champion with a 2x4 plank, allowing Raven to make the pinfall and regain the title.

No disqualification!
March 15: After Kurt Angle attacked Stone Cold Austin's wife, Debra, on *RAW*, Austin had his chance for revenge in a No Disqualification Match. The match was typically violent, with Austin relishing his opportunity to inflict pain on Angle. The finale was chaotic: The Rock (Austin's upcoming *WrestleMania* opponent) arrived in the ring and hit Angle with his Rock Bottom move, only to be hit by a Stone Cold Stunner in return. Austin then pinned the prone Angle for the victory.

Triple H provocation

March 22: In the lead-up to the Triple H vs. Undertaker match at *WrestleMania*, Triple H and Big Show attacked Undertaker's brother Kane in the middle of the ring on *SmackDown*. While under armed guard in the backstage area, Undertaker looked on horrified. He attacked his captors and ran down to the ring, still in handcuffs, to defend his brother. However, a handcuffed Undertaker was no match for Triple H and Big Show, and Undertaker was brutally dealt with, even being hit with a sledgehammer.

March 22: "The cerebral assassin" Triple H gives Kane his signature Pedigree move onto a steel chair—even though their match is officially over.

Elsewhere in WWE...

March 26: The last-ever episode of WCW *Monday Nitro* featured a simulcast with WWE's Mr. McMahon on *RAW* announcing that he had purchased WWE's main competitor, WCW. Mr. McMahon's son Shane appeared later in the episode to announce that he had in fact stolen WCW from under the nose of his father, setting up a subsequent invasion of WWE by WCW.

Hardy's brotherly helper

April 12: Despite his popularity and array of high-flying moves, few thought Jeff Hardy would defeat Triple H for his WWE Intercontinental Championship. After a back-and-forth match, it appeared as if Triple H had won, until Hardy's brother Matt ran to the ring and leveled Triple H with a chair. This allowed Jeff Hardy to unleash his signature Swanton Bomb finisher and secure his first WWE Intercontinental Championship.

April 12: Battered but not beaten, Jeff Hardy climbs onto the ropes hoping to turn the tables on Triple H

2001

April 19: Kane and Undertaker prepare to take on all comers on their way to tag team gold.

A busy night for "The Brothers of Destruction"

April 19: The opening match saw Rhyno, with Edge and Christian by his side, against Kane, who was in the ring with his brother Undertaker. Undertaker soon removed Edge and Christian, who brawled on the outside, leaving Kane to dominate Rhyno. However, Steve Austin and Triple H ran down to ringside and owing to the no-disqualification rules of a Hardcore Match, attacked Kane with steel chairs, allowing Rhyno to pin Kane and win his first Hardcore Championship.

Later, Kane and Undertaker proved that they could be described as the most unstoppable team in WWE history by defeating Edge and Christian for the World Tag Team Championships, despite interference from Triple H and Stone Cold Steve Austin, a.k.a. "The Two-Man Power Trip." This was even more impressive given the heinous attack Kane had received earlier that night from Austin and "The Game." Kane and Undertaker, "The Brothers of Destruction," didn't just win championship gold; they also won the right to face Austin and Triple H at a later date.

Long may he reign

April 26: Matt Hardy captured his first WWE European Championship in a thrilling match against the defending champion, Eddie Guerrero. The two swapped a wide variety of offense, but it was a signature Twist of Fate move in the center of the ring that sealed the championship for Hardy. He went on to hold the championship for 123 days, making him one of the longest-reigning European Champions in WWE history.

First-ever TLC Match

May 24: This episode of *SmackDown* didn't just feature the first TLC (Tables, Ladders, and Chairs) Match in the history of the show, but the first in the history of broadcast television. The WWE Tag Team Championship Four-Way Match featured The Hardy Boyz, The Dudley Boyz, Edge and Christian, and Chris Jericho and Chris Benoit, who were the current champions. This grueling yet spectacular match saw Jericho and Benoit retain their titles, with Benoit capitalizing on the carnage by climbing the ladder and grabbing the titles while his opponents were incapacitated.

May 24: Chris Jericho applies his devastating Walls of Jericho submission move to Edge on the way to retaining the WWE World Tag Team Titles alongside his partner, Chris Benoit.

The unwelcome champion

May 31: Stone Cold Steve Austin's recent cosying up to conniving WWE Chairman Mr. McMahon had lost him the love of the WWE Universe. When Austin took on Canadian Chris Benoit in front of a partisan Canadian crowd, his unpopularity was even more obvious—fueled by the fact that, prior to the match, Mr. McMahon had announced himself as the match's special enforcer. Benoit finally got his hands on Mr. McMahon, attacking him with a chair, but this gave Austin an opening, and he pinned Benoit with a roll-up to retain his championship.

INTRODUCING...

Tajiri

June 14: On his WWE debut, Tajiri defeated Crash Holly in a *King of the Ring* qualifying match under the watchful gaze of his mentor, William Regal. The Japanese Superstar would go on to win multiple titles in his WWE career, including a World Tag Team Championship and, on three occasions, the Cruiserweight Championship.

"The Japanese Buzzsaw" Tajiri strikes a pose for the WWE Universe.

Test defeats Rhyno

June 16: Test became the WWE Hardcore Champion with the help of Shane McMahon and Stacy Keibler. As the new owner of WCW, Shane McMahon had been disrupting his father's WWE programming. He influenced the show before being led away by security. A debuting Keibler distracted a smitten Rhyno, allowing Test to claim the pin.

The Dudley Boyz are back on top

June 21: The main event of *SmackDown* saw The Dudley Boyz defeat Chris Benoit and Chris Jericho to claim their fourth World Tag Team Championships. The Dudleys owed a debt of gratitude to Stone Cold Steve Austin, who attacked Benoit as he had Bubba Ray Dudley with his crossface, with the referee temporarily unconscious beside them. With Benoit incapacitated, Bubba Ray made the pin to claim the titles.

June 21: The Dudley Boyz celebrate their WWE World Tag Team Championship victory over Jericho and Benoit.

June 28: Diamond Dallas Page stands over Kane after hitting "The Big Red Monster" with a Diamond Cutter.

A message from DDP

June 28: Kane was collateral damage in front of a packed crowd at Madison Square Garden as part of the rivalry between his brother Undertaker and Diamond Dallas Page. Kane was locked in a hard-hitting match with Albert—until DDP entered the fray, hitting Kane with a classic Diamond Cutter to send a message to Undertaker. This allowed Albert to pin "The Big Red Monster" Kane and claim his first and only Intercontinental Championship.

INTRODUCING...

Torrie Wilson

June 28: Torrie Wilson made her WWE debut on *SmackDown* in a backstage segment featuring Mr. McMahon and Stone Cold Steve Austin as they looked for WCW's Booker T. The former Miss Galaxy winner would go on to forge a successful WWE career, enjoying several rivalries—most notably with Dawn Marie, which began when Marie married Torrie's father, Al Wilson, on *SmackDown*.

Torrie Wilson initially made her name on *SmackDown* as part of The Alliance invasion.

July 5: Billy Kidman hits Gregory Helms with a Springboard Bulldog move on his way to capturing the WCW Cruiserweight Championship

Momentous match, and a happy ending

July 5: This episode featured the first WCW match to be contested on *SmackDown*. With Scott Hudson and Arn Anderson on commentary and the WCW logo in the corner of the screen *SmackDown* certainly felt different. Cruiserweight Champion Gregory Helms and challenger Billy Kidman produced an entertaining match, which ended when Kidman slammed Helms into the mat to claim the title.

In addition to being two of the greatest athletes to ever set foot in the ring, Stone Cold Steve Austin and Kurt Angle showed the *SmackDown* audience that they had the ability to make them laugh, too. To cheer up Mr. McMahon, who was upset after being embarrassed on Monday's *RAW*, Austin presented him with a gift from Texas, a set of Stetsons. Austin hadn't forgotten Angle, though—he presented Angle with a tiny child's hat, making him blissfully happy.

Awesome defeat

July 12: When Jeff Hardy defeated WCW/ECW's Mike Awesome, he didn't just win the championship for himself, but for WWE in the ongoing Invasion. Hardy was assisted by an interference from former foes, Edge and Christian, who attacked Awesome with their signature Con-Chair-To finisher, allowing Hardy to claim victory.

"Tonight, we don't play fair—we play dirty!"

**The Alliance's Stephanie McMahon
(July 19, 2001)**

SmackDown's 100th episode is invaded

July 19: Leading up to *Invasion* on July 22, the conflict between WWE and the new WCW/ECW Alliance was turning very ugly. Mr. McMahon had implored Stone Cold Steve Austin to return to WWE and help WWE defeat The Alliance, and his appeals were eventually answered. Austin marched to the ring and hit both WCW Champion Booker T and ECW Champion Rhyno with a Stone Cold Stunner after they had attacked his WWE partner Kurt Angle. Then the WCW's Diamond Dallas Page appeared on the big screen and shut Austin's terrified wife, Deborah, in the trunk of his limo. Austin raced backstage to rescue her, and a mass brawl broke out there between the warring parties; meanwhile, in the ring, Angle was viciously attacked by WCW and ECW Superstars.

Stone Cold Steve Austin marks his return against The Alliance by stomping on Rhyno.

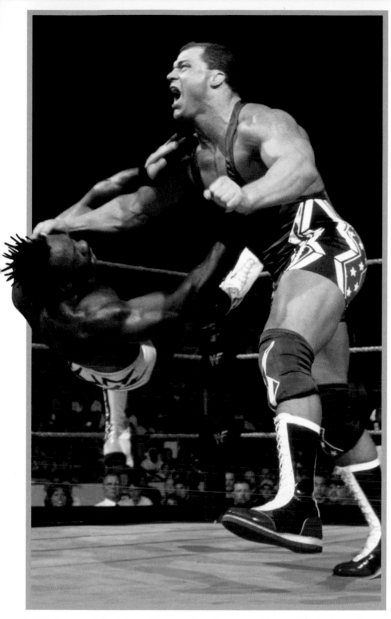

July 26: Angle attacks Booker T, providing a much-needed boost for Team WWE against Team Alliance.

Lights Out!

August 16: For the first time ever on WWE television, *SmackDown* saw a Lights Out Match between The Rock and Booker T. A Lights Out Match is designed to be a pure one-on-one confrontation, with no-disqualification and countout rules, or interference. Despite this, Shane McMahon hid under the ring and leaped out to attack The Rock with a low blow, allowing Booker T to hit The Rock with a Book End maneuver through the announce table for the win.

August 16: The Rock prepares to hit Booker T with a Rock Bottom through the announcers' table.

Kurt Angle strikes for WWE

July 26: Team Alliance had defeated Team WWE at the *Invasion* pay-per-view—thanks to the treachery of Stone Cold Steve Austin, who had turned on his WWE teammates. In this episode, Kurt Angle brought much-needed momentum back to WWE by defeating Booker T for the WCW Championship. All had looked lost for Angle when Austin ran to the ring and hit him with a Stunner. However, the Olympian recovered and wrapped Booker T in an ankle lock to claim a submission win. This was the first time the WCW Championship had changed hands on WWE programming.

Rhyno gores Jericho

August 9: Chris Jericho had just picked up a victory against Alliance member Hugh Morrus, but was ambushed by Rhyno, Morrus' fellow Alliance member, as he made his way to the backstage area. After suplexing Jericho onto the steel walkway, Rhyno gored Jericho throughout the *SmackDown* set, bringing it crashing down around him. This shocking moment showcased just how dangerous both Rhyno and The Alliance could be.

Elsewhere in WWE...

August 19: With the Invasion in full swing, *SummerSlam* featured several spectacular matches with both WWE and WCW Championships on the lineup. The main event saw The Rock defeat Booker T for the WCW Championship, while Kurt Angle retained his WWE Championship against Stone Cold Steve Austin.

Alliance clash

September 4: Despite both being members of The Alliance, there was clearly no love lost in the match between WWE Hardcore Champion Rob Van Dam and WWE Champion Stone Cold Steve Austin. In a fascinating clash of styles between the brawling "Texas Rattlesnake" and the more high-flying Van Dam, Austin appeared to have Van Dam beaten after hitting him with a Stone Cold Stunner. Austin declined to pin Van Dam and instead applied an Ankle Lock—Kurt Angle's signature move—to send a message to his nemesis, Angle. At this point, Angle's music played, distracting Austin and allowing Van Dam to win with a roll-up pinfall.

2001

September 13: During a hugely emotional episode of *SmackDown*, following the 9/11 atrocities, Mr. McMahon addresses the WWE Universe.

"America's heart
has been wounded.
But her spirit,
her spirit shines as a
beacon of freedom..."

Mr. McMahon (September 13, 2001)

The Chairman speaks out
September 13: Following the terrorist attacks of 9/11, this episode opened with WWE Chairman Mr. McMahon making a short but rousing speech to the WWE Universe. As defiant chants of "USA! USA!" rang out throughout the audience, Mr. McMahon proclaimed that this gathering, the first public assembly of its size since the attacks, sent a very simple message—that Americans would never live their lives in fear.

Meet the new Commissioner
October 11: This episode promised the announcement of a new WWE Commissioner, and it was a mystery as to who it would be. The Alliance members were squabbling in the ring when Mike Foley's music played. Following a huge ovation, the WWE Legend announced that he was the new Commissioner, and he immediately set up a match with Alliance member William Regal and WWE Superstar Kurt Angle.

Alliance Battle Royal
October 25: Members of The Alliance competed in an Over the Top Rope Battle Royal, with the winner getting a shot at Chris Jericho's WCW Championship that same night. With Booker T, Test, and Rob Van Dam as the final three superstars in the ring, Test eliminated Van Dam with a big boot to the face, which allowed Booker T to tip Test over the top rope to claim the victory. Booker T would go on to face Jericho but was ultimately unsuccessful in his quest for the gold.

Jericho is off target
November 1: In an unexpected victory for The Alliance, Booker T and Test defeated Chris Jericho and The Rock to claim the World Tag Team Championships. Jericho and The Rock appeared to be in control; however, Test ducked Jericho's dropkick from the top rope. Jericho instead connected with The Rock, and Test capitalized, following up with a kick of his own and pinning the dazed Rock to claim the victory.

November 1: The impact of an explosive Booker T chop on The Rock reverberates around the arena.

The Rock gets a People's Elbow

November 29: The Rock was in the ring with Mr. McMahon after leaping to the defense of Trish Stratus, whom Mr. McMahon seemed determined to humiliate. The Rock turned the tables on the Chairman and got him to drop his pants, before delivering his signature Rock Bottom and People's Elbow maneuvers. But then Jericho hit the ring. The Rock was hit with a low blow by Mr. McMahon, which enabled Jericho to use The Rock's own People's Elbow move on "The Brahma Bull" himself.

The "Kiss My Ass" club

December 6: Mr. McMahon was given a taste of his own medicine when The Rock forced him to join the "Kiss My Ass" club. The club had originally been set up by Mr. McMahon, who ordered its members to show their respect by kissing his ass! At first, The Rock said Mr. McMahon should kiss *his* ass, and then, to McMahon's horror, he introduced Jim Ross, whom the Chairman had recently embarrassed on *RAW*. McMahon appeared more enamored by the prospect of the next person The Rock introduced, Trish Stratus. However, The Rock's final reveal was Rikishi, and The Rock ensured that the aghast WWE Chairman joined Rikishi's Stink Face club.

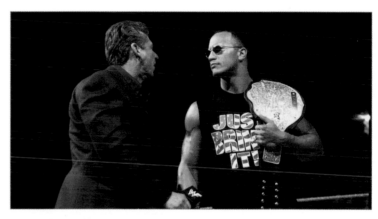

December 6: The Rock has an unpleasant surprise in store for Mr. McMahon...

In-store brawl

December 13: In one of *SmackDown*'s most famous segments, Stone Cold Steve Austin ambushed Booker T in a grocery store. Austin pelted Booker with nuts, potatoes, and coffee as Booker pleaded with "The Texas Rattlesnake" to stop. As police sirens wailed a warning, Austin made his escape, leaving Booker T in a crumpled heap on the floor.

December 13: Stone Cold Steve Austin attacks his rival Booker T in a supermarket in Bakersfield, California, causing thousands of dollars-worth of damage in the process.

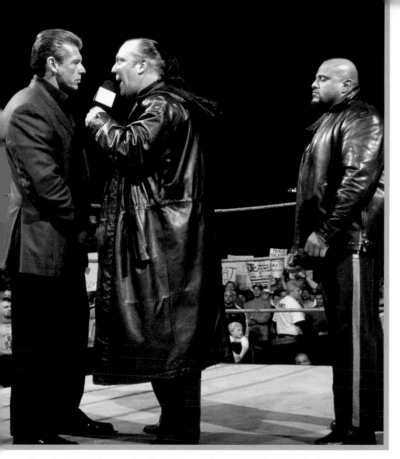

November 15: Paul Heyman gives Mr. McMahon a piece of his mind, while Tazz looks on.

"I hate your stinking guts... You stole my life, my money, my legacy."

Paul Heyman (November 15, 2001)

Strong words

November 15: In the lead-up to *Survivor Series*, former ECW owner and Alliance member Paul Heyman decided to call out WWE Chairman, Mr. McMahon. Heyman proclaimed that WWE would die at *Survivor Series*. Mr. McMahon confronted Heyman in the ring, but Heyman was not cowed, replying with a barrage of insults and accusations. However, Heyman went too far when he aimed a jibe at his former ECW employee—and now-WWE commentator—Tazz. This was a mistake, as Heyman was quickly silenced by a devastating Tazzmission hold.

Elsewhere in WWE...

November 18: *Survivor Series* saw the culmination of the WCW/ECW Alliance Invasion, when Team Alliance, featuring Booker T, Kurt Angle, Rob Van Dam, and Stone Cold Steve Austin, was defeated by Team WWE, which included Chris Jericho, Kane, Undertaker, Big Show, and The Rock.

2002

THIS WAS A huge transition year for *SmackDown*. It began with the introduction of the nWo (New World Order) and the buildup to one of the greatest *WrestleMania* events of all time, *X8*. Then, in March, WWE split into two separate brands, *RAW* and *SmackDown*. At this point, *SmackDown* began to really grow its own distinct identity, becoming the home of excellent in-ring action and young, hungry WWE Superstars. Both John Cena and Randy Orton made their debuts, and *SmackDown* also showcased emerging young Superstars, including Edge and Brock Lesnar, alongside established Superstars, such as Kurt Angle and Eddie Guerrero.

"This is not a joke. I am not a joke. I am serious. And you will not look past me..."

Chris Jericho (January 17, 2002)

War of words
January 17: Chris Jericho had beaten both The Rock and Stone Cold Steve Austin in the same night to claim WWE's first Undisputed Championship at *Vengeance* in 2001. However, Jericho felt that he was not being respected as a champion. Prior to their match at the *Royal Rumble*, Jericho ranted and raved at The Rock, demanding to be taken seriously. The Rock ranted back, telling Jericho that he was deadly serious that *he* would win. Despite this, Jericho went on to retain the WWE Undisputed Championship.

Mr. McMahon's nWo threat
January 24: Mr. McMahon had become frustrated by WWE co-owner Ric Flair, convinced that Flair was slowly "killing" the company. In a dramatic promo, Mr. McMahon claimed that the WWE was "his creation," and *he* would be the one who injected "the fatal dose of poison." As Mr. McMahon turned in his chair, this "poison" was revealed to be the infamous nWo, consisting of former WCW stars Scott Hall, Kevin Nash, and Hulk Hogan.

Diamond Dallas Page victory
January 31: DDP had won multiple championships during his WCW tenure, and on *SmackDown*, he won his first and only WWE singles championship. After a competitive match against Christian, DDP eventually hit the reigning champion with a Diamond Cutter to claim the WWE European Championship. The victory proved popular, with Page celebrating as he walked through the jubilant crowd, triumphantly holding the title aloft.

February 7: Undertaker locks Maven in a submission maneuver— just before The Rock's intervention.

An improbable win
February 7: Undertaker was dominating Maven in their match on *SmackDown*—until a decisive assist from The Rock. He ran down to the ring and hit Undertaker with a steel chair and then his Rock Bottom move. This allowed Maven to pin Undertaker, claiming an unlikely victory and the WWE Hardcore Title!

A big celebration and a revenge attack

February 21: Triple H's worst nightmare came true when his rival, WWE Undisputed Champion Chris Jericho, formed an alliance with his estranged wife, Stephanie McMahon. Triple H was so furious that he attacked them both. (Stephanie and Jericho's business partnership would carry forward to the main event at *WrestleMania X8*, when Triple H spectacularly overcame Jericho and Stephanie to win the title.)

Also in this edition, Billy and Chuck defeated the team of Tazz and Spike Dudley to claim their first WWE Tag Team Championships, and nWo were forced to read out a WWE lawyer-approved statement apologizing for recently attacking The Rock on *RAW*. They were interrupted by Stone Cold Steve Austin, who attacked them with a tire iron. Austin isolated his upcoming *WrestleMania* opponent, nWo's Scott Hall, tying him up and verbally abusing him before driving him back to the ring to give him an embarrassing beatdown as the episode ended.

February 21: Stone Cold Steve Austin attacks nWo's Scott Hall with cans of beer.

Goldust grabs his chance

February 28: Goldust took full advantage of the 24/7 defense of the Hardcore Championship rule when he defeated Maven. The youngster had just received a beatdown from Undertaker and was recovering backstage on a stretcher, when Goldust appeared, apparently concerned for his well-being. However, this was just a ruse—Goldust attacked Maven, knocking him off the stretcher and pinning him to be crowned WWE Hardcore Champion for the first time.

Hogan aligns with The Rock

March 21: Following The Rock and Hulk Hogan's Icon Vs. Icon Match at *WrestleMania X8* (which The Rock won), the Hulkster was once again a favorite of the WWE Universe. He cemented this on *SmackDown* when he ran to ringside to save The Rock, who had been attacked by Scott Hall and Kevin Nash. Hogan had the upper hand until X-Pac, in nWo colors, ran to the ring and hit Hogan with a steel chair. To add insult to injury, the new-look nWo spray-painted their logo on Hogan's back.

Also on this episode, Diamond Dallas Page (DDP) fell victim to an interference from Christian, whose attack with a set of brass knuckles gifted the European Championship to William Regal. This would be the third of four WWE European Championship reigns for Regal, putting him level with D-Lo Brown, who had also won four in 1998–1999.

March 21: DDP and William Regal battle for the WWE European Championship.

Kane makes an impression—or two

March 28: Kane may be one of the most destructive Superstars in WWE history, but he isn't usually famed for his impressions. On this occasion, however, "The Big Red Monster" had the WWE Universe in hysterics with note-perfect impersonations of both his teammate, The Rock, and Hulk Hogan, prior to their match against the nWo. Kane would then go on to claim victory for the team after hitting the nWo's X-Pac with a devastating chokeslam.

2002

April 4: The Rock locks in the Sharpshooter on Chris Jericho.

A new era and a big mistake

April 4: This episode marked the start of a new era, as *SmackDown* began to assert its own brand identity. The Rock made an immediate impact after being drafted as Mr. McMahon's number-one pick, interrupting both Chris Jericho and Kurt Angle at the opening of the show. The main event—Jericho vs. The Rock—was a fierce, chaotic battle with pride at stake. Angle interfered on behalf of Jericho, before Edge evened up the score, helping The Rock to get the win.

Previously, a mistake by Torrie Wilson, who had accompanied Tajiri to the ring, cost "The Japanese Buzzsaw" the WWE Cruiserweight Championship. Torrie had moved the title during the match, causing Tajiri to be distracted as he looked for it. Billy Kidman capitalized with a roll-up pin to become a six-time WWE Cruiserweight Champion. After the match, Tajiri berated Torrie in Japanese, leaving her distraught in the middle of the ring.

You're hired!

April 11: *SmackDown* owner Mr. McMahon conducted interviews for a new personal assistant in this episode. After he had dismissed several less-than-suitable candidates, the WWE Universe went wild as the Stacy Keibler's theme music rang out. The Chairman literally fell off his chair when Keibler started dancing on his desk. Mr. McMahon had found his new assistant!

April 18: Hogan gets the better of Angle, before suffering at the hands of his own partner, Triple H.

Triple H attacks Hulk Hogan

April 18: Tensions were simmering between Triple H and Hulk Hogan despite being tag team partners in the main event against Kurt Angle and Chris Jericho. With Triple H and Hogan due to meet for the Undisputed Championship at the upcoming *Backlash* pay-per-view, there had been a confrontation at that week's *RAW*. Things got worse on *SmackDown* when Hogan accidentally hit Triple H with a chair while aiming for Angle. Triple H retaliated later on, leveling the Hulkster with a chair as the show closed.

INTRODUCING...

Randy Orton

April 25: Randy Orton made his WWE debut on *SmackDown* with an upset victory against the veteran Bob Holly. Orton would go on to be one of the most decorated Superstars in WWE history. He became a multiple-time WWE Champion and achieved a host of other accomplishments, including the WWE Intercontinental Championship and two *Royal Rumble* victories in 2009 and 2017.

Randy Orton opens his illustrious *SmackDown* career.

Batista makes his WWE debut

May 9: He would go on to become one of the greatest Superstars in WWE history, but Batista made his WWE debut billed as Deacon Batista in a Tag Team Match alongside the Reverend D-Von (formerly of The Dudley Boyz). Batista still cut an intimidating figure, making his presence felt by distracting the referee during the course of the match. This distraction enabled Jericho to hit D-Von's opponent, Triple H, with the collection box, allowing the Reverend to collect the win.

May 9: Debuting Deacon Batista impresses fans with his formidable physical presence when accompanying the Reverend D-Von to the ring.

Two-time Cruiserweight Champ

May 16: The Hurricane became a two-time WWE Cruiserweight Champion by scoring an impressive victory in a Triple Threat Match against Tajiri and Billy Kidman. With Kidman recuperating outside the ring, Tajiri aimed a spinning kick, which The Hurricane managed to duck, allowing him to hit a chokeslam for the victory. The Hurricane would go on to hold the title for 38 days, before losing to Jamie Noble at *King of the Ring*.

Kurt Angle fools no one

May 23: After Kurt Angle had lost a humiliating Hair vs. Hair Match with Edge at *Judgment Day*, the WWE Universe was intrigued to see what Angle would look like on this *SmackDown* episode. After some delay, Angle eventually came to ringside. However, far from being bald, Angle appeared to have a full head of hair beneath his headguard. But the wig fooled nobody—it was nearly ripped off by Maven and Edge, before Christian ran to Angle's aid and safely escorted him backstage.

Triple H earns a title shot

June 6: This episode began with a 20-man Battle Royal, with the winner earning the right to face Undertaker, the WWE Undisputed Champion, at the upcoming *King of the Ring*. After defeating 18 other WWE Superstars, just Hulk Hogan and Triple H remained in the ring. After a brief brawl, the contest was undecided because both Superstars fell from the ring at exactly the same time. Mr. McMahon decided that, as they were both losers, the winner would be decided in the night's main event. Following a highly competitive match, Triple H eventually hit Hogan with his devastating Pedigree move to become the number one contender for Undertaker's championship.

Hair today, gone tomorrow

June 13: Hulk Hogan and Triple H took on the team of Kurt Angle and Undertaker in one of the most star-studded main events in *SmackDown* history. The match itself ended with Triple H being disqualified for attacking Undertaker with a sledgehammer, but there were plenty of incidents after the bell. Hogan and Triple H both attacked Angle, with Triple H pulling Angle's singlet down to reveal his underwear. This distraction allowed Hogan to complete Angle's humiliation by tearing off Angle's wig and putting it on himself, before executing a leg drop on Angle and posing with Triple H, as the show drew to a close.

May 23: Edge whips a bewigged Kurt Angle against the ropes before trying to expose the newly shorn Olympian.

June 13: Kurt Angle tries to conceal his bald head after Hulk Hogan removes his wig.

July 4: Edge and Hulk Hogan prove youth and experience is a winning combination.

Edge tag teams with his hero

July 4: Edge got to achieve a boyhood dream by teaming with Hulk Hogan in their match for the WWE Tag Team Championships. All-American Hogan received an incredible ovation on this episode. Despite a valiant effort from the current champions, Billy and Chuck, they were no match for Hulk Hogan and Edge. The new team hit a combined Big Boot on Chuck, before individually hitting him with a Big Leg Drop. Edge followed up to make the pin and capture the championships.

Meet the new *SmackDown* GM

July 18: After announcing Eric Bischoff as General Manager of *RAW*, Mr. McMahon used this episode to announce the new General Manager of *SmackDown*. Despite initial skepticism, Stephanie McMahon won over the *SmackDown* roster and crowd with a rousing speech. She then further endeared herself to fans by throwing Eric Bischoff, who had been trying to lure The Rock to *RAW*, out of the building.

July 18: Stephanie McMahon shakes her father's hand as she is announced as the new *SmackDown* GM.

INTRODUCING...

John Cena

June 27: John Cena made an impactful WWE debut on *SmackDown* when he took on Hall of Famer Kurt Angle by answering an open invitation from the Olympian. Young Cena may have lost, but he fought hard—much to the admiration of the locker room and wider WWE Universe. Cena would go on to be one of the greatest WWE Superstars of all time, becoming a multiple-time WWE Champion and competing in many legendary *WrestleMania* main events.

More than 16 years after his debut, John Cena is still enthralling WWE fans to this day.

Lesnar defeats a legend

August 8: The main event was a battle between the generations as Hulk Hogan took on the emerging Brock Lesnar. Lesnar had put his WWE Undisputed Championship opportunity at *SummerSlam* up for grabs; however, this wouldn't prove a risk, since Lesnar dominated Hogan in a manner few had seen before. He defeated Hogan with a bear hug and sent a message to the WWE Universe by attacking Hogan with a chair and leaving him in a heap.

"Before the night is through, The Rock and Brock will collide!"

The Rock (August 22, 2002)

Brock meets The Rock

August 22: Manager Paul Heyman boastfully introduced "the next big thing," Brock Lesnar, to the WWE Universe, and they proceeded to belittle The Rock, Lesnar's upcoming opponent at *SummerSlam*. The Rock appeared on the ramp to have his say—and was jumped by Chris Benoit and Eddie Guerrero, while Lesnar snickered. The Rock later recovered to claim a tag team victory, alongside Edge, against Guerrero and Benoit.

INTRODUCING...

Rey Mysterio

July 25: Wearing his trademark *luchador* mask, Rey Mysterio made his WWE debut on *SmackDown* with a fine victory over Chavo Guerrero. He ended the match with a typically acrobatic springboard Hurricanrana. Mysterio would go on to amass a huge array of accomplishments in WWE, including winning the World Heavyweight Championship on two occasions.

Only 5 ft 6 in (1.68 m) tall and 175 lbs (79 kg), Rey's speed and skill brought him wins over much larger opponents.

A Cage Match to remember

July 25: Stephanie McMahon's first main event match as *SmackDown* General Manager was to pit two of *SmackDown*'s brightest young stars, Chris Jericho and Edge, against each other in a Cage Match. It turned out to be one of the greatest matches in the blue brand's history. The two rivals' monumental contest ended when Edge escaped the cage and jumped to the floor, just ahead of Jericho, who was crawling through the cage's open door. Edge had little chance to celebrate. After the bell, he was attacked by Test, Christian, Lance Storm, and a recovered Jericho, before John Cena and Rey Mysterio ran down to even up the odds.

Elsewhere in WWE

August 25: In one of the best *SummerSlam* events of all time, Brock Lesnar defeated The Rock to become the WWE Undisputed Champion. The show also saw the return to action of the great WWE Superstar Shawn Michaels after a four-year absence, who defeated Triple H in an unsanctioned Street Fight.

A No. 1 Contenders Tournament

August 29: Following his famous victory at *SummerSlam*, the Undisputed Champion Brock Lesnar became exclusive to *SmackDown*. The blue brand's General Manager, Stephanie McMahon, wasted no time capitalizing on this development. She kicked off this episode by setting up a No. 1 Contenders' Tournament for the championship—much to the excitement of the WWE Universe. That tournament's bruising battle was eventually won by Undertaker, who defeated both Chris Benoit and Kurt Angle, before riding off on his Harley-Davidson chopper.

August 29: Undertaker celebrates becoming the number one contender for the championship.

July 25: Using the steel cage as a weapon to hurt and wear down his opponent, Edge suddenly gets the better of Chris Jericho.

Battle of the newbies

September 5: Both Brock Lesnar and Randy Orton were new to WWE, but they were at very different stages in their careers. This may have only been Lesnar's rookie year, but he was already the Undisputed Heavyweight Champion and the clear favorite to win. Despite this billing, Orton ran Lesnar close in an entertaining match, which the champion eventually won with his F-5 finisher.

A wedding hitch and a rematch

September 12: The wedding of Billy and Chuck was far from joyous. After a touching promo, it transpired that the two weren't gay and that the whole thing had been orchestrated by their manager, Rico, as a publicity stunt. The elderly Justice of the Peace then ripped off his prosthetic mask, revealing himself to be *RAW* GM, Eric Bischoff. As he restrained a shocked Stephanie McMahon, Rico turned on Billy, allowing Bischoff's *RAW* henchmen, Three Minute Warning, to pulverize Chuck and then slam Stephanie.

On the same episode, Kurt Angle and Rey Mysterio topped their entertaining match at *SummerSlam* with an all-time classic rematch. In a wonderful clash of styles between Angle and the high-flying Mysterio, this captivating back-and-forth encounter eventually finished with Angle making a devastating Angle Slam from the top rope, getting the pin, and gaining the win.

September 26: Eddie Guerrero grapples with Edge during their No Disqualification Match.

September 12: Billy and Chuck are all smiles before their wedding ceremony goes drastically wrong.

Match with no rules

September 26: This brutal contest saw the conclusion of a long rivalry between Edge and Eddie Guerrero. The pair had just faced each other at the *Unforgiven* pay-per-view, where they had pulled out all the stops. The WWE Universe watched in awe as the two rivals used steel chairs and other weaponry and hit moves that would have finished off lesser opponents. This epic match eventually concluded when Edge hit Guerrero with his Edgecution finisher from the top of a ladder to seal the victory.

2002

Undertaker rules

October 17: After defeating Chuck Palumbo with an F-5, Brock Lesnar was immediately ambushed by Undertaker. Undertaker, who was wearing a cast on his arm, used it as a weapon, brutally attacking Lesnar and any WWE official who tried to pull them apart. Eventually, a dazed Lesnar was escorted from the ring by his manager, Paul Heyman, as Undertaker ruled the ring.

A blue brand classic

October 24: With such an array of talent on show, Edge and Mysterio vs. Los Guerreros was likely to be a good match. However, this fast-paced, high-flying encounter far exceeded expectations, proving a superb showcase both for themselves and the *SmackDown* brand. Mysterio and Edge won when Mysterio hit Chavo with a top-rope leg drop while the referee's back was turned, allowing Edge to make the pin.

Cena steals the show

October 31: This Halloween special saw the Superstars enjoying a backstage costume party. Cena, who was still finding his feet during his rookie year, was dressed as Vanilla Ice and used the episode as an opportunity to showcase his freestyle rapping abilities. His rap was so successful that it sowed the seed for his latter "Doctor of Thuganomics" persona, an important stepping stone in his phenomenal WWE career.

October 17: WWE officials recoil as Undertaker uses the cast on his broken hand as a weapon.

A Two Out of Three classic

November 7: Edge and Rey Mysterio were able to triumph over the WWE Tag Team Champions, Chris Benoit and Kurt Angle, in this memorable Two Out of Three Falls Match. Edge and Mysterio won the first fall, but Angle and Benoit then evened the score. The match was eventually won when Benoit accidentally hit Angle with a diving headbutt, which allowed Mysterio to clear out Benoit and Edge to claim the pinfall on Angle.

November 7: Rey Mysterio gives Kurt Angle a dropkick during their Two Out of Three Falls Match.

October 31: John Cena channels his inner Vanilla Ice for the WWE Universe.

Thanksgiving brawl

November 28: Brock Lesnar, who had attacked Big Show the previous week against the express wishes of Stephanie McMahon, was suspended at the start of this Thanksgiving Special. His suspension did not prevent him from making an unexpected return later that night to once again brutalize Big Show and showcase his awesome strength by hitting the 500-lb goliath with an F-5 through the announce table. Lesnar's real fury was directed at Paul Heyman, who had betrayed him when aligning with Big Show at *Survivor Series*. The episode closed with Lesnar chasing Heyman into the backstage area, before Stephanie McMahon and a group of police officers put a stop to his pursuit.

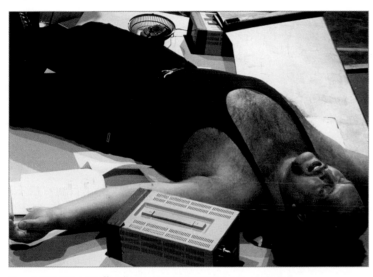

November 28: A dazed Big Show lies amid the wreckage of the announce table.

"I'm first class. And right now, I'm all business."

Stephanie McMahon (December 12, 2002)

Scott Steiner snubs *SmackDown*

December 12: Stephanie McMahon had been attempting to persuade Scott Steiner—"the hottest free agent in sports entertainment"—to sign a *SmackDown* contract for weeks, literally rolling out the red carpet for him. Steiner proclaimed that he couldn't trust Stephanie because she had spurned his romantic advances, and he declared his loyalty to *RAW* instead. The sight of *RAW* General Manager, Eric Bischoff, gleefully greeting Steiner as he walked away rubbed salt into Stephanie's wounds.

December 12: Stephanie McMahon tries to persuade Scott Steiner to sign with *SmackDown*.

Elsewhere in WWE

December 15: At *Armageddon*, Kurt Angle defeated Big Show to be crowned WWE Champion. Triple H faced Shawn Michaels in the main event, a Three Stages of Hell Match, to be crowned World Heavyweight Champion.

Heyman and Angle's goal

December 19: Recently crowned WWE Champion Kurt Angle used this episode of *SmackDown* to announce Paul Heyman as the new head of his management team. Hugely successful, as well as being selfish and manipulative, the manager came down to the ring to a chorus of boos from the crowd. He embraced Angle, before telling the WWE Universe that the two men had hatched the plan a week before *Armageddon* and had been conspiring together to win the WWE Championship.

2003

THIS WAS AN intriguing year for *SmackDown*, with a mix of established Superstars, such as Hulk Hogan, Roddy Piper, and Undertaker, mixing with emerging athletes, like Rey Mysterio, John Cena, and Brock Lesnar. *SmackDown* continued to grow as a brand, further establishing itself as the home of fast-paced and technical in-ring action—as exemplified by September's Iron Man Match between Kurt Angle and Brock Lesnar. *SmackDown* also saw a change in General Manager. Stephanie McMahon was ousted by her own father, who in turn was replaced by Paul Heyman toward the end of the year.

February 6: Underdogs Shelton Benjamin and Charlie Haas look focused prior to their match against Los Guerreros.

A May and December wedding

January 2: WWE fans held up placards saying "Al is a fool" as *SmackDown* hosted the controversial wedding of Al Wilson, father of Superstar Torrie, and Dawn Marie. This was no heartwarming affair. First, there was the considerable age difference between Wilson and his Superstar bride. Second, during the service, Dawn Marie claimed she wanted to recite her wedding vows without her wedding dress on. In the end, both she and Al decided to strip down to their underwear. The wedding fueled the rivalry between Torrie and Dawn Marie, which intensified further when Al Wilson passed away, owing to overexerting himself on honeymoon.

Hogan and McMahon trade insults

January 23: The legendary Hulk Hogan made his return to *SmackDown* to a sustained standing ovation from the WWE Universe. A clearly emotional Hulkster announced that he had signed a new WWE contract, to more applause. The mood darkened when WWE Chairman Mr. McMahon interrupted Hogan and proceeded to insult him. Both men squared up to each other and engaged in a war of words, which ended when Hogan hit McMahon with a right hand, before standing over him and ripping open his vest in signature style.

The wrong man

February 6: The team of Charlie Haas and Shelton Benjamin defeated the formidable Los Guerreros to claim their first WWE Tag Team Championships on *SmackDown*. Despite being aligned with Kurt Angle and having Paul Heyman in their corner, the Guerreros were considered favorites, particularly after Eddie executed a trademark Frog Splash on Benjamin. However, Benjamin wasn't the legal man tagged into the match, so the referee stopped the count. While Guerrero was distracted, Haas rolled him for the pin.

Two seconds short of a win

February 27: Kurt Angle had issued a challenge to any aspiring WWE Superstar: Anyone who could last five minutes in the ring with him would get a WWE contract. A fresh-faced young man by the name of Brian Kendrick answered the challenge—and amazed and impressed the WWE Universe by almost taking Angle the distance. He missed out by a mere two seconds after receiving an Angle Slam. Kendrick would go on to have a successful WWE career, winning the WWE Cruiserweight Championship.

February 27: Kurt Angle hits Brian Kendrick with a clothesline.

Angle's double trick

March 13: Brock Lesnar seemed determined to make short work of Kurt Angle in their match for the WWE Championship. Lesnar didn't even give Angle a chance to take off his top before hitting him with a trademark F-5. However, before Lesnar could seal an easy win, he was spooked and then distracted by Haas and Benjamin outside the ring. Meanwhile, an identical figure swapped places with the prone body on the mat, and, as Lesnar went to pin Angle, he was rolled up and pinned himself! Angle had retained his championship and celebrated wildly. Lesnar had previously been attacking Kurt's near-identical brother, Eric, before the two made the switch.

"There's no way in hell I'm gonna let Hulkamania die, brothers!"

Hulk Hogan (March 20, 2003)

Mr. McMahon, the "evil genius," attacks

March 20: In a segment hosted by legendary announcer "Mean" Gene Okerlund, Mr. McMahon and Hulk Hogan met in the ring to sign the contract for their upcoming match at *WrestleMania*. Hogan arrived in the ring first to another huge ovation and defiantly declared that he would never compete again if Mr.McMahon defeated him. He then stood looking at the Titantron screen, awaiting Mr. McMahon's entrance. However, while Hogan was staring at images of Mr. McMahon, the real thing snuck up behind him and smacked him repeatedly with a steel chair. McMahon then manhandled the barely conscious Hulkster, forcing him to sign the contract in his own blood.

Elsewhere in WWE

March 30: *WrestleMania XIX* will be remembered as one of the best of all time, thanks to a series of excellent matches. Hulk Hogan defeated Mr. McMahon in a match 20 years in the making; Stone Cold Steve Austin took part in his last-ever match; and, in the main event, Brock Lesnar defeated Kurt Angle to claim the WWE Championship.

Piper's Pit makes a WWE return

April 10: "Rowdy" Roddy Piper, hosted a Piper's Pit segment with Mr. McMahon as his guest. The two traded insults at first and there was clearly tension brewing, until they agreed that they both hated Hulk Hogan. Piper had the final stinging word, however. As Mr. McMahon was leaving the ring, Piper sarcastically congratulated him on something that he, Piper, had never "achieved" himself—losing to Hulk Hogan in the ring!

April 10: Roddy Piper and Mr. McMahon insult each other during Piper's Pit.

2003

John Cena is number one
April 17: The culmination of a No. 1 Contenders' Tournament for Brock Lesnar's WWE Championship saw Chris Benoit take on John Cena. The more experienced Benoit was a heavy favorite going into the match. However, it was Cena who claimed the victory, after countering Benoit's offense for a sudden pinfall.

Show of strength
April 24: Guest commentator John Cena used the opportunity to attack Brock Lesnar in his match against A-Train. Lesnar appeared to have the match won after hitting A-Train with his signature F-5, until Cena jumped into the ring and leveled Lesnar with a right fist wrapped in a chain. Cena then hit Lesnar with an Attitude Adjustment to show his dominance over the champion.

May 1: Mr. America, a.k.a. Hulk Hogan, owns the ring as the fans cheer.

Mr. America bests Mr. McMahon
May 1: Fans were left in little doubt as to the real identity of Mr. America, for the masked Superstar strutting to the ring for a Piper's Pit segment bore a striking resemblance to Piper's old rival Hulk Hogan. The resemblance prompted Piper's rage and also provoked Mr. McMahon to come to the ring. McMahon used his position as WWE Chairman to fire Mr. America. However, the masked Superstar proclaimed he couldn't be fired as he hadn't signed with Mr. McMahon and had an iron-clad contract with his daughter, Stephanie. McMahon, along with Piper and his sidekick, Sean O'Haire, attempted to mount an attack, but Mr. America fought them off, much to the crowd's joy.

April 24: John Cena disrespects Brock Lesnar by seizing Lesnar's title.

INTRODUCING...

Zach Gowan
May 15: Zach Gowan made his WWE debut as a fan, leaping to the defense of Mr. America during Piper's Pit. As he was attacked by Piper, his prosthetic leg was accidentally pulled off, much to the shock of the crowd. Gowan would go on to sign a full-time WWE contract and enjoy a successful career, notably clashing with the Chairman himself, Mr. McMahon.

Gowan would be the first competitor in WWE history to compete with a prosthetic leg.

Playing possum

May 29: Team Angle—Charlie Haas and Shelton Benjamin—had been pursuing the Tag Team Champions, Eddie Guerrero and Tajiri for some time. They reckoned without Guerrero's cunning. With the referee distracted, Guerrero, who had been struggling for the actual title with Haas, suddenly threw himself down on the mat. When the referee turned around, he saw Haas holding the title and Guerrero apparently lying injured. Assuming foul play, the referee disqualified Guerrero and Tajiri, enabling them to retain their titles.

Flying high with Rey

June 5: In front of a partisan hometown crowd that included his family at ringside, Rey Mysterio defeated Matt Hardy to capture the WWE Cruiserweight Championship. This main event showcased some phenomenal offense by both men, with Hardy's hard-hitting style contrasting with Mysterio's high-flying moves. Hardy seemed to have the match won after hitting Mysterio with a top rope leg drop; however, Mysterio somehow managed to kick out. Frustrated, Hardy then went for a Twist of Fate move, which Mysterio countered for a pin to capture the championship.

"A superplex just imploded the ring!"

Commentator Michael Cole (June 12, 2003)

An unforgettable impact

June 12: In one of the most famous moments in *SmackDown* history, Brock Lesnar hit Big Show—who weighed 500 lbs (226.8 kg) at the time—with a superplex from the top rope. The impact was so great that the entire ring collapsed. The fans could not believe their eyes, and medics clustered anxiously around the two men as the show went off air.

June 26: Big Show double chokeslams Brock Lesnar and Kurt Angle.

Blindsided!

June 26: After a mass brawl between all participants the previous week on *SmackDown*, a Six-Man Tag Team Match was set up to help settle their differences. The main event saw Big Show put in a dominant performance, hitting a double chokeslam on both Brock Lesnar and Kurt Angle. Mr. America then had the advantage over Big Show, until Mr. McMahon distracted him by threatening to attack his friend, Zach Gowan. This allowed Big Show to blindside Mr. America and hit him with a chokeslam for the victory.

June 12: Both Brock Lesnar and Big Show lie prone on the mat after the impact of a superplex on Big Show causes the ring to collapse.

2003

INTRODUCING...

Ultimo Dragon

June 26: Japanese high-flying legend Ultimo Dragon made an impressive WWE debut on *SmackDown* with a victory over Shannon Moore. The former WCW Cruiserweight Champion didn't hit the same heights in WWE. However, he did go on to achieve two of his dreams, performing at Madison Square Garden and also *WrestleMania*.

Ultimo Dragon celebrates his win over Shannon Moore.

Two-time winners

July 3: Former Team Angle members Charlie Haas and Shelton Benjamin stepped out of Kurt Angle's long shadow by capturing the WWE Tag Team Championships for a second time. Taking on the formidable team of Tajiri and Eddie Guerrero, Benjamin kicked Tajiri so hard he landed on a vehicle that was parked at ringside. This distracted both the referee and Guerrero, allowing Haas to roll up Guerrero for the pin.

July 3: Tajiri winces in pain after being kicked onto a parked vehicle by Shelton Benjamin.

Revenge of "The Deadman"

July 17: John Cena showed an unprecedented level of disrespect in the lead-up to his match with Undertaker at *Vengeance*. Cena cut an aggressive rap against Undertaker in a graveyard, taking several personal shots at "The Deadman" and even urinating on a gravestone. Undertaker didn't waste much time putting Cena in his place, riding to the ring on his chopper and attacking the upstart before he scrambled to the safety of the backstage area.

Elsewhere in WWE

July 27: The *SmackDown*-branded pay-per-view *Vengeance* treated fans to the crowning of two new WWE Champions. Eddie Guerrero claimed the vacant United States Championship, and Kurt Angle got the better of Brock Lesnar and Big Show in a Triple Threat Match to become WWE Champion.

August 14: Brock Lesnar looks pleased with himself after aligning with the most powerful man in WWE, Mr. McMahon, at the expense of his former friend, Kurt Angle.

Mr. McMahon's new friend

August 14: Brock Lesnar had shocked fans during his match with Mr. McMahon the previous week by turning on his friend Kurt Angle, who was guest referee. It was time for Lesnar to explain himself. Lesnar explained that Angle ceased to be his friend when he took the WWE Championship from him at *Vengeance*. The crowd booed as Lesnar explained that he had just been using Angle, much to Mr. McMahon's glee.

Undertaker buries all comers

August 28: Undertaker saw off Brock Lesnar and Big Show to become the number one contender for Kurt Angle's WWE Championship the following week on *SmackDown*. At the climax of this hard-hitting match, Lesnar was about to superplex Big Show from the top rope, when Undertaker got underneath Lesnar and hit him with a devastating Last Ride for victory. Lesnar would get his revenge on Undertaker on next week's episode, when his interference handed Angle victory over "The Deadman."

Parking lot brawl

September 11: Eddie Guerrero put his United States Championship on the line in a brutal Parking Lot Brawl against John Cena, his rival. Cena opened proceedings with a rap about Guerrero, who then gained an early advantage by using his championship title as a weapon. The clash eventually ended when Eddie's nephew, Chavo, struck Cena from behind, allowing Eddie to hit a Frog Splash from the roof of an automobile for the pin.

Here come the iron men

September 18: For the first time in network television history, *SmackDown* played host to a 60-Minute Iron Man Match. This epic encounter, with Brock Lesnar challenging the WWE Champion Kurt Angle, would be remembered as one of the blue brand's greatest matches. Lesnar dominated the majority of the contest, leading Angle five falls to two with just 14 minutes remaining. Angle showed immense courage to pull that back to five falls to four with just seconds left on the clock as he applied his devastating Ankle Lock to Lesnar. The comeback would fall heartbreakingly short, with Lesnar refusing to submit and holding on to become the new WWE Champion.

September 18: Kurt Angle applies the Ankle Lock to Brock Lesnar in their 60-Minute Iron Man Match.

Elsewhere in WWE

September 21: The RAW-branded pay-per-view *Unforgiven* was notable for Goldberg winning his first World Heavyweight Championship with a victory over Triple H. Had Goldberg lost, he would have been forced to retire. Christian also defeated Chris Jericho and Rob Van Dam in an entertaining Triple Threat Match to retain his Intercontinental Championship.

August 28: Undertaker lifts Brock Lesnar for a chokeslam on his way to victory.

2003

September 25: Tajiri employs the Leg Scissors in an attempt to wear down Rey Mysterio.

Beware the red mist

September 25: In an entertaining match between two excellent technicians, "The Japanese Buzzsaw," Tajiri eventually overcame the popular Cruiserweight Champion, Rey Mysterio. Tajiri had accidentally incapacitated the referee by hitting him with a spin kick meant for Mysterio, so another official had to run to the ring and take over. While this new official was checking on his colleague, Tajiri spat red mist in Mysterio's eyes, temporarily blinding him and getting the pin.

Angle mocks Cena

October 17: *SmackDown* opened with the music of John Cena; however, it was Kurt Angle who came to the ring, dressed in his rival's street clothes. Angle delivered a rap pretending to be Cena but sending him up at the same time, much to the fans' amusement. A little person dressed in Angle's ring gear then appeared, chased "John Cena" out of the ring, and then made him tap out to an Ankle Lock, as Angle predicted Cena would at the upcoming *No Mercy* event. The real Cena furiously arrived—to be hit with a low blow by Angle's accomplice. Angle then completed Cena's humiliation by chucking him out of the ring.

Paul Heyman is the new GM

October 23: After defeating his own daughter, Stephanie, at *No Mercy*, Mr. McMahon had finally achieved his aim of getting her fired as *SmackDown* General Manager. Mr McMahon shocked the WWE Universe by announcing the new GM would be none other than the former owner of ECW, Paul Heyman. His first act was to set up a Triple Threat main event, which saw Undertaker defeat Brock Lesnar and Big Show.

The Basham Brothers captured their first WWE Tag Team Championships in an upset victory against Los Guerreros. While the referee was checking that their injured manager, Shaniqua, was okay, Danny Basham hit Eddie Guerrero with a night stick for an easy three count. This would be the first of two WWE Tag Team Championship reigns for the Basham Brothers.

October 17: John Cena grimaces in pain after being hit by a low blow from "mini Kurt Angle."

A pre-Survivor Series advantage

October 30: Brock Lesnar and Big Show used their main event match against the Acolytes Protection Agency (APA)—Bradshaw and Faarooq—as a chance to dismantle Team Angle prior to *Survivor Series*. After carrying out a vicious attack with a steel chair to both Bradshaw and Faarooq, Angle and Benoit ran to APA's rescue. They were soon overwhelmed, however, when the gigantic Matt Morgan and Nathan Jones arrived and pulverized them. The show finished with the awesome sight of Lesnar, Big Show, Morgan, and Jones raising their hands in victory.

Elsewhere in WWE

November 16: The co-branded *Survivor Series* saw Goldberg successfully defend his World Heavyweight Championship against Triple H in the main event and Mr. McMahon, with the help of Kane, defeat Undertaker in a Buried Alive Match.

"A monster shows no compassion… My brother was a FRAUD!"

Kane (November 20, 2003)

Kane's eulogy

November 20: After seemingly burying his brother, Undertaker, alive at *Survivor Series*, *RAW* Superstar Kane was a special guest on *SmackDown* at the behest of WWE Chairman Mr. McMahon. Kane delivered a twisted eulogy to his brother, decrying him for becoming less of a monster and more of a man. Their bitter rivalry would eventually resurface at *WrestleMania XX*, in a match that would mark the return of a more demonic Undertaker.

Thanksgiving showcase

November 27: *SmackDown*'s Thanksgiving Special opened with the entire roster at ringside. They were addressed by General Manager Paul Heyman, who announced that the winner of the upcoming Battle Royal Match would face Brock Lesnar for his WWE Championship that same night. After most of the Superstars ganged up on the mighty Big Show to eject him from the ring, the final two, Chris Benoit and John Cena, both tumbled over the top rope and hit the ground at the same time, concluding the Battle Royal. Big Show and Brock Lesnar then entered the ring and knocked out both Benoit and Cena. Paul Heyman proclaimed that Cena and Benoit would now have to face off to win the right to face Lesnar the following week.

Lesnar retains his title

December 4: Following the previous week's Battle Royal, Chris Benoit won the right to face Champion Brock Lesnar after forcing John Cena to submit. Benoit duly faced Lesnar in a grueling main event. Lesnar won by smacking Benoit's knee with a steel chair and following up with a leglock submission hold. Benoit did not tap out but instead passed out from the pain, to Lesnar's anger.

Defeat for a hometown hero

December 11: Brock Lesnar forced Rey Mysterio, the master of the 619 move, to challenge him by mocking Mysterio's hometown, San Diego. Despite his size disadvantage, Mysterio took Lesnar to the absolute limit, before being forced to submit after being put in a devastating hold by the WWE Champion.

Christmas in Baghdad

December 25: As part of its ongoing support for US forces, WWE aired its first-ever Tribute to the Troops when the *SmackDown* roster traveled to Camp Victory to put on a show for servicemen and women. It was a huge success, with the main event featuring Stone Cold Steve Austin and John Cena defeating Big Show with an Attitude Adjustment. This edition concluded with Stone Cold leading WWE's heartfelt thanks for the brave sacrifices that the troops made each and every day.

December 25: Mr. McMahon confronts Santa—none other than his old nemesis Stone Cold Steve Austin— before receiving a Stone Cold Stunner..

2004

THE BLUE BRAND went through some exciting changes this year, owing to some intriguing lottery picks and three different General Managers—Paul Heyman, Kurt Angle, and Teddy Long. *SmackDown* also witnessed the high-flying excellence of Rey Mysterio, the emergence of JBL, and the greatness of Eddie Guerrero, who dominated the start of the year as WWE Champion. John Cena began to emerge as a bona fide Superstar, cementing *SmackDown's* tradition for fostering young, hungry Superstars, and there were several outstanding contests during the year— not least an outstanding Cage Match between Eddie Guerrero and JBL with the WWE Championship at stake.

Rey Mysterio starts with a bang

January 1: *SmackDown* started 2004 in style, with the opening match seeing Rey Mysterio defeat Tajiri and claim his WWE Cruiserweight Championship. The match itself was an excellent display of high-flying moves and technical wrestling, which eventually finished when Mysterio surprised Tajiri with a Hurricanrana for the pinfall. The crowd gave Mysterio a standing ovation as he celebrated his victory.

January 1: Rey Mysterio hits Tajiri with a cross body in their entertaining championship match. Mysterio would go on to end Tajiri's almost one-hundred-day reign.

Guerrero is number one

January 29: After winning the 2004 *Royal Rumble*, Chris Benoit set his sights on Triple H's *RAW*-based World Heavyweight Championship. This left no obvious challenger for *SmackDown's* Brock Lesnar's WWE Championship. As a result, General Manager Paul Heyman set up a 15-Man Royal Rumble Match to decide the number one contender. The winner would face the champion at the upcoming *No Way Out* pay-per-view. Eddie Guerrero finally came out on top, after eliminating Kurt Angle.

January 29: Guerrero knocks Angle to the floor to become number one WWE Championship contender.

February 26: Eddie Guerrero grudgingly gives himself up to the police after being set up by Kurt Angle.

Redemption win
February 5: The popular duo of Rikishi and Scotty 2 Hotty seized the opportunity to become WWE Tag Team Champions by defeating the Basham Brothers. The win was revenge for Rikishi and Scotty 2 Hotty after they had been blindsided by the Bashams on a previous episode of *SmackDown*. The match was won when Rikishi hit Doug Basham with a Samoan Drop, to the delight of the WWE Universe.

A war of words
February 12: In the buildup to their WWE Championship Match at *No Way Out*, the champion Brock Lesnar and Eddie Guerrero engaged in a heated exchange. It started out with Lesnar dancing to a mariachi band in the ring before Guerrero interrupted proceedings. Guerrero gave a highly emotional speech, in which he revealed his battles with addiction and the struggles he had to come through to get to this point in his WWE career. The crowd cheered wildly as Guerrero stood up to Lesnar and proclaimed that the WWE Championship symbolized redemption for him and his family. Guerrero would go on to defeat Lesnar at *No Way Out,* to become WWE Champion for the first time.

A familiar challenger
February 19: Eddie Guerrero's first match as WWE Champion was against a familiar foe, his nephew Chavo, with Kurt Angle as the special guest referee. The two men had a hard-fought match in the main event, both clearly able to anticipate each other's offense. What Guerrero didn't anticipate, however, was his former friend, Kurt Angle turning on him. Guerrero appeared to have the match won after hitting Chavo with a Frog Splash, but Angle refused to make the count. Instead, he viciously attacked Guerrero, and the show closed to a chorus of boos from the WWE Universe.

"I attacked Eddie Guerrero for America!"

Kurt Angle (February 26, 2004)

The champion goes to jail
February 26: Kurt Angle used this episode to explain his reason for his attack on Eddie Guerrero the previous week. Angle explained to the WWE Universe that he had turned on his former friend because it was the right thing to do. He claimed he had not done this to benefit himself but on behalf of the WWE Universe. Angle further went on to explain that as a former addict, Guerrero was simply not fit to be WWE Champion. Furious, Guerrero rushed to the ring to attack Angle. Angle ran toward the backstage area, and a wall of police officers prevented Guerrero from pursuing him. Under the instruction of General Manager Paul Heyman, the cops then escorted the champion to jail for assault.

Guerrero wins, Undertaker returns
March 18: After defeating both Shelton Benjamin and Big Show in a series of Gauntlet Matches, Rey Mysterio earned a championship opportunity that same evening. Despite having taken part in two matches already, Mysterio put on a great show. Guerrero eventually won by capitalizing on a missed leg drop from Mysterio, rolling up the challenger for the pinfall.

In the lead-up to the WWE Superstar Draft, General Manager Paul Heyman proclaimed that no man would stand in his way when building a new *SmackDown* roster. Suddenly, the lights lowered, the bell tolled, and Undertaker, accompanied by his manager Paul Bearer, made a dramatic entrance and Tombstoned Heyman.

2004

> "I am proud to say that the new General Manager of *SmackDown* is... me, Kurt Angle!"
>
> **Kurt Angle (March 25, 2004)**

March 25: New *SmackDown* GM, Kurt Angle, addresses his newest recruit, Booker T, after making him a surprise addition to the roster.

Angle's "blockbuster news"

March 25: During the annual WWE Superstar Draft three days earlier, *SmackDown* General Manager Paul Heyman had been drafted to *RAW*. In this episode, Kurt Angle entered to the music of new *SmackDown* Superstar Triple H and announced himself as the new GM. Ignoring the fans' skeptical comments, Angle claimed that he had made a great sacrifice by putting his in-ring career on hold to take the role. He then stunned the WWE Universe by revealing that he had traded Triple H back to *RAW* in exchange for the Dudley Boyz and Booker T.

INTRODUCING...

JBL

March 25: Although John Bradshaw Layfield had been a WWE Superstar for several years, he reintroduced himself on *SmackDown* as JBL. On March 25, 2004, the financial tycoon arrived, sporting a ten-gallon hat and a suit and tie, ushering in a new era for the tough Texan. "The Loudmouth Longhorn" would go on to capture the WWE Championship at the *Great American Bash* in June and hold the championship for the remainder of the year.

JBL radiates supreme confidence on his *SmackDown* debut.

Booker T assaults Van Dam

April 15: Booker T showed a distinctly mean streak when taking on his former tag team partner Rob Van Dam in the main event. Van Dam's arms were tangled in the ropes, but instead of allowing the referee to untangle Van Dam, Booker T rained blows on his defenseless opponent. After repeated warnings, the match official had no choice but to disqualify Booker T. However, that didn't stop the assault, which continued long after the bell.

April 15: Booker T gets Rob Van Dam in a tangle, before earning himself a disqualification for a vicious attack on "Mr. Monday Night."

April 22: Charlie Haas and Rico celebrate their Tag Team Championship win with Miss Jackie.

Charlie Haas and Rico are crowned

April 22: With his regular partner, Shelton Benjamin, transferred to *RAW*, Charlie Haas needed a new teammate. Much to the surprise of Haas, Rico was unveiled as his partner immediately before their match against the Tag Team Champions, Rikishi and Scotty 2 Hotty. Despite being less than pleased to be partnered with the flamboyant Rico, the team combined well and defeated their opponents to capture the gold.

> "My career is over—and you think it's funny!""
>
> **Kurt Angle (April 29, 2004)**

Angle loses the crowd

April 29: After a brutal backstage attack by Big Show two weeks prior, Kurt Angle returned to *SmackDown* in a wheelchair. The WWE Universe was surprised to see the General Manager back so soon but showed no sympathy for his injuries. Angle's sorrowful announcement that he would never be able to compete in the ring again was greeted with loud cheers. With tears in his eyes, Angle then began to harangue the WWE Universe for their sarcastic responses. His complaints were drowned out by the crowd chanting: "You suck!"

The Champ is a chump

May 6: When Cruiserweight Champion Chavo announced an open challenge to the whole *SmackDown* locker room, he wasn't expecting Texan Superstar Jacqueline to answer the call. She hit the overconfident champ with a low blow behind the referee's back and followed up with a roll-up pinfall for a surprise win.

May 6: Jacqueline answers Chavo Guerrero's challenge for his Cruiserweight title.

JBL takes advantage

May 20: WWE Champion Eddie Guerrero, Rey Mysterio, and Rob Van Dam seemed to be in control in their match against JBL and the Dudley Boyz. However, Guerrero, feeling the effects of his brutal match with JBL at *Judgment Day* the previous Sunday and a backstage attack by JBL, suddenly appeared off-balance and unwell. While Guerrero was on the mat being attended to by the official, JBL tagged himself in and pinned him for a sneak victory. Immediately afterward, paramedics and WWE officials attended to the injured champion, while JBL celebrated.

2004

June 17: The Dudley Boyz use all their experience to gain an unfair advantage and claim the WWE Tag Team Titles.

A distraction, and an interference

June 17: This proved to be a night when two titles changed hands. The Dudley Boyz—Bubba Ray Dudley and D-Von Dudley—kicked off proceedings by sneakily defeating the popular team of Charlie Haas and Rico. Haas was distracted outside of the ring when their manager, Jackie Gayda, was inadvertently knocked off the apron; Bubba Ray seized his chance to use the ropes to pin Rico, whose free leg was being held by D-Von.

The second championship change of the night saw Rey Mysterio make short work of the WWE Cruiserweight Champion, Chavo Guerrero Sr., despite an attempted interference by the former champion, Chavo. Mysterio's array of acrobatic moves was simply too much for "Chavo Classic," and Mysterio defeated him with a trademark 6:19 and springboard leg drop for the pin.

Angle gets his way

July 8: General Manager Kurt Angle had arranged with the WWE Board that, should his bitter rival John Cena lay hands on him, Cena would suffer dire consequences. Sadly for Cena, this is precisely what happened in his main event United States Title Match against Booker T. Cena was trying to clothesline Booker, when Booker ducked. Unable to stop his momentum, Cena tumbled out of the ring and accidentally fell onto Angle. Although Cena won the match by disqualification when Roman Reigns interfered, Angle used his new powers to strip Cena of his championship for attacking him. The WWE Universe were furious as Angle achieved his secret agenda of taking Cena's title away.

Who was that masked man?

July 15: The WWE Championship was defended in a cage for the first time in *SmackDown* history, with JBL emerging triumphant after a grueling encounter. JBL owed his victory to an interference from a mysterious masked man, El Gran Luchador, who grabbed Guerrero as he climbed the cage, allowing JBL to escape and reach the ground first for the win. Guerrero subsequently unmasked the mystery man, who was revealed to be none other than the current *SmackDown* General Manager Kurt Angle.

Teddy Long's reign begins

July 29: The previous week WWE Chairman Mr. McMahon had fired a not-at-all-injured Kurt Angle from his cushy post as General Manager. On this episode, Mr. McMahon broke up an in-ring brawl between possible contenders for the vacant United States Championship and appointed Teddy Long GM. Long's first act was to set up an Eight-Man Elimination Match for the US Title. Long would become the longest-serving GM in WWE history, becoming a WWE Hall of Fame member in 2017.

Booker T later overcame a combination of René Duprée, Rob Van Dam, John Cena, Luther Reigns, Kenzo Suzuki, Charlie Haas, and Billy Gunn to capture the United States Championship. In an intriguing match, full of contrasting styles, the final three men remaining were John Cena, Rob Van Dam, and Booker T. Booker prevented Van Dam from pinning Cena by hitting Van Dam with a Five Star Frog Splash and then finished him off with a signature Scissors Kick for the win.

Eddie Guerrero's auction antics

August 5: Leading up to his match with Kurt Angle at *SummerSlam*, Eddie Guerrero was accompanied to the ring by the *SmackDown* Divas: Dawn Marie, Sable, and Torrie Wilson. They had come to help drive up the prices for some Kurt Angle memorabilia that was being auctioned for charity on WWE.com. Guerrero used his role as auctioneer to poke fun at Angle, sitting in Angle's wheelchair, joking about his plaster cast, and getting the Divas to sign a defaced Angle portrait.

A Summer Games Relay

August 12: *SmackDown* saw Team Cena take on Team Booker T in the first-ever Summer Games Relay Match. The rules were complex: the match was split into five-minute periods. If no winner emerged at the end of the first period, the team that had won the toss—in this case, Team Booker—was allowed to relay in another team member, giving them the advantage of the fresh man. If the member of Team Cena could make it through the next period, he would be allowed to relay in another member of his team and so on until the finish. Eventually, Cena rolled up Booker T for the win.

August 12: Booker T hits Rob Van Dam of Team Cena with a scissor kick.

Elsewhere in WWE

August 15: Co-branded between *SmackDown* and *RAW*, *SummerSlam* saw John Cena defeat Booker T for the United States Heavyweight Championship and JBL retain his WWE Championship against Undertaker, while Kurt Angle returned to action with a victory over his rival, Eddie Guerrero. The highlight of the *RAW* matches was Edge defeating Chris Jericho and Batista to retain the Intercontinental Championship.

September 9: Big Show lifts Nunzio with ease, before hitting him with a chokeslam.

Big Show's rip-roaring return

September 9: When a Lumberjack Match between Eddie Guerrero and Kurt Angle descended into a full-on brawl, the crowd was stunned as Big Show made an early return to *SmackDown*. He strode purposefully to the ring and began attacking members of the roster at random. The gigantic Superstar hit Bob Holly with a chokeslam, cleared the ring of The Dudley Boyz, and eventually overcame all 20 Lumberjacks, including Rey Mysterio, John Cena, and Rob Van Dam as the episode went off air.

2004

Fifth Anniversary Special

September 23: WWE Chairman Mr. McMahon opened the Fifth Anniversary show promising highlights of past events and many more future thrills. The show saw Undertaker defeat former Ministry members Gangrel and Viscera, as well as Torrie Wilson and Dawn Marie being defeated by 81-year-old veteran Superstars The Fabulous Moolah and Mae Young. The show finished with Kurt Angle rendering Big Show motionless with a tranquilizer dart and then shaving his head!

INTRODUCING...

Carlito

October 7: The swaggering Puerto Rican Carlito enjoyed a stunning debut on *SmackDown*, defeating John Cena for the United States Championship. Carlito would subsequently relinquish the title to Cena but go on to have a highly successful WWE career, including a reign as Intercontinental Champion and a winning tag team run with his brother, Primo.

Carlito's *SmackDown* debut concludes with him putting on John Cena's own chain, after using it to defeat the reigning United States Champion.

Mysterio misses out

October 14: In a *SmackDown* airing from Manchester, England, Rey Mysterio defeated 19 other WWE Superstars in a Battle Royal to win a shot at the United States Championship, held by Carlito, later that night. In a close match, Carlito retained his title by using the ropes for leverage as he pinned the popular Mysterio, much to the WWE Universe's disappointment.

Heidenreich is let loose

October 21: The intimidating Heidenreich, accompanied by Paul Heyman, made his way to the ring in a straightjacket for his match with Shannon Moore. Moore put in a gutsy display, but was no match for the massive Heidenreich, who overpowered him with a series of devastating maneuvers. Heidenreich had proven himself so dangerous that, following his victory, he had to have the straightjacket put back on him as he exited the ring.

Team Angle vs. Team Guerrero

November 11: Members of Team Guerrero took on members of Team Angle in a series of matches. First up, Eddie Guerrero and Rob Van Dam defeated Mark Jindrak and Luther Reigns with a simultaneous double Frog Splash. The main event between Kurt Angle and Big Show finished in a disqualification after members of Team Angle attacked Team Guerrero's Big Show, hoping to soften him up for the two teams' upcoming match at *Survivor Series*.

November 11: Big Show writhes in pain after being blindsided by members of Team Angle.

November 18: Cena throws Carlito at the guard rail on the way to reclaiming the United States Championship.

Night of Champions

December 30: General Manager Teddy Long opened proceedings by proclaiming that this episode would see each champion defend his title against an opponent of his choosing. John Cena defended his United States Championship against René Duprée and Funaki retained his Cruiserweight Championship against Spike Dudley. The main event saw Rey Mysterio and Rob Van Dam successfully defend their Tag Team Championships against their friends Eddie Guerrero and Booker T in an entertaining match full of trickery as well as in-ring action.

John Cena's winning return

November 18: After being put out of action for several weeks by Carlito, John Cena made his return to *SmackDown* to gain revenge and recapture the United States Championship. Cena showed his brutal side, even using a steel chair before the opening bell had sounded. Once the bell rang, Cena hit Carlito with a signature Attitude Adjustment for the victory. Cena's triumph was short-lived, however, as Carlito's associate, Jesús, attacked him from behind, and Jesús and Carlito then gave the new champ a kicking.

Cheating the cheaters

December 9: The crowd went wild as the high-flying duo of Rob Van Dam and Rey Mysterio defeated Kenzo Suzuki and René Duprée to capture the WWE Tag Team Championships. Despite their status as fan favorites, Van Dam and Mysterio used some questionable tactics to win, with Van Dam holding Mysterio's arm for extra momentum as Mysterio pinned Suzuki. However, this was seen as retribution, as Suzuki and Duprée had previously cheated to retain the championships at *No Mercy* in October.

Elsewhere in WWE

December 12:
This *SmackDown* exclusive pay-per-view saw several impressive matches, including Big Show defeating Kurt Angle, Luther Reigns, and Mark Jindrak in a Handicap Match. The main event saw JBL retain his WWE Championship against the formidable trio of Undertaker, Booker T, and Eddie Guerrero.

December 30: Rey Mysterio hits Eddie Guerrero with a typically high-flying maneuver.

2005

THIS WAS A year in which several of the younger Superstars of *SmackDown* really made their mark. John Cena, Batista, Carlito, and MNM in the Tag Team division helped to give the blue brand its own distinct identity and demonstrated the evolution of WWE. *SmackDown* also saw one champion leave, in John Cena, and another, Batista, arrive, following the annual draft lottery and the show's move from Thursday to Friday nights. Sadly, the tragic passing of Eddie Guerrero in November overshadowed the end of the year, with the whole of WWE mourning the loss of one of its most beloved and greatest Superstars.

Heyman in a casket
January 6: Paul Heyman's mouth got him into trouble when he tried to negotiate his client, Heidenreich, out of a Casket Match with Undertaker at *Royal Rumble*. General Manager Teddy Long said that if Heidenreich and Heyman defeated Undertaker in tonite's scheduled *SmackDown* contest, then he would reverse the stipulation. Heidenreich went into battle alongside a distinctly nervous Paul Heyman. When Undertaker called for two caskets to be brought to ringside, Heidenreich took fright and left Heyman to fend for himself. Undertaker tombstoned the hapless Heyman and shut him in a casket for the win.

The last man standing
January 27: With *Royal Rumble* on the horizon, no one was more pleased than Big Show to witness two of his rivals for the Royal Rumble Match beating each other into submission here on *SmackDown*. Both JBL and Angle fought incredibly hard; JBL kicked a chair into the face of Angle, only to be hit with it by Angle before he crashed to the mat. The match ended in a draw when both men failed to answer the ten count.

First-ever Tokyo broadcast
February 10: This episode had a distinctly international flavor, being broadcast from Tokyo, Japan. The show was anchored around the WWE Championship No. 1 Contenders' Tournament, in which John Cena defeated Orlando Jordan in the quarterfinals. The main event was another quarter final match between Kurt Angle and Rey Mysterio. The match itself was a technical masterclass and was eventually won by Angle when he applied a devastating Ankle Lock to Mysterio.

> ### Elsewhere in WWE
> **January 30:** At *Royal Rumble*, Batista earned the right to a World Championship Match at *WrestleMania* 21 by winning the Royal Rumble Match, finally eliminating John Cena. Elsewhere, Edge defeated Shawn Michaels in an entertaining bout, and Undertaker defeated Heidenreich in a Casket Match.

February 16: *RAW* Superstar Batista makes an impact on *SmackDown* by destroying JBL's limousine.

Batista, the limo crusher
February 17: The rivalry between JBL and *RAW*'s Batista was escalating. On Monday's *RAW*, JBL had lured Batista outside and tried to run him over with his limousine. On this *SmackDown* episode, Batista got his revenge. JBL and his Cabinet stable were in the ring, when Batista appeared on the Titantron screen and destroyed JBL's limo, before being chased away by the Cabinet. Afterward, Big Show came to ringside to confront JBL, whom he was facing at *No Way Out*, and found himself outnumbered by the Cabinet. Batista ran to Big Show's aid, much to the crowd's joy.

January 6: Undertaker rolls Paul Heyman toward a casket before slamming it shut to seal victory.

February 24: John Cena crowns WWE Champion JBL with his own portrait to spoil the Texan's party.

> ## "I am a champion that you people, quite honestly, can never be like, but you can always admire!"
>
> ### JBL (February 24, 2005)

A Celebration of Excellence

February 24: Following the successful defense of his WWE Championship at *No Way Out*, JBL held a typically self-aggrandizing Celebration of Excellence on *SmackDown*. The celebration featured the Cabinet presenting JBL with an oil painting of himself, much to the champion's delight. An angry Big Show came to the ring to bring the celebration to a close but found himself outnumbered by the Cabinet. It looked like Big Show would be on the wrong end of a beating, until JBL's upcoming opponent at *WrestleMania*, John Cena, ran to the ring to even up the score.

March 3: JBL attacks John Cena, allowing his Chief of Staff, Orlando Jordan, to steal the victory.

Orlando Jordan—United States Champion

March 3: Defending his United States Championship, John Cena appeared to have JBL's Chief of Staff, Orlando Jordan, beaten after hitting him with his signature FU. Interference from The Basham Brothers distracted both Cena and the official, allowing JBL to hit Cena with the championship belt from the ring apron, where he had been hiding. This allowed Orlando Jordan to claim an easy pin and claim the United States Championship.

Kurt Angle's mind games

March 17: In the buildup to their match at *WrestleMania 21*, Kurt Angle was determined to prove to Shawn Michaels that he was the better man. After Michaels and Marty Jannetty had reformed The Rockers on *RAW* on Monday, Angle wanted to send a message to Michaels by defeating his tag team partner on *SmackDown*. Jannetty put up a valiant effort in a back-and-forth match but eventually succumbed to Angle's signature Ankle Lock submission move.

March 17: Marty Jannetty writhes in pain as Kurt Angle cinches in his Ankle Lock.

Sensational and sexy

March 24: Before their confrontation at *WrestleMania 21*, Kurt Angle had promised to achieve every one of Shawn Michaels' career milestones in just four weeks. He had won a Ladder Match and defeated Michaels' former partner, Marty Jannetty; however, this *SmackDown* episode saw something special. Angle first entered the arena to the strains of "The Heartbreak Kid" Shawn Michaels' theme song, "Sexy Boy." He then amazed the crowd by introducing Michaels' former manager, Sensational Sherri. The pair then performed a hilarious version of Michaels' theme song, entitled, "Sexy Kurt."

2005

London wins a Battle Royal

March 31: Paul London claimed his first and only WWE Cruiserweight Championship by the unusual method of winning a Battle Royal. Chavo Guerrero came to the ring as champion, but the final two men standing were Billy Kidman and Paul London. Kidman appeared to have eliminated London when he threw him over the ropes; however, London held on to the ropes, preventing his feet from touching the floor. He then eliminated Kidman with a Hurricanrana over the top rope.

March 31: Paul London's acrobatic skills are too much for Billy Kidman and Akio to handle.

Elsewhere in WWE

April 3: *WrestleMania* 21 will be remembered for John Cena defeating JBL for the WWE Championship and Batista defeating Triple H for the World Heavyweight Championship. Kurt Angle also defeated Shawn Michaels via submission in a classic match, and Akebono defeated Big Show in a Sumo Match.

"It's been said I'm not a Superstar because I put myself on the same level as those I fight for."

John Cena (April 7, 2005)

Cena finds his voice

April 7: After defeating JBL for the WWE Championship at *WrestleMania 21*, John Cena made a triumphant return to *SmackDown*. Cena was met with a standing ovation from the crowd as he celebrated his victory over "wrestling god" JBL. Cena defiantly stated that the WWE establishment thought he was "a thug," who didn't talk or "fit the dress code" of past champions, adding that they had better lock the doors of the country club because, "the champ is here!"

April 7: John Cena celebrates his title win with the WWE Universe.

MNM's multiple attacks

April 21: Having only recently started their WWE careers, MNM—Johnny Nitro, Joey Mercury, and their manager Melina—made a real impact by capturing the WWE Tag Team Championships on this *SmackDown* episode. MNM had clearly set their sights on defeating the Champions, Eddie Guerrero and Rey Mysterio, previously attacking Rey on Carlito's Cabana interview segment and spray-painting "MNM" on the hood of Eddie's fancy lowrider automobile. Their victory was a massive upset and not gained fairly, with Melina jumping on Guerrero outside the ring, allowing Mercury and Nitro to double-team Mysterio for the pin.

May 12: Big Show doubles up in pain after taking a bite of Carlito's poisoned apple.

Carlito's poisoned apple

May 12: Carlito used his Cabana interview segment to recruit Big Show. The Puerto Rican Superstar claimed that he needed some extra muscle and that Big Show could use his brains to help his career, following his loss to Akebono at *WrestleMania 21*. Big Show said he didn't want to play second fiddle and turned Carlito down. This led to a war of words, which ended with Big Show grabbing an apple from Carlito's hand and biting into it. He then collapsed in agony—the apple was poisoned—and Carlito attacked him.

The Winner's Choice

May 26: The main event featured a Winner's Choice Battle Royal, where the winner would get to face an opponent of his choosing on the following week's show. Kurt Angle triumphed against 19 other Superstars, including Heidenreich, Carlito, Booker T, Eddie Guerrero, and Rey Mysterio, finally eliminating Mysterio with an Angle Slam. Instead of picking WWE Champion John Cena or even his current nemesis, Booker T, as his upcoming opponent, Angle shocked the WWE Universe by choosing Booker's wife, Sharmell!

Holding out for a hero

June 9: WWE Champion John Cena had been drafted to *RAW*, leaving *SmackDown* without a champion. JBL seized this opportunity to try to convince General Manager Teddy Long that, based on his past successes, he should be awarded a new Championship. Long flatly denied JBL's request and declared that a new title, the *SmackDown* Championship, would be set up. Long also announced new draft picks across the next few weeks, including Chris Benoit, Randy Orton, and Christian.

JBL's worthless title

June 30: JBL thought he had won the first-ever *SmackDown* Championship when he defeated Undertaker, Christian, Chris Benoit, Booker T, and Muhammad Hassan in a Six-Man Match. His joy was short-lived, however, as Teddy Long arrived in the ring to declare that the *SmackDown* Championship was no longer necessary. This was because, for his final draft pick, he would be bringing the World Heavyweight Champion Batista over to *SmackDown* from *RAW*.

June 30: JBL looks on in horror as *SmackDown* GM Teddy Long announces that his final draft pick is World Heavyweight Champion Batista.

"Dominick, next week, is going to legally be my son!"

Eddie Guerrero (August 4, 2005)

August 4th: Rey Mysterio attempts to comprehend the news that his fierce rival, Eddie Guerrero, is the biological father of his son, Dominick.

A question of paternity

August 4: The bitter rivalry between Rey Mysterio and Eddie Guerrero became highly personal during Christian's Peep Show interview. Guerrero claimed that Mysterio's son, Dominick, was legally and biologically his. Mysterio begged Guerrero to leave Dominick out of their conflict, but Guerrero refused, claiming that he had always longed for a son. Mysterio then appealed to Guerrero's competitive nature by challenging him to a match to decide who should look after Dominick.

Seventeen days later, following a hard-fought Ladder Match at *SummerSlam*, Mysterio defeated Guerrero, putting an end to this distressing custody wrangle.

A message from "The Deadman"

August 11: In the run-up to their match at *SummerSlam*, Randy Orton promised to defeat one of Undertaker's legendary opponents on *SmackDown*. In what was Orton's first match since *WrestleMania 21*, the crowd was surprised when the Ugandan giant Kamala, alongside his handler Kim Chee, made his way to the ring. Kamala put up a good fight, but eventually Orton struck with a devastating RKO. However, before he could pin Kamala, the lights went out and smoke filled the ring as the letters on the big screen went from RKO to RIP, much to Orton's horror.

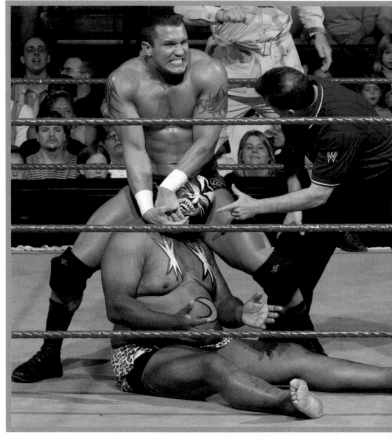

August 11: Randy Orton applies a head-twisting submission hold to Kamala.

INTRODUCING...

Mr. Kennedy

August 25: Mr. Kennedy made his *SmackDown* debut defeating Funaki—but not before cutting off ring announcer Tony Chimel and making his own introduction. This would become a trademark of Mr. Kennedy, who would go on to have a successful WWE career, capturing the United States Championship and winning the Money in the Bank briefcase in 2007.

Superconfident Mr. Kennedy would enjoy high-profile rivalries with various Superstars, including Shawn Michaels and Edge.

Friday night spectacular

September 9: The first *SmackDown* episode in its new Friday time slot was, to date, one of the greatest in the show's history. It opened with the Legion of Doom defending their WWE Tag Team Championships against young upstarts, MNM, and featured Undertaker confronting Randy Orton as part of their escalating rivalry. Eddie Guerrero then took on Rey Mysterio in a spectacular Cage Match, which ended with Guerrero preferring not to take the easy option of exiting the cage for the win in favor of hitting Mysterio with a Frog Splash for the pinfall. The show was rounded off with a hugely physical Bullrope Match, which saw Batista defend his World Heavyweight Championship with a last-gasp victory over JBL.

"The Deadman" vs. "The Legend Killer"

September 16: The legendary Undertaker defeated "The Legend Killer" Randy Orton in an enthralling main event. The match was hugely competitive. Orton used every trick in the book, including having a casket delivered to ringside that turned out to contain an Undertaker lookalike. Orton appeared to have the advantage when his father, "Cowboy" Bob Orton, distracted Undertaker; however, "The Deadman" was able to kick out from Orton's RKO finisher and deliver a Tombstone piledriver for the victory.

September 16: Undertaker looks bemused when presented with an effigy of himself during his main event battle with Randy Orton.

Piper beats the odds

October 7: "Rowdy" Roddy Piper was at a numerical disadvantage when taking on Randy Orton and his father, Bob, in a Handicap Match. The Ortons were in a dominant position, with Randy so confident that he tagged his 54-year-old father in to make the winning pinfall. However, at the crucial moment, Undertaker's ominous music began to play. This distracted the Ortons, allowing Piper to roll up Bob Orton for the victory.

Elsewhere in WWE

October 9: The *SmackDown* pay-per-view *No Mercy* saw Batista retain his World Heavyweight Championship against Eddie Guerrero. In addition, JBL defeated Rey Mysterio, and Bob and Randy Orton triumphed over Undertaker in a Handicap Casket Match.

INTRODUCING...

Bobby Lashley

September 23: Bobby Lashley made short work of Simon Dean on his *SmackDown* debut. Lashley has since held the ECW Championship twice, as well as the United States Championship. A career highlight was being picked to represent Donald Trump against Mr. McMahon at *WrestleMania 23* in the Battle of the Billionaires: Lashley's victory meant that the WWE Chairman had to have his head shaved. Lashley's fine WWE career continues to this day.

Since making his WWE return in 2018, Bobby Lashley has competed in memorable matches against the likes of Roman Reigns.

Behind every successful man...

October 21: *SmackDown* kicked off with a bang with Booker T defeating Chris Benoit for the United States Championship. The match finished with Booker T's wife, Sharmell, jumping onto the ring apron and hitting Benoit with a low blow behind the backs of both Booker T and the match official. This allowed Booker to hit Benoit with a Scissors Kick for the pinfall. He celebrated his win with Sharmell, little realizing her vital role in the victory.

October 21: Sharmell and new WWE United States Champion Booker T celebrate victory.

2005

October 28: Johnny Nitro and Joey Mercury of MNM hit Legion of Doom's Heidenreich with their Snapshot.

MNM defeats the Legion of Doom

October 28: The Legion of Doom, now consisting of Heidenreich and Animal, failed to defend their WWE Tag Team Championships in a Fatal 4-Way Match against the Mexicools, MNM, and William Regal and Paul Burchill. The Legion of Doom appeared to have the bout won when they set up Paul Burchill for their Doomsday Device; however, they were distracted by The Dicks stable, allowing MNM to hit Heidenreich with their Snapshot finisher to recapture the WWE Tag Team Championships.

A tribute to Eddie Guerrero

November 18: In the wake of Eddie Guerrero's tragic passing, just five days earlier, this hugely emotional episode of *SmackDown* was entirely dedicated to his memory. The show featured Superstars from *RAW* and *SmackDown* paying tribute to their friend and colleague, as well as a series of matches. The in-ring highlight was Eddie's nephew, Chavo, defeating JBL with Eddie's signature move, the Frog Splash, to the joy of the crowd.

RAW invades *SmackDown*

November 25: After a previous invasion from the Superstars of *RAW*, Teddy Long sent out the entire *SmackDown* locker room to protect the main event, Randy Orton vs. Batista. Despite this, the *RAW* Superstars did invade, prompting a mass brawl outside the ring as the crowd in Sheffield, England, went wild. Batista did his best to fend off the *RAW* superstars, until he was overpowered by Kane and Big Show who chokeslammed "The Animal" through the announcers' table to close the show.

Elsewhere in WWE

November 27: At *Survivor Series*, Team SmackDown featuring Batista, Bobby Lashley, JBL, Randy Orton, and Rey Mysterio defeated Team RAW, consisting of Big Show, Carlito, Chris Masters, Kane, and Shawn Michaels in the main event. John Cena retained his WWE Championship over Kurt Angle, and Triple H defeated Ric Flair in a Last Man Standing Match.

November 18: Eddie Guerrero's low-rider is at ringside as the WWE Universe pays its respects.

November 29. Big Show lands a clubbing blow on Rey Mysterio during their real-life David and Goliath battle.

The bigger they come…

November 29: This hour-long *SmackDown* special aired on a Tuesday night and featured an interpromotional "David vs. Goliath" match with *SmackDown's* Rey Mysterio taking on *RAW's* Big Show in the main event. Despite giving up over 300 lbs (136 kg) in weight, Mysterio looked to have the match won after hitting Big Show with a 619 and a Frog Splash. However, Kane's interference ended the match as a no contest.

INTRODUCING…

The Boogeyman
December 2: The terrifying Boogeyman dominated Ray Gordy on his *SmackDown* debut, showing the WWE Universe just what a bizarre Superstar he could be. Famed for eating worms and carrying an oversized clock with him during his smoke-filled entrance, the Boogeyman still makes sporadic spooky WWE appearances to this very day.

No one knows when the ghastly Boogeyman will next appear on *SmackDown*.

Mysterio and Batista gain the crown

December 16: The contrasting team of "The Animal" Batista and the high-flying Rey Mysterio combined to defeat MNM for the WWE Tag Team Championships. Despite facing a well-drilled opposition, who were aided on the outside of the ring by Melina, Mysterio and Batista triumphed after Rey executed a 619 flying kick on Joey Mercury; Batista then nailed him with his signature Batista Bomb finisher for the win.

December 16: Batista and Rey Mysterio celebrate capturing the WWE Tag Team Championships.

Mark Henry lends a hand

December 30: A surprise interference from "The World's Strongest Man," Mark Henry, who had not been seen in WWE for well over a year, cost Mysterio and Batista their Tag Team Titles. With the match official rendered temporarily unconscious, Henry hit the ring and attacked Batista, slamming him in an awesome show of strength. This left the way clear for MNM's Joey Mercury to make the pin—once the referee had regained his composure—and capture the WWE Tag Team Championships.

December 30: MNM celebrate recapturing tag team gold after defeating Batista and Rey Mysterio.

October 27, 2006: The Boogeyman enters the arena, determined to cause maximum mischief and mayhem.

2006

THE YEAR OPENED with Batista forced to forfeit his WWE World Heavyweight Title owing to an injury, thus sparking a frantic battle among Superstars to claim the vacant title for their own. First, Kurt Angle made the jump from *RAW* to *SmackDown* to win the championship. Later that year, two more competitors won their first World Heavyweight Title—the inspirational Rey Mysterio and the egotistical King Booker. Batista would eventually reclaim the title and end the year as it began—with the Superstar known as "The Animal" on top. This year also saw the *SmackDown* debuts of a pair of future world champions in The Great Khali and The Miz, as well as the first appearances of Hornswoggle and MVP.

Angle's gain, and a disgusting snack

January 13: Due to an injury suffered at the hands of Mark Henry, an emotionally distraught Batista was forced to relinquish the World Heavyweight Championship. To fill this unexpected void, General Manager Teddy Long set a 20-Man Battle Royal, with the winner to become the new champion. The surprise 20th entrant, *RAW*'s Kurt Angle, made a shocking jump to *SmackDown* and took the match and the title.

Also in this episode, "Rowdy" Roddy Piper's controversial interview segment Piper's Pit had perhaps its strangest-ever moment. Piper was interviewing John "Bradshaw" Layfield (JBL) and his "image consultant" Jillian Hall and joking about a strange growth on the side of Hall's face. Suddenly the ghoulish Boogeyman crashed the party, approached the terrified Jillian, licked his lips, and, to the disgust of the crowd, proceeded to eat the growth right off her face!

January 13: The Boogeyman relishes the taste of Jillian Hall's bizarre facial growth.

"Ladies and gentlemen, I bring you my guest— The Boogeyman!"

Roddy Piper (January 13, 2006)

January 20: Massive Mark Henry's painful manhandling proves too much for Rey Mysterio.

Contrasting styles

January 20: "The World's Strongest Man" Mark Henry and high-flying Rey Mysterio faced off for the chance to challenge Kurt Angle for the World Heavyweight Championship. Mysterio thought he had the match won when he hit Henry with a Frog Splash, but Henry rolled out, delivered a World's Strongest Slam, and covered Mysterio for the win and the title opportunity.

Elsewhere in WWE

January 29: Dedicating his performance in this year's *Royal Rumble* to his fallen comrade Eddie Guerrero, Rey Mysterio made a record-breaking performance in the 30-Man Royal Rumble Match, entering at number two and lasting more than an hour to win the bout and a guaranteed main event spot at *WrestleMania 22*.

Pirate blood

February 10: Looking to impress the network executives as well as the WWE Universe, Superstar Paul Burchill turned for inspiration to his ancestors, whom he claimed were pirates. Interrupting an interview segment about the Juniors Division, Burchill showed up in full pirate regalia, including a cutlass!

The challengers pile on

February 17: After another successful title defense of his Cruiserweight Championship, Gregory Helms decided to send the challenger, Scotty 2 Hotty, a message by continuing to beat on him after the match. Helms instead received a message of his own, when the entire Cruiserweight division came down on him.

Another chance for glory

February 24: Rey Mysterio had won a shot at the World Heavyweight Championship at *WrestleMania 22* by winning the *Royal Rumble* main event. However, he lost to Randy Orton at *No Way Out*, losing his title chance as well. Mysterio came out to apologize to the WWE Universe and Eddie Guerrero's family for missing *WrestleMania*, but General Manager Teddy Long reinserted Mysterio into the title match, making it a Triple Threat.

February 17: The Cruiserweight title challengers deliver a beatdown to the champion, Gregory Helms.

2006

Everyone wants Money in the Bank

March 17: For two consecutive weeks, Finlay and Bobby Lashley clashed for a place in *WrestleMania 22*'s Money in the Bank Ladder Match, the winner of which would get a shot at the WWE Championship. On the previous episode, their bout was declared no contest when the fight spilled into the parking lot; this week, the two fought in a Lumberjack Match, and "Belfast Bruiser" Finlay cracked Lashley with a shillelagh to score the pin. Nevertheless, both Finlay and Lashley would compete for the Money in the Bank briefcase at *WrestleMania* (which was won by Rob Van Dam).

March 17: Finlay resorts to using his shillelagh to defeat Bobby Lashley.

"I'm the one that will end the Undertaker at WrestleMania!"

Mark Henry (March 31, 2006)

Remembering the fallen

March 31: Mark Henry claimed that he would end Undertaker's famous *WrestleMania* undefeated streak in their Casket Match at *WrestleMania 22* on April 2. Henry solemnly called out the names of the 13 Superstars that had fallen to Undertaker, including Kane, Triple H, Randy Orton, Ric Flair, and Big Show. (Henry's own name would soon be added to this list.)

A historic celebration

April 7: At *WrestleMania 22*, Rey Mysterio had amazed the WWE Universe by defeating Kurt Angle and Randy Orton to win the World Heavyweight Championship. In the first *SmackDown* since *WrestleMania*, Mysterio proved to be a worthy champion by hitting his opponent Randy Orton with a pair of his signature 619s and following up with a top-rope leg drop to retain his title.

INTRODUCING...

The Great Khali

April 7: Fans were enjoying a *WrestleMania* rematch between Undertaker and Mark Henry when it was interrupted by a mysterious giant. The WWE Universe soon learned his name: The Great Khali. At 7 ft 4 in (2.2 m) Khali towered over Undertaker—a mere 6 ft 10 in (2.1 m)—and proved too strong for "The Deadman." Khali competed in WWE for the better part of a decade, winning the World Heavyweight Championship in 2007.

The Great Khali makes a memorable debut by targeting Undertaker.

April 28: Kurt Angle attempts to regain the World Heavyweight Championship by making Rey Mysterio submit to his painful Ankle Lock.

A great match spoiled

April 28: To the delight of the crowd in London, England, the World Heavyweight Champion Rey Mysterio granted a title match to the former champion Kurt Angle. The two were locked in a classic bout, with Angle having Mysterio in his signature, and very painful, Ankle Lock move, when Mark Henry came to the ring and slammed former Olympic hero Angle through a table.

May 12: In a hard-hitting slugfest, Bobby Lashley outlasts his longtime rival Finlay to win their *King of the Ring* semifinal encounter.

Chasing the crown

May 12: *SmackDown* General Manager Teddy Long brought the King of the Ring tournament back after a four-year absence from WWE. Kurt Angle was injured in the first semi-final, so his opponent, Booker T, advanced to the finals. The second match was a thrilling brawl between longtime rivals Bobby Lashley and Finlay. The Irishman thought he had the match won with an illegal chair shot, but Lashley speared Finlay, securing the pin and a berth in the final at *Judgment Day*.

> "Baby, we will reign over *SmackDown*, and we will rule with an iron fist!"
>
> **Booker T (May 26, 2006)**

A spear and a crown

May 26: The United States Champion JBL was more focused on challenging Rey Mysterio for the World Heavyweight Championship than defending his own title. JBL was finally goaded into putting his own title on the line, and Bobby Lashley took advantage, pinning JBL with a powerful spear.

By defeating Bobby Lashley at *Judgment Day*, five days earlier, Booker T had earned the right to be called King of the Ring. This edition of *SmackDown* featured Booker T's official coronation, with William Regal introducing the WWE Universe to both King Booker and his wife, Queen Sharmell.

May 26: King Booker and Queen Sharmell begin their reign over their *SmackDown* kingdom.

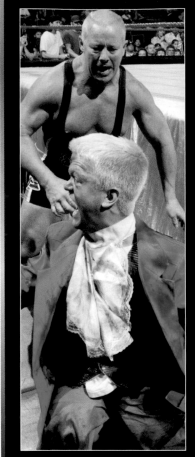

INTRODUCING...

Hornswoggle

May 26: Finlay's *SmackDown* match against Paul Burchill seemed fairly typical, until Finlay won and then looked underneath the ring. Out sprang a crazed, leprechaun-like man who attacked Burchill on Finlay's command, before returning to his "home" beneath the ring. The WWE Universe would come to know this little man as Hornswoggle, and the fiery Irishman would be a WWE staple for the next decade, winning the Cruiserweight Championship once and also being revealed as the Anonymous *RAW* General Manager.

At first it seems that only Finlay can control the troublesome Hornswoggle.

Champion's choice

June 9: Promoter Paul Heyman was relaunching the ECW brand and looking to the past to fill its roster. That included *SmackDown*'s World Heavyweight Champion, Rey Mysterio, who had made his American wrestling debut in ECW. Mysterio turned down Heyman's offer, choosing to remain on *SmackDown* instead.

Facing the King

June 30: Bobby Lashley had never competed in a Steel Cage Match before, but he decided on one to defend his United States Championship against King Booker, in order to keep his Royal Court (William Regal and Finlay) from interfering. While they still attempted to help their king, Lashley managed to win the match and defend his title.

Finlay steals the title

July 14: Defending a championship against an intense brawler like Finlay is never easy, but when Hornswoggle is involved, the task is so much more arduous. Bobby Lashley thought he had his title defense in hand, but Hornswoggle snuck a shillelagh to his partner and Finlay clocked Lashley with it, allowing him to record the pin and become the new United States Champion.

June 30: Bobby Lashley finds King Booker's cohort Finlay blocking his escape from the steel cage.

The ref is thrown, action comes in threes

September 1: After serving as an in-ring host and interviewer for months, The Miz finally made his competitive debut, facing off with WWE legend Tatanka. Tatanka controlled most of the match, until The Miz threw the ref into Tatanka and then pinned him, using the ropes for extra leverage.

Finlay thought he was defending his United States Championship against Mr. Kennedy in a one-on-one title match. *SmackDown* General Manager Teddy Long had other ideas, making the bout a Triple Threat Title Match by adding Bobby Lashley. The chaotic encounter worked to Mr. Kennedy's advantage; he pinned Lashley to win the championship.

July 28: World Heavyweight Champion King Booker drops a leg across Rey Mysterio's back en route to a successful title defense.

A championship and a crown

July 28: Rey Mysterio's four-month title reign had ended at *The Great American Bash* five days earlier, when King Booker took the championship with the help of Rey Mysterio's former friend Chavo Guerrero. Mysterio invoked his rematch clause on *SmackDown*, but, once again, Chavo attacked Mysterio, allowing King Booker to pin Rey and retain the title.

She's the greatest dancer

August 11: This year's Diva Search was down to the final four contestants, and they attempted to wow the WWE Universe and special guest judge Luke Perry in a talent show. The audience was unimpressed by three of the four competitors but approved of Layla's dance routine, so Perry declared her the winner.

Deadman standing

August 18: The Great Khali had caused quite a stir with his dominating victory over Undertaker at *Judgment Day*. "The Deadman" was ready to take their rivalry to new heights by challenging Khali to a Last Man Standing Match. Undertaker won this bruising, brutal encounter by hitting Khali with the ring steps and a steel chair.

September 1: Bidding to become United States Champion, Mr. Kennedy leaps off the top rope to slam Bobby Lashley.

2006

September 29: Edge takes advantage of an injured John Cena to spear the champion.

Cena is welcomed back

September 29: After more than a year away, John Cena made a triumphant return to *SmackDown*. To the delight of the fans, Cena teamed with "The Animal" Batista and Bobby Lashley to defeat King Booker and his royal cohorts, William Regal and Finlay.

Taking Mysterio out

October 20: The rivalry between Chavo Guerrero and Rey Mysterio took an intense turn when the two agreed to have an I Quit Match, which could only end when one competitor uttered the humiliating phrase "I quit." Guerrero managed to hang Mysterio upside down from a light support and hammer his knee with a steel chair, until Mysterio had no choice but to exclaim the two crucial words.

October 20: Chavo Guerrero peppers Rey Mysterio's knee with a series of vicious chair shots, forcing Mysterio to say "I quit!"

Three world champs—one match

October 27: WWE Champion John Cena and ECW Champion Big Show appeared on *SmackDown* on opposite sides of an enormous Tag Team Match. World Heavyweight Champion King Booker teamed with ECW's Big Show to face Cena and Booker's number one contender Batista. "The Animal" sent the Champion a message by leveling King Booker with a Batista Bomb and pinning his championship rival.

Losing Lashley

November 17: The competition for talent between *RAW*, *SmackDown*, and ECW was reaching fever pitch. ECW General Manager Paul Heyman was looking for a sixth competitor for his Elimination Chamber Match, and Bobby Lashley opted to jump from *SmackDown* and join ECW. Lashley stopped by during this edition to say goodbye and to thank Teddy Long for all the opportunities the GM had recently given him.

October 27: Batista pins World Heavyweight Champion King Booker T in tag team action, letting the King know that "The Animal" is ready to take back the title.

December 8: Jimmy Yang Wang takes out Jamie Noble on his way to becoming the number one contender for the Cruiserweight Championship.

Jimmy Wang Yang steps up

December 8: A No. 1 Contenders' Match between Jamie Noble and Jimmy Wang Yang was set to determine who would challenge Gregory Helms for the Cruiserweight Championship at *Armageddon* on December 17. This high-flying affair ended suddenly when Yang hit Noble with a moonsault to record the pin.

"The Brothers of Destruction" reunite

December 15: Two days before their *Armageddon* matches with Mr. Kennedy and MVP, Undertaker and Kane teamed up to face them in a Tag Team Match. The brothers gave Mr. Kennedy a devastating tandem chokeslam, but the sinister duo could not get a pinfall. The chaotic contest soon spilled out of the ring, leading to both teams being counted out.

Steel Cage surprise

November 24: After Montel Vontavious Porter (MVP) signed the largest contract in *SmackDown* history, the cocky Superstar demanded quality competition. General Manager Teddy Long obliged by putting MVP in a Steel Cage Match with the dangerously unpredictable Kane. MVP won, and since he was a new Superstar and Kane was a former WWE Champion, the victory was portrayed by the announcers as a major upset.

Double trouble for "The Animal"

December 1: Batista had recently captured the World Heavyweight Championship for a second time in his career at *Survivor Series*. The odds on him keeping the title seemed slim when he was forced to defend the title against both King Booker and Finlay. The two challengers could not get along, so Batista managed to retain his title by hitting Finlay with a spear and a Batista Bomb for the pin.

December 15: Brothers Kane and Undertaker unite to battle common enemies MVP and Mr. Kennedy.

2007

BATISTA BEGAN THE year as World Heavyweight Champion, but the show provided him with a formidable list of challengers, including Undertaker, Edge, and The Great Khali. Romance was also in the air, as General Manager Teddy Long's love affair with Kristal became an ongoing drama for the WWE Universe. Their romance culminated in Kristal accepting his marriage proposal, only for Long to suffer a massive heart attack at their wedding, just as they were about to exchange vows. Long's misfortune created an opportunity for his devious assistant, Vickie Guerrero, to become the new *SmackDown* General Manager.

January 5: Mr. Kennedy sets a time in the Beat the Clock challenge that no one can equal.

Up against the clock

January 5: *SmackDown* General Manager Teddy Long kicked off the year with a 16-Man Beat the Clock sprint challenge. Over the first two episodes of *SmackDown*, there would be eight matches. Whoever won their match in the fastest time would earn a World Heavyweight Championship shot. On this show, Mr. Kennedy won in the fastest time. No one beat his time the following week, so Kennedy won the title opportunity.

INTRODUCING...

Deuce 'n' Domino (and Cherry)

January 19: The *SmackDown* Tag Team division added Deuce 'n' Domino, a duo with a distinctly 1950s vibe, with their white T-shirts, blue jeans, and slicked-back hair. They were accompanied by their valet, Domino's sister Cherry, who wore a poodle skirt and often arrived at the ring on roller skates. Deuce 'n' Domino won their debut match and went on to win the WWE Tag Team Championship during their short stay in WWE.

Deuce 'n' Domino and Cherry arrive in style in their '57 Chevrolet convertible.

A *Royal Rumble* preview

January 26: *SmackDown* provided fans with a sneak preview of the *Royal Rumble* with a Six-Man Over the Top Rope Challenge Match. After Kane and The Miz were eliminated, the lights in the arena went down and a seventh competitor—Undertaker—appeared. He easily knocked out the remaining competitors.

January 26: Undertaker attacks King Booker during an Over the Top Rope Challenge Match.

February 9: Batista takes care of business by nailing Mr. Kennedy with a Samoan Drop.

Close but no cigar

February 9: After Mr. Kennedy lost a closely contested World Heavyweight Championship Match to Batista at the *Royal Rumble*, he was given another chance to dethrone "The Animal" on this episode. Kennedy was close to victory several times, but Batista hit back with a spear and a pin, managing to retain his title.

March 30: *SmackDown* GM Teddy Long (far right) ensures that Undertaker and Batista's in-ring encounter does not turn into a brawl by hiring extra security.

Unwilling partners

February 16: The WWE Universe was looking forward to two great championship matches at *WrestleMania*, but on this *SmackDown* episode, the title match participants were forced to act as tag teams. WWE Champion John Cena and his challenger Shawn Michaels beat Mr. Kennedy and MVP, while Batista and Undertaker beat Rated-RKO (Edge, Randy Orton, and their valet Lita).

McMahon's threatening message

February 23: This episode came from Rey Mysterio's hometown of San Diego. He took the opportunity to update the WWE Universe on his recovery from an injury that had sidelined him for months. Mr. McMahon interrupted Mysterio's announcement to threaten his future *WrestleMania* "Battle of the Billionaires" opponent, Donald Trump. McMahon sent his champion, Umaga, to beat up Mysterio, who thought Trump was going to win, in order to give his rival a taste of what to expect at *WrestleMania*.

The ECW Champion comes to *SmackDown*

March 2: ECW Champion and Donald Trump's designated Superstar in the "Battle of the Billionaires" Bobby Lashley came back to *SmackDown*. He didn't just come to show off his title—he defended it against Mr. Kennedy. It was a hard-fought battle, but Lashley managed to deliver a running powerslam and pin his persistent challenger.

"The Animal" and "The Deadman" face off

March 30: Just a few days ahead of their epic *WrestleMania* encounter for the World Heavyweight Championship, "The Animal" Batista and "The Deadman" Undertaker had a heated face-to-face confrontation. A phalanx of security men tried to keep them apart, but they repeatedly attacked each other. In the end, Batista got the upper hand by landing his Spinebuster move.

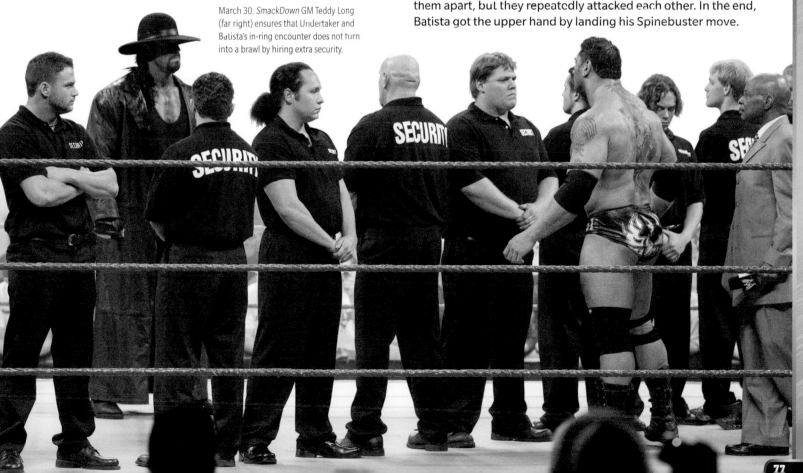

2007

May 11: Edge takes advantage of an exhausted Undertaker to cash in his Money in the Bank contract and win the World Heavyweight Championship.

"The Ultimate Opportunist" strikes

May 11: World Heavyweight Champion Undertaker and Batista fought in a Steel Cage Match. Both men escaped at the same time, meaning that Undertaker was still champion. Mark Henry then ran to the ring and attacked Undertaker, further injuring the champ. Finally, Edge, "The Ultimate Opportunist," saw his chance: Coming to the ring to cash in his Money in the Bank title opportunity, he pinned Undertaker to win the World Heavyweight Championship.

Ozzy in the house

May 18: Reality television star and former Black Sabbath frontman Ozzy Osbourne made an appearance on *SmackDown* to perform his new hit single "I Don't Want to Stop." The WWE Universe loved the performance. WWE Superstar Jillian Hall, always on the lookout for a chance to show off her vocal "talents," hoped that Ozzy would let her sing for him. Security came to Ozzy's rescue.

April 6: Undertaker makes his way to the ring with his World Heavyweight Championship.

Celebration time

April 6: On the first *SmackDown* after *WrestleMania*, two Superstars celebrated their historic wins. Mr. Kennedy bragged that he had backed up all his boasts by winning the Money in the Bank Match, and the night closed with Undertaker making his first appearance since winning the World Heavyweight Championship from Batista.

New tag team champs

April 20: Just a few months into their WWE tenure, Deuce 'n' Domino reached the pinnacle of tag team competition by winning the WWE Tag Team Championships from Paul London and Brian Kendrick. An in-match injury to London left Kendrick on his own. Their two-to-one advantage allowed Deuce 'n' Domino to make the title-winning pinfall.

May 18: Security has to step in to prevent would-be singer Jillian Hall from bothering Ozzy Osbourne.

Vickie's new job

May 25: Looking to free up some time to spend with his new girlfriend, Kristal, *SmackDown* General Manager Teddy Long decided to hire Vickie Guerrero as his assistant. She was a divisive character, and the WWE Universe was by no means happy with the choice. Over time, Long would regret his decision, too. Eventually, Vickie would take his full-time GM position, and he would be demoted to assistant GM.

May 25: Mark Henry seizes Batista outside the ring during their Fatal 4-Way Match.

A ticket for the cage

May 25: Four men thought they should be the next challenger for Edge's World Heavyweight Championship. So Teddy Long set a Fatal 4-Way Match, whereby the first man to record a decision would face Edge in a Steel Cage at *One Night Stand*. Batista delivered devastating spears to Finlay, Mark Henry, and Kane. He then flattened Finlay with a Batista Bomb to win the match and earn the opportunity.

The Chairman lets loose

June 8: Edge probably thought he'd scored a major coup when he had Mr. McMahon as a guest on his Cutting Edge interview segment. Unfortunately, the Chairman was in a bizarre mood and berated Edge, forcing him to defend his title against Batista again. Mr. McMahon also poured scorn on Teddy Long's relationship with Kristal and suspended Superstar Ashley Massaro for accidentally spilling his coffee on him.

Elsewhere in WWE

June 11: For the first time ever, a WWE draft shook up the roster of three different brands, including *RAW*, *SmackDown*, and ECW. *SmackDown* gained past and future World Champions, Ric Flair and The Great Khali, and *RAW* gained King Booker and the reigning ECW Champion Bobby Lashley.

Teddy pops the question

June 22: Amid all the chaos in WWE, *SmackDown* General Manager Teddy Long decided to take the plunge and ask his girlfriend Kristal to marry him. She did not give him an answer, fleeing the ring. However, Long caught up with her backstage, where she tried on the ring and said "Yes!"

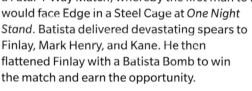

June 22: Teddy Long shares a romantic moment with the WWE Universe as he proposes to Kristal.

2007

July 20: No one looms larger than The Great Khali as 20 men fight in a Battle Royal.

Battle for the title

July 20: Kane's attack on Edge during the previous week's Mardi Gras celebration injured the champion, forcing him to relinquish the title. A 20-Man Battle Royal was held to find a new champion. Several of the competitors teamed up to eliminate Mark Henry, a former Olympic weightlifter billed as "The World's Strongest Man." In the end, The Great Khali defeated Kane and Batista to win the match and the World Heavyweight Championship.

Celebration Khali-style

July 27: A week after becoming the first Indian-born World Champion in WWE history, The Great Khali held a Punjabi-style championship celebration. Surrounded by colorful dancers, The Great Khali's advocate, Ranjin Singh, praised Khali's manifest achievements, until cut short by Batista, who demanded a match for the title.

July 13: Feeling far from festive, Kane chokeslams one of Edge's Mardi Gras celebrators.

A "monster" at the Mardi Gras

July 13: With *SmackDown* taking place in New Orleans, World Heavyweight Champion Edge celebrated his continuing reign with a Mardi Gras celebration, complete with parade characters wearing oversized *papier-maché* heads. The vibrant party was interrupted when "The Big Red Monster" Kane was revealed to be one of the characters in disguise. Only the interference of the other parade characters saved Edge from a brutal chokeslam.

July 27: The Great Khali and Ranjin Singh celebrate Khali capturing the World Heavyweight Championship.

An heir to the empire?

August 17: A week earlier, WWE Chairman Mr. McMahon had been served with a paternity suit. This not only revealed that, unbeknownst to him, he had another child; it informed him that this child was a WWE Superstar. Mr. McMahon came to *SmackDown* to see if he could find any clues to his child's identity. There were numerous suspects but no solid answers.

Elsewhere in WWE

August 26: After being sidelined for eight months with a torn quadriceps, Triple H made a triumphant return to the ring when he faced King Booker in a match to determine who was the true King of WWE. "The Game" hit Booker with a signature Pedigree move to secure the pinfall and win the match.

Rivals team together

August 31: During their extended rivalry for the United States Championship, MVP and Matt Hardy extended their battles beyond the ring, trying to one-up each other at arm wrestling, boxing, basketball, even pie eating. They briefly put their differences aside to team up and defeat Deuce 'n' Domino for the WWE Tag Team Championship.

A Belfast Brawl decider

September 14: Finlay and Kane had each won a match during their ongoing rivalry, so they met in a Belfast Brawl to settle their issues. The first time it was held, the Belfast Brawl had no countouts or disqualifications—it had to be settled with a pinfall or submission. Finlay nailed Kane with a chair and pinned "The Big Red Monster" with a signature Celtic Cross move.

"I love Kristal more than anything in the whole world."

Teddy Long (September 21, 2007)

Wedding bells for Teddy

September 21: The WWE Universe and the Superstars of *RAW*, *SmackDown*, and ECW were invited to the wedding of Teddy Long and Kristal. Jillian Hall tried to ruin things with her awful singing, and the sleazy Godfather tried to tempt Teddy to go partying, but he remained steadfastly committed to his bride. Then, just as he was about to say "I do," he suffered a massive heart attack!

September 21: Tragedy strikes when *SmackDown* GM Teddy Long collapses at his own wedding.

September 28: New GM Vickie Guerrero is all smiles as she welcomes Hornswoggle into her office.

Vickie gets a promotion

September 28: With Teddy Long still in a coma from the heart attack he suffered the week before, Mr. McMahon needed a new General Manager to keep *SmackDown* going. He selected Teddy's by now highly unpopular assistant, Vickie Guerrero—a choice that the WWE Universe loudly disagreed with.

INTRODUCING...

Drew McIntyre

October 12: On his WWE debut, Drew McIntyre faced former Tag Team Champion Brett Major. Thanks to McIntyre's partner, Dave Taylor, causing a distraction by decking Major's partner, Brian Major, McIntyre pinned Brett. Mr. McMahon declared McIntyre a future world champion, but it would take almost ten years—August 2017—for the popular Scotsman to achieve championship gold. McIntyre has also won the Intercontinental Championship, the WWE Tag Team Championship, and the NXT Championship in his WWE career.

Drew McIntyre initially trumpeted his Scottish roots by wearing a kilt to the ring.

> ## "I can feel my heart beating in my throat, but I'm so confident."
>
> Eve (October 26, 2007)

Diva Search finale

October 26: The 2007 Diva Search was reaching its dramatic conclusion. The last two contestants—Eve and Brooke—had one last chance to make their case for selection by explaining why the WWE Universe should not vote for the other competitor. The WWE Universe ultimately agreed with Eve and selected her as the contest's winner.

A partial announcer

November 2: World Heavyweight Champion Batista and Undertaker put their differences aside to battle the powerful duo of Mark Henry and The Great Khali. The unlikely partners seemed ready to put Henry and Khali down when announcer John "Bradshaw" Layfield, a.k.a. JBL, joined in, hitting Batista with a Clothesline From Hell and delivering a low blow to Undertaker.

November 2: Mark Henry and The Great Khali triumph over Undertaker and Batista.

Double trouble for the champ

November 30: Edge was given a World Heavyweight Championship Match by acting *SmackDown* General Manager (and also his girlfriend) Vickie Guerrero. The match ended in a no contest when Undertaker interfered and attacked both men. Teddy Long then returned to resume his GM role, announcing that Batista would defend his title against Edge and Undertaker at *Armageddon*.

Last demon standing

December 14: In advance of his Triple Threat Match for the World Heavyweight Championship against Undertaker and Edge, Batista was forced to face Kane in a Last Man Standing Match. Edge interfered to try to help Kane win the match, but Batista leveled Kane with a Spinebuster through the announcers' table to win the match.

December 14: Batista delivers a devastating Spinebuster to Kane right onto the announcers' table.

"I'm about to announce the biggest comeback since the Resurrection!"

JBL (December 21, 2007)

November 16: The Miz and John Morrison take advantage of the dysfunctional pairing of MVP and Matt Hardy to win the WWE Tag Team Championship.

New Tag Team Champions

November 16: Despite their ongoing rivalry in singles competition, MVP and Matt Hardy successfully defended the WWE Tag Team Championship. They finally lost their titles in a defense against ECW Superstars John Morrison and The Miz. MVP immediately demanded a rematch after the loss and The Miz and Morrison managed to defend their titles when MVP turned on Hardy.

JBL's farewell address

December 21: JBL decided to stop announcing *SmackDown* and return to the ring. However, he proclaimed that his in-ring comeback would not be on *SmackDown*, but on *RAW*. JBL wanted to get revenge on *RAW* Superstar Chris Jericho for bumping into him during Jericho's last pay-per-view match.

2008

LOVE AND HATE were in the air in 2008—and most of those emotions revolved around *SmackDown*'s power couple, Edge and Vickie Guerrero. The romance and eventual marriage of the "Rated R Superstar" and Guerrero played out on *SmackDown* over the year, as did Edge's intense rivalries with Batista, Undertaker, Triple H, and Jeff Hardy for the World Heavyweight and WWE Championships. Undertaker also had his share of epic battles with the "World's Largest Athlete," Big Show. The women's competition received a shot of extra intensity in 2008 with the addition of *SmackDown*'s own championship, the Divas Championship, and the introduction of three future champions: Natalya, Brie Bella, and Nikki Bella.

Mysterio beats the clock

January 4: For the second straight year, *SmackDown* began with a beat-the-clock challenge to determine who would face the World Heavyweight Champion at the *Royal Rumble*. Thanks to interference by Edge and the Edgeheads in Batista's and Undertaker's matches, it looked like Finlay's time would be the best. However, Rey Mysterio managed to win his match against Edge two minutes faster and so nabbed the title opportunity.

January 4: Rey Mysterio leaps from the top rope to land on Edge.

Tough love

January 11: Ever since Mr. McMahon discovered that Hornswoggle was his illegitimate child, he had decided to show his diminutive son some tough love by forcing him to fight the gigantic Great Khali on numerous occasions. On this episode, Hornswoggle had to arm wrestle Khali's interpreter, Ranjin Singh. Luckily, Hornswoggle's regular ally Finlay was looking out for him and helped him to win.

January 11: Hornswoggle arm wrestles with Ranjin Singh in an attempt to impress his father, Mr. McMahon.

February 1: Ric Flair battles MVP to hold on to his WWE career.

Just holding on

February 1: After falling out with WWE Chairman Mr. McMahon, Ric Flair's career was hanging by a thread. In November 2007, Mr. McMahon mandated that the next match Flair lost would force "The Nature Boy" to retire. MVP was the latest Superstar to try to retire Flair, but "The Nature Boy" won their match by disqualification when MVP refused to release a submission hold.

Love is in the air but so is pain

February 15: Edge had planned the perfect in-ring romantic night with Vickie Guerrero, a night that he hoped would end with him popping the question and Vickie saying "Yes!" Rey Mysterio interrupted the love fest to express his disgust with their union. The two Superstars clashed, and then Mysterio accidently landed a West Coast Pop maneuver on Guerrero, knocking her out cold.

February 15: Rey Mysterio's West Coast Pop maneuver has an unintended victim, Vickie Guerrero.

Hall of Fame generations

February 29: Winner of the 2007 Diva Search Eve Torres gave the WWE Universe a scoop, letting them know that the next two inductees into the 2008 WWE Hall of Fame would be High Chief Peter Maivia and Rocky Johnson, The Rock's grandfather and father. It was also announced that The Rock would be attending the ceremony to personally induct both men.

Steel cage peril

March 14: Less than a month before Shawn Michaels and Ric Flair were set to face off at *WrestleMania XXIV* in Ric Flair's final match, the two were forced to team up and face Edge, the Edgeheads, and Chavo Guerrero in a 4-on-2 Handicap Steel Cage Match. Undertaker appeared to try to even the odds, but the numbers were too great, and Edge escaped the cage to win the match for his side.

> "There's nothing I hate more than a loudmouth, braggart, blowhard buffoon... with his own talk show!"

Chris Jericho (March 21, 2008)

March 21: Chris Jericho returns to *SmackDown*.

The return of Y2J

March 21: *SmackDown* viewers had not seen Chris Jericho on the show for more than five years. "Y2J" made a triumphant return as the guest on MVP's talk show, The VIP Lounge. They started with some verbal sparring—MVP claiming that Jericho's return had been a failure and Jericho mocking MVP's name. Things then turned physical, and Jericho tipped over a ladder with MVP on it.

Money in the Bank preview

March 28: CM Punk and John Morrison, ECW Superstars set to compete in the Money in the Bank Ladder Match at *WrestleMania XXIV*, met in a one-on-one encounter. Morrison had Punk on the ropes early with his unique offense, but Punk fought back and managed to hit Morrison with his Go to Sleep signature move to secure the three count.

April 4: Batista berates Shawn Michaels for his role in "Nature Boy" Ric Flair's retirement.

Batista's rage

April 4: An emotional Shawn Michaels came to address the *SmackDown* audience about the recent *WrestleMania* match in which he defeated Ric Flair, forcing "Nature Boy" to retire. Before Michaels could explain himself, Batista interrupted. Batista was furious that Michaels beat Flair and argued that Michaels' huge ego prevented him from doing the right thing—letting Flair win and continue his WWE career.

INTRODUCING...

Natalya

April 4: A mysterious woman appeared to help Victoria decimate Cherry and Michelle McCool, the two finalists in *SmackDown's* Diva competition. The WWE Universe soon learned that her name was Natalya and that she was a member of the famous Hart family. In the decade that followed, Natalya won two championships.

Natalya jumps into the action to help Victoria.

April 25: Undertaker pummels Batista in a brutal No Disqualification Title Match.

Softening up the Champion

April 25: Just days before Undertaker was set to defend the World Heavyweight Championship against Edge at *Backlash*, *SmackDown* General Manager, and Edge's fiancée, Vickie Guerrero forced him to face Batista in a No Disqualification Title Match. Both men took advantage of the no-disqualification stipulation, and it seemed Batista was sure to win after he performed a Batista Bomb on the ring steps. But Shawn Michaels ran in and Superkicked Batista, allowing Undertaker to get the pinfall victory.

Three titles, one night

May 2: Assistant General Manager Teddy Long opened this action-packed episode by announcing that three titles—the WWE Tag Team Championship, the United States Championship, and the World Heavyweight Championship—would all be defended that night. The Miz and John Morrison retained their Tag Team Titles against Jimmy Wang Yang and Shannon More, and Matt Hardy retained the United States Championship vs. MVP. The World Heavyweight Title Match never happened because General Manager Vickie Guerrero stripped Undertaker of his title.

The right to fight

May 9: After stripping Undertaker of the World Heavyweight Championship the week before, *SmackDown* General Manager Vickie Guerrero began to arrange a match for the title. She determined that Undertaker would be one participant and set a Championship Chase to decide the other competitor. Batista thought that he had earned the spot after a grueling Over the Top Rope Battle Royal; however, Edge entered at the last minute and won the title opportunity.

High stakes in TLC

May 31: Edge's interview segment The Cutting Edge had a first-time guest—Undertaker. The two were set to meet in a TLC Match for the World Heavyweight Championship at the *One Night Stand* event on June 1, with the stipulation that if Undertaker lost, he would be banned from WWE. Undertaker had no interest in talking—he just wanted to get his hands on Edge. However, the remaining members of the La Familia villainous alliance—Chavo Guerrero, Curt Hawkins, Zack Ryder, and Bam Neely—then entered the ring and overwhelmed Undertaker.

Cousin Sal takes to the ring

June 6: A rivalry between "Rowdy" Roddy Piper, Santino Marella, and *Jimmy Kimmel Live* comedian Cousin Sal, in which cake was thrown in Marella's face, twice, led to a match between Cousin Sal and Santino on *SmackDown*. Marella promised to embarrass the novice competitor, but, thanks to ringside distractions from Jimmy Kimmel and Piper, Sal was able to roll up Santino for a surprise pinfall victory.

June 27: World Heavyweight Champion Edge and WWE Champion Triple H engage in a war of words.

Roster of champions

June 27: The 2008 WWE Draft was good for *SmackDown*. The blue brand added Jeff Hardy, Mr. Kennedy, Umaga, and Hall of Fame announcer Jim Ross, but the real coup was adding WWE Champion Triple H. This meant that *SmackDown* had both Edge, the World Heavyweight Champion, and Triple H, the WWE Champion, at the same time. When the two champions came face to face, it soon became clear that amicable coexistence was off the menu.

June 6: "Rowdy" Roddy Piper and Jimmy Kimmel hold up Cousin Sal's arms in victory after his surprise win.

2008

Dreaming big

July 4: With *RAW* claiming the WWE Women's Championship, *SmackDown* General Manager Vickie Guerrero thought it was high time the female competitors of *SmackDown* had a title of their own. Natalya had already earned her place in a match to crown the inaugural Divas Champion, and a Golden Dreams Match was held to determine her opponent. Michelle McCool outbattled five other competitors to earn the spot.

"Hell hath no fury over a woman scorned!"

Vickie Guerrero (July 18, 2008)

July 18: Vickie Guerrero screams when the Hardys and Triple H destroy her wedding reception.

Wedding chaos

July 18: This episode was all about the wedding of Edge and Vickie Guerrero. Their wedding ceremony happened earlier in the day, so the entire show was their wedding reception. Inevitably, things did not go smoothly—the Hardys ruined the wedding cake and Triple H showed a hidden camera video of Edge making out with wedding planner Alicia Fox. Vickie was outraged!

July 25: Dejected, Edge comes to terms with the fact that he will have to face Undertaker at *SummerSlam*.

Vickie's revenge

July 25: Edge attempted to publicly apologize to his new wife for his infidelity with their wedding planner. Vickie almost seemed prepared to forgive him, but then confessed that she had done something crazy in her anger—she had reinstated Undertaker, and Edge would have to face "The Deadman" at *SummerSlam* in a Hell in a Cell Match.

Elsewhere in WWE

August 17: *SummerSlam* 2008 was packed with incredible moments and matches for the WWE Universe. For the first time, Batista and John Cena clashed in one-on-one competition, a match won by Batista. Edge would probably rather forget the event, as not only did he lose a Hell in a Cell Match to Undertaker, but "The Deadman" chokeslammed Edge off a ladder, through the ring, and straight to hell.

INTRODUCING...

The Bella Twins

August 29: In her debut match, a rookie by the name of Brie Bella shocked the highly experienced Victoria. After being thrown out of the ring, Brie escaped under it. Victoria dragged her out, seeking a seemingly certain victory. However, to Victoria's amazement, Brie was suddenly all energy and pinned her. This pattern would be repeated for weeks, until it was revealed that, beneath the ring, Brie was switching places with her identical twin sister, Nikki. The Bella Twins became a fixture in women's competition over the years, winning three championships between them.

Brie Bella enters the ring in her debut match.

Lumberjack scramble

September 5: Just days before he would defend the WWE Championship in a Championship Scramble at *Unforgiven*, Triple H had to face The Great Khali in a Lumberjack Match. The other four competitors in the upcoming Scramble Match were Lumberjacks. Despite most of the Lumberjacks favoring Khali, Triple H managed to give the giant a Pedigree finishing move to win.

September 5: Triple H faces off with The Great Khali in their Lumberjack Match.

New Tag Team Champions

September 26: The Colon Brothers (Carlito and Primo) had only been competing as a tag team on *SmackDown* for a few weeks, but they made the most of their opportunities and gained a title opportunity against Hawkins and Ryder. The reigning champions controlled most of the match, until Primo cleverly tagged in Carlito without Zack Ryder noticing. Carlito caught Ryder unaware and pinned Ryder to win the titles.

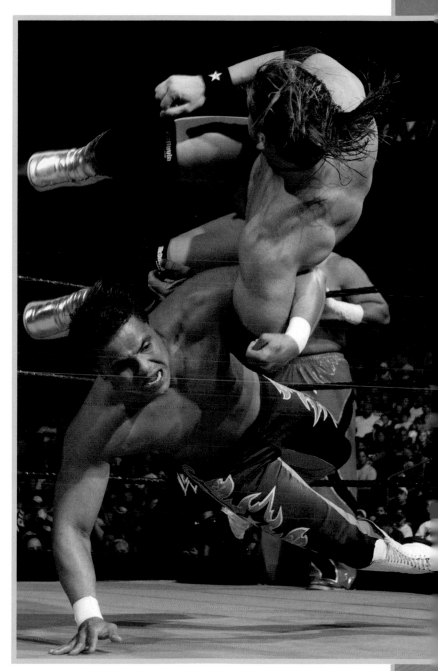

September 26: Primo (from The Colon Brothers) takes down Curt Hawkins.

New network, huge show

October 3: To celebrate the first show on its new television home, MyNetworkTV, Superstars from *RAW*, ECW, and *SmackDown* competed in all-star Champion vs. Champion Matches. WWE Champion Triple H upheld the honor of *SmackDown* by defeating World Heavyweight Champion Chris Jericho and ECW Champion Matt Hardy in a Triple Threat Match.

2008

Divas Las Vegas

October 17: With *SmackDown* emanating from the city of Las Vegas, General Manager Vickie Guerrero decided to set up a Vegas Match to determine the number one contender for the Divas Championship. Five Superstars competed in the match, in which the first competitor to grab a pair of fuzzy pink dice hanging off a pole would win. In the end, Maria was able to outwit the competition and earn the title opportunity.

The Khali Kiss Cam

October 24: The WWE Universe got to see a very different side of The Great Khali in this episode. The giant and his interpreter talked about all the letters from women wanting to kiss the "Punjabi Playboy." The duo then launched the Khali Kiss Cam, which located women in the audience looking for a smooch from The Great Khali.

Halloween horror

October 31: On this special Halloween edition, Chavo Guerrero saw his nightmares come true when he had to face Undertaker in a Casket Match. Undertaker's rival Big Show appeared at the top of the entrance ramp, but his interference only seemed to anger "The Deadman," who nailed Guerrero with a Tombstone Piledriver and rolled him into the casket for the victory.

October 31: Undertaker rolls Chavo Guerrero into a casket in order to win his match.

"What a baleful contest for the anatomies of both these two magnificent athletes!"

Commentator Jim Ross (December 5, 2008)

Settling matters in a steel cage
December 5: The months-long rivalry between Big Show and Undertaker came to a head in this Steel Cage grudge match. Big Show repeatedly slammed Undertaker into the unforgiving walls of the cage and leveled Undertaker with a Superplex. But "The Deadman" would not stay down; he locked Big Show in a Hell's Gate submission maneuver, forcing him to tap out.

Street Fight epic
December 12: At *Armageddon*, both Triple H and Jeff Hardy were set to challenge Edge for the WWE Championship. However, the two challengers seemed more interested in tearing each other apart than getting their hands on the champion. So *SmackDown* General Manager Guerrero set up a Street Fight between the two of them. The action soon spilled out of the ring, but Edge himself then interfered, resulting in a no contest draw.

November 21: Brie and Nikki Bella wave to the crowd as they arrive for their debut Tag Team Match.

Twin magic
November 21: For weeks, Brie Bella had been tricking her opponents and winning matches by secretly switching places with her twin sister, Nikki. Once their ruse was discovered, the twins decided to pair up in tag team matches. In their debut match, they defeated Victoria and Natalya.

Elsewhere in WWE

November 23: John Cena suffered a herniated disc in his *SummerSlam* encounter with Batista, and normally that kind of injury leads to six months of rehab. However, Cena made a miraculous comeback and, less than three months later, defeated Chris Jericho for the World Heavyweight Championship at *Survivor Series*.

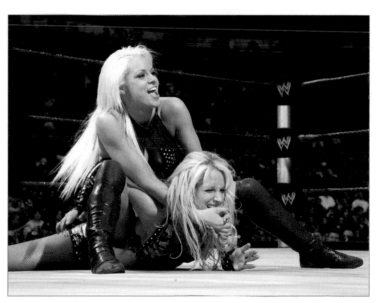

December 26: Maryse grips Michelle McCool in a painful submission hold.

A new Divas champion
December 26: Michelle McCool had held the Divas Championship since July, but she was scheduled to defend the title against Maryse, with Maria serving as special guest referee. Michelle thought that she had won the match and chose to argue with the official about a two count, allowing Maryse to catch the distracted champ with a kick to the head, get a three count, and become the new Divas Champion.

2009

A QUESTION EVERYONE was asking in 2009 was "Who is the face of *SmackDown*?" As past holders of the World Heavyweight Championship for extended periods of time, Edge, CM Punk, and Undertaker thought they could make that claim, but others, such as fan favorites Jeff Hardy, Rey Mysterio, and Triple H, and the egomaniacal Chris Jericho thought themselves worthy as well. It was clear that some people would do anything to reach the top, as the year was bookended by a pair of shocking betrayals. At the beginning of the year, Matt Hardy turned on his brother, Jeff, and, at the year's end, Batista threw away his friendship with Rey Mysterio.

January 2: Michelle McCool blindsides her former friend Eve after Eve lets her guard down.

McCool loses her cool
January 2: A week after attacking her former friend Maria, Michelle McCool apologized to Maria as well as to backstage interviewer Eve Torres. However, her apology was as fake as McCool's friendship with Eve. McCool kicked and punched Eve as she was leaving the ring and then slammed her into the guard rail and ring apron.

Triple duty for "The Game"
January 9: The WWE Universe had enjoyed Triple H mocking *SmackDown* General Manager Vickie Guerrero on the first episode of 2009, but she got her revenge by forcing him to compete in three matches on the same show. He beat John Morrison in a Tables Match and outlasted The Miz and Chavo Guerrero in a Handicap Match; however, Big Show finally took out "The Game" in a Last Man Standing Match with his Knockout Punch finisher.

WWE Champion Jeff Hardy and his girlfriend Beth were the victims of an accident earlier in the week when an unknown assailant drove their car off the road. Hardy promised to return to *SmackDown* the following week, ready to defend his WWE title at the *Royal Rumble* against Edge.

"If my survival means Jeff's total destruction, then so be it!"

Matt Hardy (January 30, 2009)

A brother's betrayal

January 30: For months, Jeff Hardy had suffered attacks by an unknown individual, and most of the WWE Universe assumed that Edge was the perpetrator. The truth, however, was far more chilling. Jeff's brother Matt explained to the WWE Universe that he was tired of looking after his younger sibling and that he'd turned against him, most recently by causing Jeff to lose the WWE Championship to Edge at the *Royal Rumble* on January 25.

Clearing the Chamber

February 6: Vladimir Kozlov, undefeated in singles competition, was able to outlast 15 other competitors to win an Over the Top Battle Royal and earn a spot in the Elimination Chamber Match for the WWE Championship. Kozlov gave a dominant performance, single-handedly eliminating the last four competitors: The Great Khali, Primo, Carlito, and R-Truth.

February 13. The Miz and Morrison win the right to take the Bella Twins out on Valentine's Day

Battling for a Valentine's Day date

February 13: Two months before they would battle at *WrestleMania XXV* to unify the World and WWE Tag Team Championships, The Miz and Morrison faced off against Carlito and Primo for very different stakes—the right to take the Bella Twins on a Valentine's Day date. To the Bellas' disappointment, The Miz and Morrison defeated the Colon brothers to win the match and the date!

"You've crossed the line, Orton. One you can't come back from!"

Triple H (February 20, 2009)

Orton out of order

February 20: Winning the *Royal Rumble* earned Randy Orton a shot at the WWE Championship at *WrestleMania* against Triple H, but Orton made the battle intensely personal by physically attacking Triple H's father-in-law, Mr. McMahon, and his brother-in-law, Shane McMahon, as well as "putting his hands" on his wife, Stephanie McMahon. Interviewed by commentator Jim Ross, Triple H promised that Orton would face the gravest consequences for harming the mother of his children.

MVP gets the title back

March 20: For most of the previous two years, the United States Championship was held either by MVP or Shelton Benjamin. Benjamin risked his eight-month reign by defending the title against MVP, who had held it for almost a year in 2007 and 2008. MVP won the title a second time by hitting Benjamin with his Playmaker finisher and following up by pinning him.

February 6: Vladimir Kozlov celebrates the victory that earns him a spot in the Elimination Chamber.

March 27: Shawn Michaels continues his mind games with his *WrestleMania* opponent Undertaker, dressing like him, but all in white.

The anti-Undertaker

March 27: The WWE Universe was expecting a dramatic Undertaker entrance, but instead of dark druids lining a path for the man in black, the druids and their accompanying Superstar were clad in white—Shawn Michaels was appearing as the anti-Undertaker. He then explained the ways he and his *WrestleMania* opponent were similar, and also their crucial differences, which he said would lead to the end of Undertaker's *WrestleMania* streak.

April 10: John Cena tries to goad Edge into starting a physical altercation with him.

> "I hate you! Hate is a strong word, but it sums up everything I feel for you, Cena!"
>
> Edge (April 10, 2009)

On Edge's list

April 10: On his first Cutting Edge interview show since losing his World Heavyweight Championship at *WrestleMania 25*, Edge had John Cena as his guest. It was a bitter pill for the host to swallow as he shared a laundry list of reasons why he hated John Cena, including the fact that Cena had the most important thing in the world to Edge—the World Championship.

April 24: Shane McMahon and Batista come together to defeat the Legacy in tag team action.

Batista beats Rhodes, Big Show floors Undertaker

April 24: The McMahon family gained a valuable ally in Batista for their ongoing war with Randy Orton and his Legacy teammates. Batista teamed with Shane McMahon against Cody Rhodes and Ted DiBiase. There was a rocky moment when Shane crashed into Batista on the apron, but "The Animal" stayed focused and planted Rhodes to the mat, allowing McMahon to capture the pin.

This year, the WWE draft sent Big Show to *RAW* but, before leaving, he promised to defeat Undertaker in his last *SmackDown* match. Undertaker tried his Old School maneuver, but Big Show countered with a thunderous right hand and then followed up with another to win.

A slap from Sherri Sheppard

May 1: MVP had a famous admirer in his corner when talk show *The View*'s co-host, Sherri Sheppard, accompanied him to the ring for his United States Championship defense against Dolph Ziggler. Sheppard certainly helped MVP's cause by arguing with Ziggler and even slapping his face, giving the champ time to recover from Ziggler's attacks. MVP then knocked away a dropkick and nailed Ziggler with his signature Playmaker to retain his title.

May 1: Sherri Sheppard, wearing a stylish robe, accompanies MVP to the ring for his title match against Dolph Ziggler.

No one owns the blue brand

May 15: The show opened with Chris Jericho and Edge arguing that they were *SmackDown*'s biggest stars, so General Manager Teddy Long decided they should settle matters with a match. Nothing was settled, however, as the encounter descended into chaos and was called a no contest, thanks to Jericho using a steel chair and interference from Jeff Hardy, CM Punk, Umaga, and Rey Mysterio.

Getting the better of Layla

May 29: The ongoing rivalry between Eve Torres and Layla was becoming rather one-sided. Eve had bested Layla in a Dance Off and an Arm Wrestling Match (on May 1 and May 8, respectively). When they met this time, Layla hoped to get some revenge. She hit Eve with a cross body, but Eve rolled through it to pin Layla and continue her dominant streak in encounters between the two.

May 29: Layla drives a knee into the small of Eve's back—but Eve later bounces back to win the match.

2009

June 5: Both Edge and Jeff Hardy are willing to add a degree of risk to their verbal confrontation by holding it high above the ring.

Ladder confrontation

June 5: Just days before their Ladder Match for their World Heavyweight Championship, Edge, the Champion, invited his challenger, Jeff Hardy, onto his Cutting Edge talk show. Hardy was willing to talk, but it had to be atop a 15-foot (4.6-meter) high ladder. Hardy regretted this precondition when Edge hit him with his title and sent him crashing to the ring below.

Cash-in success

June 12: CM Punk was looking to celebrate his newly won World Heavyweight Championship with the WWE Universe, but they sided with Jeff Hardy, who came out demanding a rematch for the title. Hardy was not the only one looking to challenge Punk that night—Edge also wanted his contractual rematch for the title as well. But Punk would face neither. Edge and Hardy were forced to face each other that night, a bout Edge won via disqualification.

June 12: CM Punk proudly displays his title, but the WWE Universe is in no mood to celebrate with him.

Evaluating the General Manager

June 26: Mr. McMahon's appearance on *SmackDown* was bad news for General Manager Teddy Long. The Chairman of WWE insisted that Long needed to impress him with his decisions. As a main event, Long set up a Cage Match involving Edge, Chris Jericho, Rey Mysterio, and Jeff Hardy, with CM Punk as special guest referee. The WWE Universe loved the frantic action, but Mr. McMahon told Long he was on probation.

Elsewhere in WWE

June 29: During his brief ownership of RAW, Donald Trump introduced the concept of rotating guest General Managers. Each week, a new celebrity from music, movies, sports, or more would come in and run the show for the night. Throughout 2009, guest GMs included Shaquille O'Neal, Snoop Dogg, Mark Cuban, Timbaland, and more.

July 3: At first, CM Punk and Jeff Hardy work together in their tag team match, but their animosity soon emerges.

My rival, my partner

July 3: Despite the intense rivalry between CM Punk and Jeff Hardy over the World Heavyweight Championship, *SmackDown* General Manager Long decided to shake things up by forcing them to team up against the Unified Tag Team Champions, Edge and Chris Jericho. At first, Punk and Hardy managed to surprise the WWE Universe by working well together, but their teamwork soon broke down, and Hardy abandoned Punk, who was then Speared and pinned by Edge.

Intercontinental rivals

July 10: Chris Jericho was already sporting two titles as one half of the Unified Tag Team Champions, but he was looking to add a third by challenging Rey Mysterio for the Intercontinental Championship. Jericho tried to make the most of his size advantage, but Mysterio used his speed to hit Jericho with a variety of aerial moves, eventually pinning "Y2J" with a top-rope springboard moonsault.

New partner wanted

July 17: Edge ruptured his Achilles tendon, sidelining him for months. Rather than feel sympathy for his tag team partner's injury, Chris Jericho lambasted Edge for being their championship team's weak link. Jericho refused to forfeit his Unified Tag Team Championship, vowing to find a stronger partner than Edge.

Kane's mind games

August 14: Wanting to knock the massive Great Khali off his game in advance of their *SummerSlam* encounter, Kane kidnapped his interpreter, Ranjin Singh (who it turned out, was actually Khali's brother). Kane mentally tortured Singh, forcing Khali to seek him out. Once Khali found his brother, Kane ambushed Khali with a lead pipe.

July 10: Rey Mysterio drives his body into a prone Chris Jericho during his successful title defense.

September 4: John Morrison hits his Starship Pain maneuver en route to defeating Rey Mysterio.

Morrison's starship to the title

September 4: John Morrison, "The Shaman of Sexy," was given the opportunity to snare gold when he was granted a shot at Rey Mysterio's Intercontinental Championship. The two traded spectacular moves in and out of the ring, and there were numerous near falls. Finally Morrison managed to nail Mysterio with Starship Pain and record the pin, becoming the new champion.

Batista's choice and Long's wild ride

September 18: Batista's *RAW* contract had expired, making him a free agent. For "The Animal," choosing which brand to sign with was a no-brainer—he wanted to return to *SmackDown*. Chris Jericho arrogantly confronted him on his first day back, claiming he was "the base" of *SmackDown*. Batista responded by saying, "To be the Man, you've got to beat the Man." Batista had the last laugh, using a Batista Bomb to defeat Jericho that same night.

After being part of a conspiracy that robbed Undertaker of the World Heavyweight Championship at *Breaking Point*, Teddy Long was fearful that "The Deadman" would seek revenge. The *SmackDown* General Manager's instincts were correct. When Teddy looked to leave the arena in his limo, Undertaker was behind the wheel, and he took Long for a terrifying ride.

Welcome to the future

September 25: Mr. McMahon has always had an eye for talent, and he was sure he'd identified a future World Champion—*SmackDown*'s Drew McIntyre. The WWE Universe did not think much of Mr. McMahon's proclamation and neither did R-Truth, who came down to the ring and brawled with the arrogant Scot. It took three referees to pull them apart.

August 28: Jeff Hardy tries to escape the cage, but CM Punk hangs on to him.

Loser Leaves

August 28: The rivalry between CM Punk and Jeff Hardy extended beyond the World Heavyweight Championship and became intensely personal over their very different lifestyle choices. It was clear that *SmackDown* wasn't big enough for both of them, so the two were set to meet in a Steel Cage Match, where the winner got the title and the loser was forced to leave *SmackDown*. Punk successfully defended his title and sent Hardy packing.

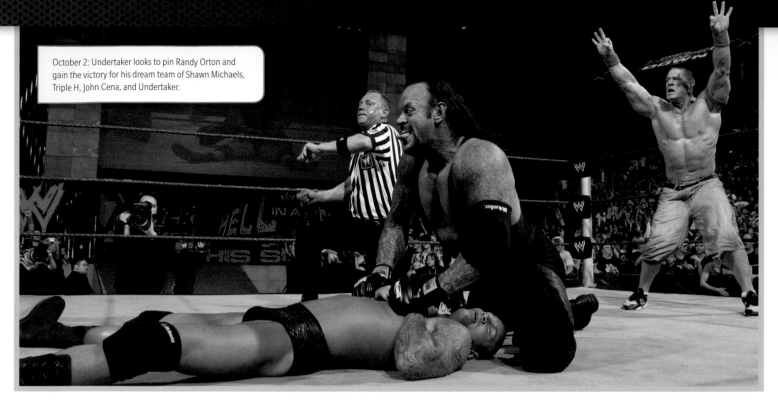

October 2: Undertaker looks to pin Randy Orton and gain the victory for his dream team of Shawn Michaels, Triple H, John Cena, and Undertaker.

"Finally, on the show he started, the show he put on the map, the show that was named after him... Finally, The Rock has come back to *SmackDown*!"

The Rock (October 2, 2009)

Tenth anniversary spectacular

October 2: To honor ten years of *SmackDown*, WWE celebrated in and out of the ring. Not only did a party rage all night, The Rock delivered a taped interview highlighting the blue brand's first decade. To close the show, the team of Undertaker, John Cena, Shawn Michaels, and Triple H defeated a quartet of CM Punk, Randy Orton, Ted DiBiase Jr., and Cody Rhodes in the most star-studded Eight-Man Tag Team Match in *SmackDown* history.

Meet Team *SmackDown*

October 16: *SmackDown* needed a team to face the *RAW* squad at *Bragging Rights*. Teddy Long made Chris Jericho captain, but Kane decided that he would be co-captain with Jericho. The other five spots were decided by qualifying matches during the night. They went to Dolph Ziggler, Cryme Tyme, Eric Escobar, and Drew McIntyre, although all five were replaced the following week, by Finlay, R-Truth, Matt Hardy, and the Hart Dynasty.

A sudden reverse

October 23: CM Punk challenged Undertaker in a Submission Match for the World Heavyweight Championship, and things didn't look good for "The Deadman," as Punk had his own hand-picked officials, Scott Armstrong and Teddy Long, at ringside. The plan seemed to be working when Punk slammed Undertaker repeatedly with a chair, but before Punk could make him tap out to his Anaconda Vice, Undertaker reversed it into a Hell's Gate and recorded a submission victory to retain the title.

October 23: Despite a stacked deck, Undertaker retains the World Heavyweight Championship.

2009

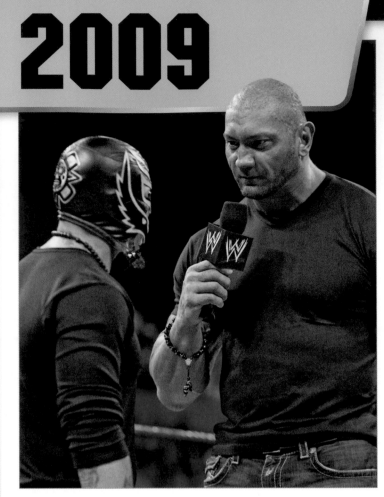

October 30: Batista refuses to explain himself to his former friend Rey Mysterio.

Batista's betrayal

October 30: Rey Mysterio came to *SmackDown* looking for answers. His former best friend, Batista, had recently betrayed and attacked him after a match in which they both failed to defeat Undertaker for the World Heavyweight Championship. Instead of giving reasons for his behavior, Batista came to the ring and threatened to hurt Mysterio again, unless he went away.

Battling the brothers

November 20: The Brothers of Destruction, Kane and Undertaker, reunited to face Unified Tag Team Champions Jeri-Show in a non-title match. Jericho and Big Show isolated Kane, working over "The Big Red Monster" and preventing him from tagging in Undertaker. The action spilled out of the ring, and, when it was clear that the official had completely lost control, the match ended as a no contest.

November 20: Chris Jericho finds himself in the unenviable position of being stuck between Kane and Undertaker.

INTRODUCING...

Luke Gallows

November 27: CM Punk, looking to promote his Straight Edge Society—whose members had to forswear smoking, drinking, and drugs—introduced the WWE Universe to Luke Gallows, his disciple. Formerly known as Festus, Gallows became a devoted follower of Punk and the first member of Punk's cult. Freed from Punk's influence, Gallows would later form a successful tag team partnership with Karl Anderson that won championships around the world, including the *RAW* Tag Team Championships in 2017.

CM Punk claims that his Straight Edge Society has turned Luke Gallows' life around.

Mickie Grabs Her Chance

December 4: A Triple Threat Match was set to determine the number one contender for Michelle McCool's Women's Championship. Natalya, Mickie James, and Beth Phoenix were all ready to win the match and claim the opportunity. Phoenix thought she had the match won when she hit Natalya with her Glam Slam, but the opportunistic James drop-kicked Phoenix out of the ring and pinned Natalya to earn the title opportunity.

December 4: Beth Phoenix looks to dominate both Mickie James and Natalya and become the number one contender for the Women's Championship.

Street-fighting men

December 11: Former best friends Batista and Rey Mysterio met in a Street Fight. Batista may have thought his massive size and power would give him a decisive advantage, but Rey used his speed to keep Batista out of the ring and off his feet. The tide eventually turned when Batista assaulted Rey with the ring steps, a camera cable, and even the announcers' desk. Back in the ring, Batista blasted Rey with a steel chair to win the match.

December 25: D-Generation X gets into the holiday spirit with their unofficial mascot, Hornswoggle.

A DX Christmas, and Mysterio takes on Undertaker

December 25: D-Generation X—Shawn Michaels and Triple H—gave the WWE Universe a bonus Christmas present by defending their Unified Tag Team Championships against the Hart Dynasty. A combination of a Sweet Chin Music move from Michaels and a Triple H Pedigree on David Hart Smith allowed the duo to snag the victory and retain the titles. Official D-X mascot Hornswoggle then joined them in the ring for a holiday celebration.

A week after beating Batista to become the number one contender for the World Heavyweight Championship, Rey Mysterio looked to record another defeat of a much larger opponent—the Champion, Undertaker. Mysterio tried to gain an advantage with hit-and-run moves, but Undertaker—124 lbs (56.2 kg) the heavier man—grabbed Mysterio and tossed him around like a rag doll. Mysterio briefly changed the momentum, but "The Deadman" had the contest in his pocket, until Batista interfered and attacked Undertaker. Mysterio leveled both men with his 619 kick, and the match ended in a disqualification.

October 2, 2009: After forming a star-studded team with John Cena and D-Generation X, Undertaker celebrates his team's victory over CM Punk, Randy Orton, and Legacy.

2010

THROUGHOUT 2010, the WWE Universe was consistently amazed to see how ruthless Superstars were prepared to be to attain their goals. Whether it was CM Punk expanding his cultlike Straight Edge Society, Kane attacking his own brother Undertaker in order to put him out of commission, Alberto Del Rio injuring in-ring competitors, or Dolph Ziggler dating *SmackDown* Consultant Vickie Guerrero to gain a career advantage, it seemed that the Superstars of *SmackDown* would stop at nothing to reach the top.

A celebrity apprentice
January 8: General Manager Teddy Long congratulated Maria for becoming a cast member of the new season of the *Celebrity Apprentice* TV show, knowing that she would represent *SmackDown* well. Vickie Guerrero also complemented Maria but implied that she would have been a much better choice—if only she hadn't been far too busy to appear on it.

A great escape
January 15: When their match to determine the number one contender to Undertaker's World Heavyweight Championship the previous week did not produce a winner, Batista and Rey Mysterio met in a Steel Cage to settle the matter. Rey tried to escape the cage early, while "The Animal" Batista seemed more focused on punishing Mysterio inside the cage than escaping from it and winning the match. Batista's overconfidence was his downfall. He lifted Mysterio onto his shoulders and tried to slam him against the side of the cage, but, with the last of his strength, Mysterio managed to clamber out of the top of the cage to win and become the number one contender at the upcoming *Royal Rumble*.

February 5: New Champion Mickie James finds a temporary ally in her ongoing war with Lay-Cool— Beth Phoenix. However, Phoenix really has her sights set on winning James' title for herself.

"I accept Straight Edge into my life... I accept CM Punk as my savior!"
Serena (January 22, 2010)

INTRODUCING...

Serena
January 22: CM Punk was looking for another member for his Straight Edge Society, his militant cult promoting abstinence from drinking, smoking, and drugs. A woman suddenly jumped out of the audience and begged for his help... Serena became the third member of his society and, to prove her loyalty, was prepared to let Punk shave her head. For the next eight months, Serena would be a mainstay of the Straight Edge Society. She departed WWE in August 2010 but returned in 2017 to compete in the inaugural Mae Young Classic tournament, where she lost in the second round.

Serena has her head shaved by CM Punk as his "disciple" Luke Gallows looks on.

Beating back the bullies
February 5: Since being traded to *SmackDown*, Mickie James had been bullied by WWE Women's Champion Michelle McCool and her BFF Layla. Mickie finally gained revenge at *Royal Rumble* by taking the title from McCool. On *SmackDown*, James celebrated winning the Championship and formed an impromptu team with Beth Phoenix to defeat McCool and Layla.

February 23: WWE launched NXT, a new show designed to find WWE's next great Superstar. Eight rookies were paired with WWE Superstars in a weekly competition that ran for 15 weeks, until one rookie remained. That winner would receive a WWE contract and a title opportunity. Wade Barrett won the first season, and the format would run for four additional seasons before NXT evolved into the third WWE brand, alongside *RAW* and *SmackDown*, that it is today.

Edge spears Jericho, McCool kicks James

February 26: Chris Jericho's dream of main-eventing *WrestleMania* was seemingly dashed when Edge eliminated him to win *Royal Rumble*. But Jericho found another way, winning the World Heavyweight Championship in the *SmackDown* Elimination Chamber. Edge announced that he would be challenging Jericho at *WrestleMania XXVI,* and the two had a war of words on *SmackDown,* which turned physical when Edge Speared the champion.

Former WWE Women's Champion Michelle McCool got her rematch for the title against Mickie James and stacked the deck in her favor by having Vickie Guerrero appointed special guest referee. Steadfastly biased, Guerrero refused to make the three count when James rolled McCool. Instead, Guerrero slapped James, and while they were shouting at each other, McCool caught James with a kick to the jaw to win back the title.

February 26: Chris Jericho is not dressed for competition when he is ambushed by Edge.

Birthday party pooper

March 12: To honor his daughter Aliyah's ninth birthday, Rey Mysterio brought his entire family to the ring, where the WWE Universe sang "Happy Birthday"—until CM Punk and his Straight Edge Society rudely interrupted proceedings. Punk challenged Rey to a match at *WrestleMania,* as well as a match that night. Punk continued to taunt Mysterio and his family, until Rey left, eager to get his loved ones out of harm's way.

March 12: The threatening, black-clad figure of CM Punk looms over Rey Mysterio's frightened family, spoiling daughter Aliyah's birthday celebrations.

SmackDown vs. RAW

March 26: *SmackDown* opened with a 10-Man Tag Team Match, pitting the five *WrestleMania* Money in the Bank competitors from *SmackDown* against their *RAW* counterparts. The question stood as to how well the teams would work together, but both teams cooperated out of brand loyalty. Drew McIntyre managed to win for the *SmackDown* team by pinning Christian.

Swagger cashes in

April 2: Chris Jericho opened this episode by bragging how he'd successfully defended the World Heavyweight Championship against Edge at *WrestleMania XXVI*. He compared the WWE Universe to Edge, calling both losers, which led Edge to come out and beat up and spear Jericho. Seeing the ideal opportunity, Jack Swagger cashed in his Money in the Bank Title opportunity, pinning Jericho to become the new World Heavyweight Champion.

April 2: Jack Swagger opens his bid for the World Heavyweight Championship by laying out Chris Jericho with his Money in the Bank briefcase.

The 2010 WWE Draft

April 30: As ever, WWE was shaken up by the annual draft, which saw Superstars change places between *SmackDown* and *RAW*. *SmackDown* lost Chris Jericho and Edge to *RAW*, but saw its own influx of talent, gaining Kofi Kingston, Cody Rhodes, and MVP. Most worrisome for World Heavyweight Champion Jack Swagger was that Big Show had jumped over from *RAW* to *SmackDown*. Big Show immediately declared his aim of taking Swagger's title.

May 14: Kofi Kingston executes a Boom Drop on Christian, hoping to win the Intercontinental Title.

Almost, but not quite

May 14: The previous week, General Manager Teddy Long suspended Drew McIntyre and stripped him of the Intercontinental Championship for gross insubordination. In this episode, Kofi Kingston and Christian fought in the finals of a tournament to crown a new champion. Kingston won the match and the title —or so he thought. Suddenly, McIntyre appeared with a note from WWE Chairman Mr. McMahon, overruling Long, reinstating McIntyre, and returning the title to him.

Two-on-one for the title

May 14: Beth Phoenix was set to face Rosa Mendes in a non-title match, but *RAW* General Manager and *SmackDown* Consultant Vickie Guerrero came out and changed things up—forcing Phoenix to defend the WWE Women's Title against both members of LayCool (Layla El and Michelle McCool) at the same time. Phoenix held the pair off as long as she could, but eventually the numbers game caught up with her, and Layla pinned her to win the title.

Fatal 4-Way qualification

May 28: Just weeks before a new WWE event, *Fatal 4-Way*, was set to debut, *SmackDown* General Manager Teddy Long needed to determine the three men Jack Swagger would defend his World Heavyweight Title against. Big Show was given one spot, and the other two were determined by a pair of exciting matches that saw CM Punk defeat Kane and Undertaker overcome Rey Mysterio.

June 4: To honor the fallen Undertaker, a group of druids bring an empty casket into the arena.

Who hurt Undertaker?

June 4: To the solemn sound of chanting monks, a group of druids slowly carried a casket to the ring. A blinding flash of light illuminated the auditorium entrance, and the shaven-head figure of Kane arrived in the ring. He told the druids to open the casket, which was revealed to be empty. Seething with fury, Kane mourned Undertaker, his brother, telling the WWE Universe that he'd found him in an unresponsive, vegetative state. Kane vowed that he would not rest until he had taken revenge on those responsible for the attack on his brother.

> "My brother will rise from the dead no more—gone is the Undertaker!"
>
> **Kane (June 4, 2010)**

Long vs. "The Chosen One"

June 18: For months, Drew McIntyre felt he was being treated unfairly by General Manager Teddy Long. With the backing of Chairman Mr. McMahon, who had presented McIntyre as a future World Champion, McIntyre forced Teddy Long to face him in the ring; otherwise Long would be fired. Long was at a distinct disadvantage, as he had never been an in-ring competitor. Nevertheless, he bravely appeared. After threatening to tear Long apart, McIntyre made him get on his knees, acknowledge that he was "The Chosen One," and then pinned him with a foot on his chest. Long escaped further humiliation when Kofi Kingston and Matt Hardy interfered on his behalf. Aided by ten security men, McIntyre took out all his pent-up fury on them, to a chorus of boos from the WWE Universe.

June 18: General Manager Teddy Long searches in vain for any trace of clemency or goodwill in Drew McIntyre's menacing gaze.

2010

Alberto Del Rio

June 25: The WWE Universe had its first glimpse of the arrogant Mexican aristocrat Alberto Del Rio, who liked to boast about his great honesty, integrity, and superior intelligence. A few months later, Del Rio would finally compete in the ring and prove to be a brutal opponent, injuring both Rey Mysterio and Christian. With his personal ring announcer, Ricardo Rodriguez, Del Rio became a main-event mainstay in WWE, winning the WWE Championship, the United States Championship, and the World Heavyweight Championship, as well as the 2011 *Royal Rumble*.

Suave Alberto Del Rio presented himself as a new, superior kind of Superstar.

Bad news for dad

July 16: Kane continued his search for the person or persons responsible for the attack on his brother Undertaker. His latest suspect was Jack Swagger. To prove his innocence, Swagger brought his father to the ring and showed a series of photos that gave him an iron-clad alibi for the day Undertaker was attacked. However, Kane was not convinced. He attacked Swagger, and also gave Swagger's father a Chokelsam and a Tombstone.

Elsewhere in WWE

July 18: Thanks to its popularity, the Money in the Bank Match was moved from *WrestleMania* to its own pay-per-view. This first-ever event had two Money in the Bank Matches, one for *RAW* Superstars and one for *SmackDown* Superstars. Kane won the *SmackDown* opportunity and cashed it in immediately after Rey Mysterio's successful title defense against Jack Swagger. Kane became the first star to use a Money in the Bank title opportunity the same day he won it. He duly defeated Mysterio to become World Champion.

Ziggler's first title

August 6: Dolph Ziggler finally managed to secure a title for himself when he defeated Kofi Kingston for the Intercontinental Championship. Kingston must have thought he had the match won after nailing Ziggler with his Trouble in Paradise move, but Ziggler's girlfriend, Vickie Guerrero, distracted the official, allowing Ziggler time to recover. He then hit Kingston with his Zig-Zag finisher to claim the Intercontinental Championship.

July 16: Jack Swagger's helpless father wishes he had stayed home as he feels the full force of Kane's anger.

Del Rio makes an impression

August 20: After months of promo videos proclaiming his matchless skills and abilities, the WWE Universe finally got to see Alberto Del Rio in action when he challenged his Mexican countryman Rey Mysterio in the main event. Mysterio managed to hit some of his signature acrobatic offense, but Del Rio forced Mysterio to tap out to his Cross Arm Breaker.

August 20: Alberto Del Rio connects with a dropkick on Rey Mysterio during Del Rio's debut match.

Return of "The Deadman"

August 27: Kane's continued efforts to find the party responsible for attacking Undertaker masked a shocking, dark secret—*he* was the one who had attacked his brother! But Kane hadn't finished the job, and Undertaker returned to *SmackDown* to confront his treacherous sibling. Undertaker called Kane a "diseased soul," unworthy of holding the World Heavyweight Title, adding that he would come for Kane's title when he wanted it.

August 27: Undertaker comes to the ring looking to confront his brother Kane.

Will Hornswoggle speak?

September 17: *SmackDown* General Manager Teddy Long took several controversial steps in an effort to get Hornswoggle to speak. A few weeks back, electroshock therapy had not worked, so Long sent Hornswoggle back to school, hoping a nun could teach him the basics of speech. It didn't take very long for Hornswoggle's antics to make the nun give up and exclaim that he didn't need lessons—he needed an exorcism!

Defending their titles

September 24: The makeshift team of "Dashing" Cody Rhodes and "The Chosen One" Drew McIntyre put their newly won WWE Tag Team Titles on the line against the previous champions, the Hart Dynasty. The Harts were in control early, but McIntyre drove Tyson Kidd into an exposed turnbuckle to reverse the momentum. McIntyre finished Kidd off with his Future Shock maneuver to secure the three count for his team and retain the championship.

September 24: Rhodes and McIntyre celebrate their defense of the WWE Tag Team Championship.

2010

October 1: Edge proves to the WWE Universe that the Swagger Soaring Eagle has emphatically landed.

Disrespecting the eagle

October 1: To celebrate *SmackDown*'s move to the SyFy Network, Jack Swagger returned to Oklahoma City to crown himself "King of Oklahoma." He also brought his own personal mascot, the Swagger Soaring Eagle. Edge interrupted to say that both Swagger's coronation and his mascot were stupid, and he emphasized his point by spearing the mascot!

The *Bragging Rights* team

October 15: The second annual *Bragging Rights* event pitted the best of *RAW* against *SmackDown*'s top Superstars. *SmackDown* GM Teddy Long wanted his brand to win the trophy for a second straight year, so he set qualification matches to build the best possible team. Joining *SmackDown* team captain Big Show were match winners Rey Mysterio, Jack Swagger, Alberto Del Rio, Edge, Tyler Reks, and Kofi Kingston.

Undertaker's revenge

October 22: With both *SmackDown* and *RAW* looking to gain momentum heading into *Bragging Rights*, this episode's main event pitted *SmackDown*'s World Heavyweight Champion Kane against *RAW*'s Champion, Randy Orton. The match was hard to call—then Undertaker's ominous bell sounded and the arena was momentarily plunged into darkness. When the lights came back on, Orton snuck up behind Kane, hit him with his RKO finisher, and left with the title. As Kane strode around the ring, the bell tolled again and Kane's vengeful brother Undertaker rose up, ripping through the canvas and dragging Kane down to "Hell."

October 22: Kane discovers that the bell is tolling for him as his vengeful brother Undertaker rises through the canvas.

November 19: Kaval uses every last drop of his strength and skill to pin Ziggler.

NXT rookie shocks the show

November 19: NXT Season 2 winner Kaval saw his WWE career get off to a rocky start, as he was winless since joining the *SmackDown* roster. The prospect of a first victory seemed dim when he had to face Intercontinental Champion Dolph Ziggler. Kaval seemed close to victory with a couple of near falls, but Ziggler thought it was over when he rolled up Kaval, but Kaval reversed the hold into a pinning combination, grabbing his first win.

The Nexus arrives

November 5: While much of their destruction occurred on *RAW*, the Nexus would also come to raise havoc on *SmackDown*. *SmackDown* rivals were forced to put their differences aside to face the Nexus in a 10-Man Tag Team Match. Those rivalries caused some intersquad squabbling among the *SmackDown* side, with Kane fighting Big Show and Edge, but eventually Edge speared David Otunga to win the match for team *SmackDown*.

Sheamus is the king

November 26: For the first time in four years, WWE was set to crown a new King of the Ring. *RAW* had four first-round matches, and so did *SmackDown*. Kofi Kingston defeated Jack Swagger; Drew McIntyre pinned MVP; Cody Rhodes defeated Rey Mysterio; and Alberto Del Rio outlasted Big Show. Unfortunately for *SmackDown*, the winner of the tournament was *RAW*'s Sheamus.

An interference and a grudge

December 17: New WWE Champion The Miz made a special appearance on *SmackDown* to face Rey Mysterio. Thanks to some interference by Alberto Del Rio, The Miz got the drop on Mysterio and pinned him to win the match.

Frustrated by Del Rio's involvement, General Manager Teddy Long scheduled a tag team match featuring The Miz and Del Rio against Mysterio and Edge for this very night. This became a no contest when Kane came out and attacked his bitter rival. Edge was the number one contender for Kane's World Heavyweight crown and had been messing with Kane's head by kidnapping Paul Bearer, Kane's father and manager. Not even a sizable squad from the *SmackDown* locker room could pull these two enemies apart.

Sealed with a kiss, smacked with a chair

December 21: On a special live episode of *SmackDown*, John Cena faced both Dolph Ziggler and Ziggler's girlfriend Vickie Guerrero in a Handicap Match. Guerrero felt that Cena had disrespected her and demanded that her boyfriend Ziggler defend her honor. Ziggler almost had Cena beat, until Guerrero became involved, allowing Cena to get a second wind, give Ziggler his signature Attitude Adjustment, and get the pin. Cena celebrated by giving Vickie a great big kiss, and then CM Punk arrived, smacked Cena with a steel chair, and left him gasping on the mat.

December 21: Vickie Guerrero tries to pull John Cena off her boyfriend Dolph Ziggler during their 2-on-1 Handicap Match.

2011

TWO MAJOR VOIDS had to be filled on *SmackDown* in 2011: one lasted most of the year; the other resulted in a permanent loss. The latter occurred when Edge, a mainstay of the show for most of its existence, was forced to retire owing to a medical issue. The other disappearance was Undertaker, who went absent from the WWE ring after defeating Triple H at *WrestleMania XXVII*. Happily, "The Deadman" would return in 2012. The loss of Edge, however, led to a number of Superstars attempting to step up and take his spot, including his former tag team partner, Christian, as well as Randy Orton, Mark Henry, Big Show, and Daniel Bryan.

January 7: Kofi Kingston hits Dolph Ziggler with his signature Trouble in Paradise kick during their battle for the Intercontinental Championship.

Last man standing
January 7: The first *SmackDown* match of 2011 saw Edge defend his World Heavyweight Championship in a Last Man Standing Match against Kane. The object of the match was to so incapacitate one's opponent that he could not answer the official's ten count. The two Superstars battled in and out of the ring and also in the arena itself, and Edge had to resort to repeatedly bashing Kane's knee with a chair to keep Kane down and win the match.

Kofi Kingston's busy night
January 7: Kofi Kingston was looking to become a three-time Intercontinental Champion when he challenged Dolph Ziggler for the title. Kingston hit Ziggler with a high cross body off the top turnbuckle to secure the pin and win the match. Ziggler's girlfriend, assistant General Manager Vickie Guerrero, then ordered that Ziggler should get an immediate rematch; however, Kofi managed to win that contest as well to keep the title.

Meet The Corre
January 21: On the previous week's *SmackDown*, Wade Barrett had taken on Big Show, receiving aid from his former Nexus teammates Justin Gabriel and Heath Slater, as well as the massive Ezekiel Jackson. The quartet introduced themselves on this edition of *SmackDown* as The Corre, a group that promised to do such damage and cause such chaos that the behavior of The Nexus would pale in comparison.

January 7: Edge spears Kane in a brutal battle to retain his World Heavyweight Championship.

Kelly Kelly comes through

February 4: The odds of Edge retaining his World Heavyweight Championship seemed slim, thanks to the scheming of acting General Manager Vickie Guerrero. She forced Edge to team with Kelly Kelly against the trio of Dolph Ziggler and LayCool (Layla and Michelle McCool). Edge would lose his title if either he or Kelly Kelly were pinned. Kelly Kelly ruined Guerrero's plan by spearing and pinning Layla. Enraged, Vickie Guerrero promptly fired Kelly!

February 4: Against the odds, Kelly Kelly proves that she's no "weak link" by pinning Layla and saving Edge's championship title.

A 12-man battle

February 18: The 600th Episode kicked off with a huge 12-Man Tag Team Match featuring the participants of the two upcoming Elimination Chamber Matches. Edge led his team of John Morrison, John Cena, Rey Mysterio, Randy Orton, and R-Truth to victory over Kane, Drew McIntyre, CM Punk, King Sheamus, Dolph Ziggler, and Wade Barrett when he pinned Ziggler after a Spear.

Vickie loses a match and her job

February 25: Vickie Guerrero had been abusing her power for years, but karma finally caught up with her. In January, General Manager Teddy Long had been attacked. On this episode, Long wrangled a confession from Guerrero that her boyfriend Ziggler had been involved. Long fired Ziggler, but gave Vickie a chance to save her job if she and Drew McIntyre could defeat Kelly Kelly and Edge. They couldn't, and Vickie's employment was terminated.

March 11: Entering to his Motörhead theme tune "The Game," Triple H radiates menace.

"Let me show you, Deadman, what I do!"

Triple H (March 11, 2011)

No more Mister Nice Guy

March 11: A few days after Undertaker announced that his match against Triple H at *WrestleMania* would be No Holds Barred, "The Game" entered the arena to remind "The Deadman" that he would not fail to stop Undertaker—as Shawn Michaels had in the previous two *WrestleManias*—because he would bring his most twisted, brutal side to the match.

Christian and Del Rio in a Cage

March 18: Just a few weeks before Alberto Del Rio was set to challenge Edge for the World Heavyweight Championship at *WrestleMania XXVII*, Del Rio faced Edge's best friend Christian in a Steel Cage. Christian won the battle when he climbed out of the cage first to win the match, but ended up losing the war when an enraged Del Rio bashed him repeatedly and Brodus Clay attacked Edge as he came out to help Christian.

March 18: Edge suffers a steel chair beating at the hands of Brodus Clay as Alberto Del Rio looks on approvingly.

2011

March 25: Barrett gets ready to deliver his Wasteland finisher on Intercontinental Champion Kingston.

Barrett wastes the champ

March 25: Kofi Kingston was looking to defend his Intercontinental Championship against Wade Barrett, but unfortunately, he had to deal with the rest of The Corre as well. Heath Slater prevented Kingston from hitting Barrett with his Trouble in Paradise move, and the distraction allowed Barrett to nail the champion with his Wasteland finishing move to win the match and take the title.

A ladder to glory

April 15: A previously unsuspected medical ailment forced Edge to retire and relinquish the World Heavyweight Title. After Edge had taken his leave with a heartfelt farewell speech, General Manager Teddy Long set a 20-Man Battle Royal to determine who would face number one contender Alberto Del Rio in a Ladder Match for the vacant championship at *Extreme Rules*. Christian won and would go on to capture the title a few weeks later.

Titles for Big Show and Kane

April 22: The Corre's Heath Slater and Justin Gabriel learned what a massive undertaking defending their Tag Team Championships would be when they were challenged by the gigantic duo of Kane and Big Show. Corre teammate Ezekiel Jackson tried to help the beleaguered champions, but Kane tossed him out of the ring, allowing Big Show to chokeslam Slater, pin him, and win the Tag Team Titles for himself and Kane.

INTRODUCING...

Jinder Mahal

April 29: The 2011 draft wasn't the only event to bring new Superstars to *SmackDown*. Jinder Mahal introduced himself backstage to fellow countrymen Ranjin Singh and The Great Khali. Mahal would soon be competing in both *SmackDown* and *RAW* rings. He would reach the apex of his career in 2017, when he defeated Randy Orton for the WWE Championship, a title he held for almost six months.

Proud of his Punjabi Sikh heritage, Jinder Mahal came to call his signature slam finisher The Khallas—Hindi for "Finish."

The annual shakeup

April 29: Once again, the rosters of *SmackDown* and *RAW* were turned upside down, thanks to the annual WWE draft. On the televised portion of the draft, *SmackDown* gained Randy Orton, Mark Henry, and Sin Cara, but they lost Rey Mysterio, Alberto Del Rio, and Big Show. The online portion of the draft was even better for the blue brand, as it gained three former or future World Champions: Daniel Bryan, Sheamus, and The Great Khali.

April 29: Randy Orton shows off a little blue brand pride after being drafted to *SmackDown*.

Thrown to the lions

May 6: After winning the World Heavyweight Championship for the first time in his 17-year career at *Extreme Rules*, Christian did not have long to celebrate his emotional win, as Mark Henry, The Great Khali, and Randy Orton all stepped up to challenge Christian. GM Teddy Long placed the decision in the hands of the WWE Universe, who selected Orton. Randy made good on the choice, pinning Christian that night to become new World Heavyweight Champion.

Nothing cheesy about Brie

May 20: More than a month into her WWE Divas Championship reign, Brie Bella faced a stern challenge in the form of Natalya. Brie was challenged by impressive technical wrestling moves by Natalya, but Brie managed to counter with a submission maneuver. Natalya grabbed the momentum with an elevated suplex, but Brie finished Natalya off by ramming her into the turnbuckle, giving her an X-Factor facebuster, and pinning her.

May 20: Brie Bella gets to work on Natalya's left arm on the way to her successful title defense.

A loser's revenge

May 27: Ever since Rey Mysterio broke his nose, Cody Rhodes wore a protective mask to protect his face. He also shielded himself from having to see the uglier (in his opinion) members of the WWE Universe by having his assistants pass out paper bags to cover their faces before his matches. Perhaps Cody should have focused more on his opponent, as Daniel Bryan forced Rhodes to submit. Sore loser Rhodes then attacked Bryan and left him lying with a paper bag over his head.

May 27: An irate Cody Rhodes puts a paper bag on dazed Daniel Bryan's head.

June 3: Special guest referee Christian starts out impartial but can't help interfering in the match between Sheamus and Orton.

June 24: Ezekiel "Big Zeke" Jackson gives Wade Barrett a thunderous slam on the way to victory.

A special guest spoils Sheamus' party

June 3: Randy Orton was looking to defend his World Heavyweight Championship against Sheamus; unfortunately for Sheamus, Orton's other championship rival, Christian, stepped in as the special guest official. Christian seemed to be playing fair until Sheamus accidently ran into him. Then Christian refused to count a pinfall by Sheamus and hit "The Celtic Warrior," allowing Orton to nail Sheamus with an RKO to win the match.

It's torture when teammates meet

June 24: Less than a week after winning the Intercontinental Championship, Ezekiel Jackson's first title defense was against the previous champion and his former Corre stablemate Wade Barrett. Barrett tried to gain an early advantage with a blindside attack before the match had even started. He seemed to be in control for much of the match, until Jackson came back with a series of powerful clotheslines and his Torture Rack submission move to win the match and retain the title.

A very sore loser

July 1: Mark Henry was given the opportunity to face Randy Orton in a non-title match that, if Henry won, would lead to a shot at the World Heavyweight Championship. "The World's Strongest Man" took full advantage, decimating Orton with a series of power moves. Suddenly, Big Show's music hit, distracting Henry long enough to allow Orton to hit an RKO and win the match by count out. A furious Henry destroyed the AV equipment and beat up a technician.

Money splits partners

July 15: Three-time Tag Team Champions, Heath Slater and Justin Gabriel, saw their partnership dissolve when both qualified for the *SmackDown* Money in the Bank Ladder Match. Slater felt his former partner was holding him back, so they met one-on-one in this episode. They were evenly matched, but Gabriel was able to hit his 450 Splash off of the top rope to pin Slater and win the bout.

Champion vs. champion

July 22: In a rare bout, the Intercontinental Champion Ezekiel Jackson and the World Heavyweight Champion Christian met in a non-title match. Jackson impressed the WWE Universe by nailing Christian with a series of power moves, but Christian's veteran savvy allowed him to outsmart Jackson, hit his Killswitch finisher, and win the match.

July 22: Two champions, one winner—and this time it's Christian, despite Jackson's best efforts.

Meet the new boss

July 29: New Chief Operating Officer (COO) of WWE, Triple H, addressed the World Heavyweight Championship situation, which Christian had won from Randy Orton by getting Orton disqualified. Triple H was interrupted by Christian, who was looking to establish a working relationship with the new boss. Triple H didn't take kindly to the interruption, calling it a "slap in the face," and informed Christian he would be facing Randy Orton in a no-disqualification, No Holds Barred Title Match at *SummerSlam*.

A title at the crossroads

August 12: Cody Rhodes challenged Ezekiel Jackson for his Intercontinental Championship. It seemed that Rhodes would not be able to overcome the champ's power after Jackson delivered several scoop slams, but Rhodes used a combination of a Ted DiBiase distraction, an illegal hit with his protective mask, and his Cross Rhodes finishing maneuver to pin Jackson and capture the Intercontinental Championship.

Victory goes to the strongest

August 19: *SmackDown* General Manager Teddy Long set a 20-Man Battle Royal to determine the number one contender for Randy Orton's World Heavyweight Championship. Mark Henry chose to destroy competitors both in an out of the ring. Sheamus and Wade Barrett tried to work together to eliminate Henry, but "The World's Strongest Man" held on, finally eliminating Sin Cara to win the match and the title opportunity.

August 19: Amid the chaos of a 20-Man Battle Royal, Mark Henry dominates the center of the ring.

A special surprise for Christian

August 26: With *SmackDown* emanating from Calgary, Alberta, Canada, it made perfect sense to have the city's favorite son Bret "Hit Man" Hart serve as a special guest General Manager. The WWE Universe expressed its approval when he scheduled the whining Christian to face Randy Orton in a Steel Cage Match on the following week's *Super SmackDown Live*.

Conflict on The Cutting Edge

September 16: Edge's talk show, The Cutting Edge, returned with World Heavyweight Champion Randy Orton and his challenger Mark Henry as guests. Edge asked Orton how he could handle such a physical force of nature like Henry and asked the World's Strongest Man why he'd never won "the big one" in his career. Eventually, the talking ceased and the two began brawling in the ring, as the entire *SmackDown* locker room piled in.

September 16: Incensed by being called "The world's strongest failure," Henry slams Orton.

"I want things to be so much better—not just for me, but for everybody!"

CM Punk (August 30, 2011)

Punk takes on the boss

August 30: Once he became COO, Triple H tried to focus on business issues and stay out of the ring. CM Punk made that impossible by running down "The Game," as well as his family and friends. The two decided to settle matters in the ring, so on this *SmackDown* edition, they signed a contract for their *Night of Champions* clash. While they both agreed to the match, the war of words got intensely personal during the signing.

August 30: Triple H accuses CM Punk of disrespecting him, his family, and the WWE.

No escaping the lumberjacks

September 23: Christian tried to convince WWE COO Triple H that *he* was the leader of the *SmackDown* locker room and the rightful World Heavyweight Champion, not the current holder, Mark Henry. Triple H gave him the chance to prove both claims by making a Lumberjack Match for the title. Christian did not get the help he was hoping for, as none of the lumberjacks would support him. Henry gave Christian the World's Strongest Slam and pinned him to emphatically retain his title.

Secret meetings

September 30: The relationship between management and labor in WWE had deteriorated since Triple H took over as COO. His top lieutenant, Executive Vice President of Talent Relations John Laurinaitis, came to *SmackDown* and held secret meetings with some of the most disgruntled Superstars. "The Game" confronted his underling about this "betrayal," but Laurinaitis claimed he was only trying to help smooth over any problems.

October 14: The ring can barely contain the mayhem of *SmackDown*'s celebratory 41-Man Battle Royal.

Big Show's big return

October 7: Mark Henry's rise to the World Heavyweight Championship began by inducting Big Show into his so-called Hall of Pain. Henry broke Big Show's ankle, putting "The World's Largest Athlete" on the shelf for four months. On this episode, Show returned looking for revenge and Henry's title. When Henry refused to grant him a title opportunity, Big Show slammed the champ through the announcers' table.

October 7: Big Show returns from injury, determined to prove to champion Mark Henry that he really is a Weapon of Mass Destruction.

WWE's biggest-ever Battle Royal

October 14: To celebrate *SmackDown* becoming the second-longest running episodic TV show in history (passing the Western series *Gunsmoke* and trailing only *RAW*), *SmackDown* held the biggest Battle Royal in WWE history, with the winner of the 41-Man Match getting a title opportunity of his choosing that night. Randy Orton outlasted everyone else, eliminating The Miz to get a shot at World Heavyweight Champion Mark Henry.

Mask vs. Mask Match

October 21: For months, the WWE Universe had been seeing double with Sin Cara, as it seemed as if the masked luchador had an evil doppelganger. Eventually, Sin Cara Azul and Sin Cara Negro chose different color masks and met in a "loser must unmask" match. The original Sin Cara, Azul, forced his double to submit and remove his mask.

October 21: Sin Cara Azul proudly displays the mask of his vanquished rival Sin Cara Negro. Unmasking an opponent is held to be the ultimate victory among *luchadores*.

Big Show interferes

November 4: Mark Henry continued to deny Big Show a title opportunity, so Big Show decided to back another challenger—Daniel Bryan. The *SmackDown* Money in the Bank briefcase holder faced Henry in a non-title match, and Big Show interfered, knocking out Henry with a KO punch. Show tried to get Bryan to cash in his title shot, but before he could, Henry recovered and delivered a World's Strongest Slam on Bryan.

November 11: Barrett shows Randy Orton the ropes, and Orton doesn't like what he sees.

Battle of the captains

November 11: Randy Orton and Wade Barrett each assembled 5-man teams for a traditional 5-on-5 Survivor Series Elimination Match, but first the two captains met in one-on-one competition. The match was physical and intense, with Barrett planting Orton on the mat with a devastating slam. Orton seemed to reverse the momentum with a second-rope superplex, power slam, and a draping DDT, but Barrett stole the match with a rollup.

An unfair cash-in

November 25: Injured World Heavyweight Champion Mark Henry came to the ring to complain about Big Show injuring him at *Survivor Series*, resulting in him not being able to compete for medical reasons. Big Show added injury to injury by knocking Henry out. Daniel Bryan then ran out with his Money in the Bank briefcase, cashed it in, and pinned the comatose Henry to win the title. However, General Manager Teddy Long reversed the decision, since Henry had not been medically cleared to compete.

A Christmas miracle

November 29: The holidays came early to a special live edition of *SmackDown*. Special guest host Mick Foley arranged for a series of holiday-themed matches, including an "All I Want For Christmas" Battle Royal, with the winner getting to make a wish that would be granted by Santa Claus. Against all odds, and thanks to Sheamus' intervention, Hornswoggle won and Santa later granted him his dearest wish: the ability to talk!

November 29: Hornswoggle dances with glee after winning a chance to meet Santa Claus.

Cody replaces Booker

December 9: The WWE Universe was used to Booker T serving as a commentator, but Cody Rhodes, angry at being badmouthed by Booker over several weeks, made that impossible by attacking him before the show started. Rather than force the *SmackDown* announcing crew to perform shorthanded, Rhodes stepped in, saying that he could easily replace Booker T on the show.

Bryan's title under threat

December 23: Daniel Bryan came to the ring to celebrate his new World Heavyweight Championship, but Big Show and Mark Henry were already in the ring arguing who should get first crack at Bryan's title. Big Show congratulated Bryan for defeating him for the title, but Henry, the previous champion, just wanted to squash Bryan like a bug.

Falls count anywhere

December 30: One of the most intense recent rivalries on *SmackDown* closed with a Falls Count Anywhere Match in the main event. Wade Barrett and Randy Orton took their match all over the arena, including backstage. The match had a shocking conclusion, with Barrett throwing Orton down a flight of stairs. Perhaps realizing that he'd gone too far, Barrett then ran off.

December 30: Barrett looks on as his bitter rival Orton groans in pain at the bottom of the staircase.

December 23: Big Show and Mark Henry argue over who should get the first shot at Daniel Bryan's title.

2012

IN MANY WAYS, 2012 on *SmackDown* was the year of Sheamus. He won the 2012 *Royal Rumble* and decided to challenge World Heavyweight Champion Daniel Bryan at *WrestleMania*. After winning the title, Sheamus defended it against all comers for most of the year, until finally losing to Big Show late in the year. Bryan's title loss at *WrestleMania* was just the start of his drama—he, along with Kane, was forced to take anger management classes, which eventually led to the duo forming Team Hell No. Power at the top proved to be volatile as well. After guiding a losing team at *WrestleMania*, Teddy Long was forced out as *SmackDown* General Manager, and *RAW* General Manager John "People Power" Laurinaitis took over *SmackDown* as well. But "People Power" didn't last long, and Laurinaitis was fired and replaced by WWE Hall of Famer Booker T.

Fighting for a job
January 6: As Zack Ryder was now the United States Champion, he felt he could no longer serve as assistant to *SmackDown* General Manager Teddy Long. Superstar Santino Marella was eager to fill the role, but Long said he first had to beat Drew McIntyre in a match. Marella hit McIntyre with his signature Cobra maneuver, securing the position of Assistant General Manager, and putting Drew McIntyre's employment on *SmackDown* in deep jeopardy.

A gigantic accident
January 13: Daniel Bryan had his work cut out defending his World Heavyweight Championship against the massive Big Show—especially as the match stipulation was that it would be a no countout and no disqualification match. Bryan tried using a chair to get an advantage; enraged, Big Show chased Bryan around the ring, accidentally flattening Bryan's girlfriend, AJ Lee. Big Show was devastated by his clumsiness, and the match was stopped so AJ could receive medical attention.

January 13: A distraught Big Show doesn't know what to do after running into AJ Lee and knocking her down.

January 20: The Lumberjacks for the World Heavyweight Championship Match were supposed to stay outside the ring, but instead they swarmed the competitors inside.

Lady Luck rules *SmackDown*

January 20: With *SmackDown* broadcasting from "Sin City" Las Vegas, chance played a crucial part in matchmaking. Superstars had to spin the wheel to set their matches. Sheamus and Wade Barrett met in a Tables Match, Santino Marella defeated Drew McIntyre in a Blindfold Match, and Mark Henry's title match against Daniel Bryan became a Lumberjack Match—that turned into a massive Superstar brawl. This allowed Bryan to escape with his title.

Talking out of turn

February 3: *SmackDown* General Manager Theodore Long announced who would be challenging for Daniel Bryan's World Heavyweight Championship at *Elimination Chamber*. One participant, Mark Henry, was not happy and demanded a one-on-one title match. Long did not like Henry's attitude; he took Henry out of the Elimination Chamber Match and then suspended him!

> "You wanna know someone who's done a lot more damage than Big Show? You, Cole!"
>
> **AJ Lee (February 10, 2012)**

AJ speaks her mind

February 10: About a month after she was inadvertently injured by Big Show, AJ Lee returned for an interview with commentator Michael Cole. AJ explained that she believed Big Show did not mean to hurt her. She also claimed that Cole himself had done untold damage to her boyfriend Daniel Bryan, herself, and the entire Diva division with his unrelenting negativity on commentary, and that the WWE Universe would be better off if he just shut up!

Orton's replacement

February 17: *SmackDown* lost one of its Elimination Chamber Match competitors just a week before the event, owing to a concussion suffered by Randy Orton. To fill the spot, General Manager Teddy Long created a wild card Battle Royal, open to any member of *SmackDown*, *RAW*, or *NXT*. Long's own assistant, Santino Marella, outlasted the field to earn a place in the Elimination Chamber.

Two champions meet

February 21: On a special live *Super SmackDown*, both *SmackDown* and *RAW* tried to prove their superiority in a match pitting the blue brand's World Heavyweight Champion Daniel Bryan against the red brand's Champion, CM Punk. Ironically, each General Manager ordered the match to be restarted after their respective Champions had apparently won, so neither man could claim victory.

February 21: World Heavyweight Champion Daniel Bryan drives a knee into WWE Champion CM Punk.

2012

March 16: Kane takes particular joy in sharing how he plans to destroy Randy Orton at *WrestleMania*.

GM for a day

March 9: The WWE Universe knew there was the odd chance of seeing a Steel Cage Match close an exciting night of action. But in this episode, a Steel Cage Match for the United States Championship opened the show, with Santino Marella defending the title against Jack Swagger. Vickie Guerrero tried to interfere on Swagger's behalf, but it backfired, and she slammed the cage door on him, allowing Santino to escape the cage and retain his title.

Less than a month before a *WrestleMania* contest to determine which General Manager would take over both shows, John Laurinaitis was made General Manager for the night on *SmackDown*. He made a strong argument that he was the man to run both shows by opening the night with a Steel Cage Match for the United States Championship. Santino Marella managed to successfully defend his title against former champion Jack Swagger.

The Viper vs. The Big Red Monster

March 16: For weeks, Randy "The Viper" Orton had been stalked by Kane, "The Big Red Monster." Orton was usually the hunter, not the hunted, so Orton came to the ring looking for an explanation. Surprisingly, Kane obliged—Kane explained that he had decided that WWE was not big enough for both of them and he wanted to decimate Orton. However, he wanted to do it on his terms, and that meant waiting until *WrestleMania*.

Big Show's *WrestleMania* promise

March 30: For weeks, Cody Rhodes had been mocking the *WrestleMania* record of Big Show, his challenger for the Intercontinental Championship. But in a passionate interview, "The World's Largest Athlete" guaranteed that this year's *WrestleMania* would be different. He was going to create his own special *WrestleMania* moment in 2012 by knocking the mouthy Rhodes out and taking his Intercontinental Championship.

INTRODUCING...

Ryback

April 6: A monstrous new member of the *SmackDown* roster made his debut on this episode, crushing his competition that night. Known as Ryback, he would defeat one, two, or three competitors in a match, always demanding that the WWE "Feed Me More!" His impressive winning streak throughout 2012 earned him title matches against CM Punk—which Punk had to cheat to win. However, Ryback did capture the Intercontinental Championship during his four-year stay in WWE.

Ryback brought an intensity to the ring that quickly established his WWE career.

Layla's first title defense

May 4: After winning the Divas Championship at *Extreme Rules*, Layla made her first appearance on *SmackDown* in more than a year. She faced stiff competition in the form of Natalya, who was angry that Layla had gained a title opportunity after a year on the shelf. Natalya's physical power gained her an early advantage, but Layla nailed the Canadian Superstar with a Neckbreaker to win.

April 10: Sheamus celebrates victory with "Mean" Gene Okerlund and other WWE Legends.

May 4: Layla pins Natalya to retain the Divas Championship Title.

An improbable tag team partnership

April 10: On a special Old School episode, John Laurinaitis—the new General Manager of both *RAW* and *SmackDown*—put new World Heavyweight Champion Sheamus in a Tag Team Match against Daniel Bryan and Alberto Del Rio. Keeping with the night's theme, the new General Manager paired Sheamus with former announcer "Mean" Gene Okerlund. Despite having to do all the work, Sheamus pinned Bryan to win the match and then celebrated with all the various WWE Legends present.

A one-on-one advance

May 11: Sheamus knew that he would have his hands full with three championship contenders at *Over the Limit*, but in this episode's main event he got to focus on just one of his rivals—Chris Jericho. Sheamus rained a series of clubbing blows on Jericho's chest, but "Y2J" used kicks and submission holds to turn the tide. The Champion almost submitted to "Y2J"'s Walls of Jericho finisher, but Alberto Del Rio suddenly burst into the ring and attacked both men, making the match a no-contest draw.

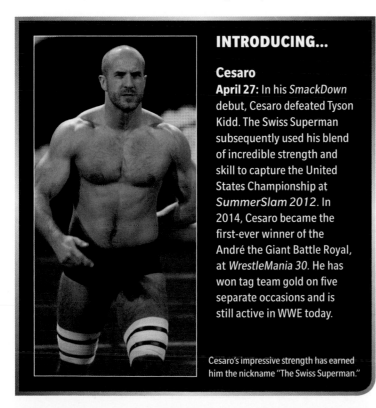

INTRODUCING...

Cesaro

April 27: In his *SmackDown* debut, Cesaro defeated Tyson Kidd. The Swiss Superman subsequently used his blend of incredible strength and skill to capture the United States Championship at *SummerSlam 2012*. In 2014, Cesaro became the first-ever winner of the André the Giant Battle Royal, at *WrestleMania 30*. He has won tag team gold on five separate occasions and is still active in WWE today.

Cesaro's impressive strength has earned him the nickname "The Swiss Superman."

May 11: Chris Jericho looks to soften up World Heavyweight Champion Sheamus with a Walls of Jericho maneuver in advance of their title match.

May 18: Santino Marella brings down Cody Rhodes with a "Cobra-enhanced" clothesline.

Battle of the title holders

May 18: Champion met Champion on *SmackDown* when the Intercontinental Champion, Cody Rhodes, faced off against the United States Champion, Santino Marella. Rhodes used a hammerlock and dropkick to take an early advantage in the match, but Santino was able to kick out of a pinfall attempt. He then hit Rhodes with his signature Cobra Strike and grabbed the win.

Three men in a battle

May 25: To determine the next challenger for Sheamus' World Heavyweight Championship, the General Manager's Executive Administrator, Eve, set up a massive Triple Threat Match for this episode's main event: Randy Orton vs. Kane vs. Alberto Del Rio, with the winner challenging for the championship. At first, Del Rio and Kane worked together against Orton, but that partnership quickly dissolved and the two attacked each other. Orton thought he'd won the match with an RKO move, but Del Rio sneakily grabbed the pin and earned the title opportunity.

May 25: Looking to become the number one contender, Randy Orton levels Alberto Del Rio with a DDT.

June 8: Brodus Clay and the Funkadactyls celebrate another Clay victory with a post-match dance.

Brodus joins the blue brand

June 8: While most Superstars were now free to appear on *RAW* and *SmackDown,* General Manager John Laurinaitis banned Brodus Clay from *RAW*, making him a permanent member of *SmackDown*. Unhappy about the ban, Clay decided to take his anger out on his *SmackDown* opponents. Accompanied to the ring by two dancers known as the Funkadactyls, Brodus started with a dominating victory over Derrick Bateman, crushing him with a devastating splash.

Cena's knockout appearance

June 15: *RAW*'s John Cena wasn't supposed to be on *SmackDown*, but he rushed over to confront Big Show after "The World's Largest Athlete" challenged him. But when Cena came to the ring, General Manager Laurinaitis explained that he had sent Big Show home to avoid a physical confrontation. Cena took out his anger and frustration on Laurinaitis instead, knocking him unconscious.

Shooting for Money in the Bank

June 29: In both this and the next episode, Superstars were slated to compete in the annual *Money in the Bank* qualifying matches. On this show, Damien Sandow, Tyson Kidd, Christian, Santino Marella, and Tensai all won their matches to advance to *Money in the Bank*. The following week, Cody Rhodes and Dolph Ziggler also qualified.

July 23: The longest-running weekly episodic television program in history, WWE RAW aired its landmark 1,000th episode, and the WWE Universe was not disappointed. The night was packed with exciting matches, strange events, and historic returns, as the world was treated to reunions of both D-Generation X and the Brothers of Destruction, a wedding between Daniel Bryan and AJ, and The Rock "laying the smackdown" on Big Show, before The Rock was unexpectedly attacked by WWE Champion CM Punk.

And the new General Manager is...

August 3: John Laurinaitis had been fired as General Manager of *SmackDown* and *RAW* at *No Way Out* on June 17, creating a leadership void that needed to be filled. Mr. McMahon appeared on *SmackDown* to announce the new General Manager—Booker T. A popular choice with the crowd, the former World Heavyweight Champion promised that *SmackDown* was "about to blow up," and he set matches for the night featuring Sheamus, Tensai, Alberto Del Rio, and Randy Orton.

Bizarre love triangle

July 3: Daniel Bryan and CM Punk were not just rivals for the WWE Championship—they were also competing for the affections of AJ Lee. In what was supposed to be a one-on-one interview between Lee and Michael Cole, Lee was unable to clarify her position before being interrupted by both Bryan and Punk. She then muddied the waters further by passionately kissing both men.

Rey's back and Slater's down!

July 20: Almost a year after being sidelined with an injury, Rey Mysterio returned to *SmackDown*, where he was confronted by Alberto Del Rio (the Superstar that originally injured him) and Dolph Ziggler. To even the odds, Sheamus came out to support Mysterio, leading to a Tag Team Match in the main event. Mysterio and Sheamus won by disqualification when Del Rio's personal ring announcer, Ricardo Rodriguez, tried to change the course of the match by grabbing Sheamus' leg.

For weeks, Heath Slater had tried to make a name for himself by taking on WWE legends on *RAW*, but had gotten nowhere. He hoped that trying his luck on *SmackDown* would lead to victory. His opponent was one half of the legendary Road Warriors tag team—Animal. Unfortunately for Slater, he fell victim to a power slam and an elbow drop, and Animal quickly pinned him.

August 3: Booker T takes the reins of *SmackDown*, promising to give the WWE Universe all the excitement they crave.

2012

Return of the Highlight Reel

August 10: For the first time in two years, Chris Jericho welcomed the WWE Universe to his Highlight Reel interview show. Jericho's scheduled guest, Dolph Ziggler, refused to appear, and his representative Vickie Guerrero came out instead. Jericho decided to interview her. Their verbal sparring led to Ziggler sneaking up on Jericho and slamming him with his Money in the Bank briefcase.

A unique job interview

August 17: Both Kaitlyn and Eve wanted to become the assistant to new *SmackDown* General Manager Booker T. To decide the issue, Booker pitted them against each other in a match, with the winner getting the position. After recent successes in the ring, Kaitlyn was confident, but Eve was able to pin her and earn the plum position in Booker T's new administration.

Fighting for their rights

August 24: Both Alberto Del Rio and Randy Orton thought they had legitimate claims to be the next man to challenge Sheamus for his World Heavyweight Championship. General Manager Booker T decided to let them settle matters in the ring with a No. 1 Contenders' Match. Orton almost nailed Del Rio with his RKO move, but Alberto managed to hold on to the ropes and then get "The Viper" to tap out to his Cross Armbreaker maneuver.

A *WrestleMania* rematch

September 14: Daniel Bryan was granted a non-title match against World Heavyweight Champion Sheamus who, just a week earlier, had had his devastating Brogue Kick finisher banned by General Manager Booker T for the injuries it had caused. The title was not on the line, but Bryan was eager to prove that his 18-second loss to Sheamus at *WrestleMania* was a fluke. Not only did Bryan survive much longer, but he also came close to pinning the champion several times, before he finally tapped out of Sheamus' Texas Cloverleaf move.

August 17: Eve pins Kaitlyn, earning the right to become the assistant to General Manager Booker T.

Monster and Goat unite

September 21: While Kane and Daniel Bryan were Tag Team Champions, they were still not a functional unit, as the two constantly argued that each by himself was the "Tag Team Champion." Coming together to face a common enemy of the duo of Damien Sandow and Cody Rhodes in a Lumberjack Match finally put "The Big Red Monster" Kane and "The Goatface" Bryan on the same page.

"The Viper" gets bitten

September 28: Big Show was back on *SmackDown* with one aim in mind—he wanted the World Heavyweight Championship. He was given an opportunity to earn the shot, facing Randy Orton in a No. 1 Contenders' Match in the main event. Orton was at a disadvantage, as Alberto Del Rio, hoping to take Orton's place in the contest, had attacked "The Viper" backstage, injuring his ribs. Orton bravely went ahead with the match, but Big Show ruthlessly targeted his ribs and chokeslammed him twice to win.

Showoff vs. champ

October 5: WWE Champion CM Punk felt that no one was giving him the respect he deserved. He decided to teach one particularly disrespectful Superstar, Dolph Ziggler, a lesson in the night's main event. Ziggler gave the champion all he could handle, including snaring a two-count after slamming Punk off the top rope. But Ziggler missed a corner splash, and Punk turned that into a Go To Sleep maneuver for a pinfall victory.

Kick vs. punch

October 12: Looking to settle the argument over which move was more devastating—Sheamus' Brogue Kick or Big Show's Knockout Punch—*SmackDown* General Manager Booker T brought in a device designed to measure the power of each. Sheamus's kick was recorded at 1,322 lbs per sq in (92.9 kg per sq cm). At first, Show refused to participate, but he eventually clocked the machine, and it measured an astounding 1,809 lbs per sq in (127.2 kg per sq cm).

October 5: Both Dolph Ziggler and CM Punk probe their opponent, looking for an early advantage in their match.

October 12: Big Show demonstrates the power of his punch by setting a record on Booker T's machine.

2012

October 26: With Eve incapacitated, Kaitlyn and Layla double-team Aksana.

Tag team turmoil
October 26: For over a month, Kaitlyn had been trying to find out who attacked her at *Night of Champions*, costing her a title opportunity. On *SmackDown*, she thought she finally had proof— a text message between Eve and Aksana planning the attack. While they continued to deny the charges, Booker T organized a tag team match between them and the team of Kaitlyn and Layla. Eve managed to snag the win, when Layla mistakenly kicked her partner Kaitlyn, knocking her out and allowing Eve to pin Kaitlyn.

Three guests for the price of one
November 2: The Miz's talk show segment, Miz TV, returned to *SmackDown* with the former World Heavyweight Champion Sheamus as a guest, but the interview did not remain a one-on-one affair for long. After The Miz had insulted Kofi Kingston, the man himself appeared and mocked the host for not winning the Intercontinental Championship in their last encounter. Big Show then interrupted to remind Sheamus that he had taken the World Heavyweight Championship from him at *Hell in a Cell* on October 28.

Fighting all over the arena
November 6: The rivalry between Alberto Del Rio and Randy Orton reached such a fever pitch that the ring could not contain the two competitors, and they met in a Falls Count Anywhere Match. They battled throughout the arena, even onto the concourse and concession stands. Del Rio tried to hit Orton with a steel chair while Orton was prone on the ring steps, but Orton moved and gave Del Rio an RKO onto the steps to win.

Also in this episode, Kofi Kingston defended his Intercontinental Championship against the previous champion, The Miz. Kingston prevailed in this evenly contested bout with a high-cross body manuever off the top rope. The Miz sportingly offered to shake the champion's hand, but Kingston gave The Miz a dropkick.

Rumors of romance
November 23: Once again, Miz TV talk show opened *SmackDown*, this time with John Cena as The Miz's guest. He quizzed Cena about his relationship with former *RAW* General Manager AJ Lee. Cena seemed uncomfortable with this line of questioning, but he did admit he had feelings for AJ, who also came out for the interview. Dolph Ziggler and Vickie Guerrero tried to stir the pot, but Cena refused to take the bait.

November 6: Kofi Kingston and The Miz brawl outside the squared circle.

130

December 7: Hornswoggle and The Great Khali make perhaps the strangest tag team pairing in WWE history.

Little and large together

December 7: The Great Khali was ready to take on Primo and Epico in tag team competition. Khali's partner, Hornswoggle, was the complete physical opposite to Khali. Nevertheless, the mismatched duo worked well together. Khali took out both Primo and Epico with a devastating clothesline move and massive body chops. The diminutive Hornswoggle then tagged in and pinned Epico with his signature Tadpole Splash move.

Enter the Hounds of Justice

December 14: Since their debut at *Survivor Series*, The Shield had dispensed their own brand of justice to those they deemed "unworthy." On this episode, they came to *SmackDown* and attacked Randy Orton in the backstage area, putting him out of action with a dislocated shoulder. On the TitanTron video screen, The Shield then announced that they planned to deal with Team Hell No and appeared in the arena ready for a match.But when Ryback joined Team Hell No in the ring, The Shield decided to forego an evenly matched, three-on-three fight.

Tag team turmoil

December 18: Bearing in mind the ongoing rivalry between John Cena and Dolph Ziggler, and Sheamus' battles with World Heavyweight Champion Big Show, General Manger Booker T set up a mighty Tag Team Match that pitted Cena and Sheamus against Ziggler and Big Show. For much of the match, Show and Ziggler controlled the action, but once Cena began turning the tide, Big E Langston interfered and battered Cena. As a result, Ziggler and Big Show were disqualified.

One last chance

December 28: Former WWE official Brad Maddox had abandoned his position to chase his dream of becoming a WWE Superstar. He had failed so far, but Booker T gave him one last chance—all he had to do was win a match to earn a contract. Unfortunately for Maddox, his opponent was "The Celtic Warrior," Sheamus. Maddox never stood a chance; Sheamus dominated the match and easily pinned him.

December 18: AJ Lee skips with delight to see the devastation wrought by Big E Langston at the expense of John Cena.

2013

CHAMPIONSHIPS HAVE ALWAYS been important in WWE, but perhaps never more important than in 2013. The year centered on the WWE and World Heavyweight Championships, kicking off with Alberto Del Rio basking in the glow of his own World Championship win. 2013 saw The Rock regain the WWE Championship after ten years; it also celebrated the longest-reigning WWE Champion, Bruno Sammartino, returning home to WWE and his induction into the Hall of Fame; finally, the year ended with the unification of the World Heavyweight and WWE Championships into the WWE World Heavyweight Championship.

On a rocky road

January 11: After ten years away, The Rock returned to *SmackDown* in his hometown of Miami in order to hype his upcoming WWE Championship Match against CM Punk at *Royal Rumble*. But a pair of young Superstars, Damien Sandow and Cody Rhodes, who called themselves Team Rhodes Scholars, were less than impressed. They insulted The Rock's intelligence, which he countered by slamming both of them to the mat and following up with a People's Elbow move.

At the beginning of the show, *SmackDown* General Manager Booker T announced that World Heavyweight Champion Big Show would defend the title against Alberto Del Rio in a Last Man Standing Match. Del Rio used the match's no-rules format to his advantage, throwing the steel ring stairs at Big Show twice and then dumping the announcers' table on top of his fallen body. Big Show couldn't respond to the referee's ten count, giving Del Rio the win and the championship.

January 11: The Rock calls out that he's come "home" to *SmackDown* and Miami.

January 4: Randy Orton declares that he's entering the Royal Rumble Match.

Out for vengeance

January 4: Randy Orton had suffered an attack by the three members of The Shield three weeks earlier. On this episode of *SmackDown*, he declared he would get his revenge on the so-called "Hounds of Justice." Furthermore, and perhaps more importantly to Orton, he announced that he was entering the Royal Rumble Match, in an attempt to win a shot at the winner's main event match at *WrestleMania*.

Del Rio's fiesta

January 18: To celebrate his World Heavyweight Championship win one week earlier, Alberto Del Rio held a "Championship Fiesta." A mariachi band played, a Latina dancer performed, and Alberto Del Rio rejoiced—until Big Show, Big E Langston, and Dolph Ziggler showed up to spoil the party. Ziggler promised to cash in his Money in the Bank opportunity to snatch Del Rio's title.

January 18. Alberto Del Rio celebrates his title win with an in-ring fiesta.

A certain Swagger

February 1: *SmackDown* General Manager Booker T was proud of the upcoming Elimination Chamber Match he had set up featuring former World Heavyweight Champions. However, Jack Swagger, not seen in WWE since the previous September, was disgusted that, as a former World Champion, he had not been given a spot. Booker told Swagger that if he won a match later that night on *SmackDown*, he would qualify for the Elimination Chamber—a feat Swagger duly accomplished.

Competing for the chamber

February 8: After nine months out of action, rehabbing an injury, Mark Henry returned to *SmackDown*, angry at having been left out of the former World Champions' Elimination Chamber Match. General Manager Booker T told Henry that he could be in the Chamber Match if he beat Randy Orton in this edition of *SmackDown*. Henry's superior strength was too much for Orton, and Henry entered the Chamber.

February 8: Mark Henry employs his considerable weight to punish Randy Orton.

February 15: Big Show floors Chris Jericho with a big right hand.

Wars of words

February 15: Chris Jericho had returned to WWE to compete in the former World Champions Elimination Chamber Match the following Sunday and confronted Big Show, who was facing Alberto Del Rio for the World Heavyweight Championship at the *Elimination Chamber* pay-per-view Sunday as well. On this edition of *SmackDown*, Jericho mocked and challenged his former friend to a match, which Big Show won with a knockout punch.

The following Sunday at *Elimination Chamber*, The Rock and CM Punk were set to battle for the WWE Championship. Four days earlier, on *RAW*, Punk had won the WWE Title from The Rock. On this episode, they traded insults, with The Rock warning Punk that, at *Elimination Chamber*, Punk would receive a beating that would haunt him for the rest of his life.

Elsewhere in WWE

February 17: At *Elimination Chamber*, Jack Swagger managed to defeat Mark Henry, Daniel Bryan, Randy Orton, Chris Jericho, and Kane inside the mammoth steel chain structure to earn a World Heavyweight Championship Title opportunity at *WrestleMania* 29. The Shield defeated John Cena, Sheamus, and Ryback. In the main event, The Rock retained the WWE Championship against CM Punk.

March 22: Fandango brags over his vanquished opponent, Chris Jericho.

INTRODUCING...

Fandango

March 1: Ballroom dancing may seem like an unusual start for a WWE Superstar, but for Fandango, it was the perfect preparation. Dancing his way to the ring for his *SmackDown* debut, Fandango and his rousing entrance music thrilled the WWE Universe. In years to come, Fandango would join with Tyler Breeze to form a tag team called Breezango, who are best known as WWE's "Fashion Police."

Fandango joins *SmackDown*, promising the WWE Universe will never forget his name.

Social Media *SmackDown*

March 1: WWE has always been at the forefront of technology and entertainment and this week's episode was called "Social Media *SmackDown*." The WWE Universe used social media to interact with the show. Viewers could express their opinions and even vote on opponents and stipulations for matches.

Remember the name

March 22: For weeks, Chris Jericho had mocked Fandango by pretending to forget how to pronounce his name. In this edition, Fandango had had enough. He knew Jericho was mocking him on purpose and attacked him, following Jericho's losing match against Jack Swagger. Fandango screamed, "What's my name!" as he pummeled "Y2J."

Strange partners

March 29: Sheamus, Randy Orton, and Big Show didn't get along, but after weeks of being separately attacked by The Shield, the trio joined forces against The Shield at *WrestleMania*. In this episode of *SmackDown*, Sheamus, Orton, and Big Show launched a surprise attack on Shield members Roman Reigns and Seth Rollins before they could even enter the ring.

March 29: Big Show and Randy Orton attack Roman Reigns and Seth Rollins in the audience area.

Elsewhere in WWE

April 6: Bruno Sammartino was the longest-reigning WWE Champion in history, holding the title for nearly eight years. He had not been seen in WWE for 30 years when it was announced that he would be inducted into the WWE Hall of Fame on April 6, 2013.

Cash-in celebration

April 12: Four days earlier on *RAW*, Dolph Ziggler cashed in his Money in the Bank Championship opportunity and won the World Heavyweight Championship from Alberto Del Rio. On this edition of *SmackDown*, Ziggler held a celebratory party for himself and his friends AJ Lee and Big E. The fun was interrupted by Chris Jericho, who challenged Ziggler to a match later that night. Ziggler accepted and, with a little blindside help from Big E, pinned Jericho.

Burying The Shield

April 26: The Shield seemed unstoppable, proving their dominance by conquering countless Superstars. Undertaker— in his first *SmackDown* match in three years—sought to bury The Shield by facing Dean Ambrose. Undertaker fought off the other members of The Shield and forced Dean Ambrose to submit to his Hell's Gate hold, but the other members of The Shield immediately attacked him. The trio finally slammed Undertaker through the announcers' table.

April 26: The Shield gives Undertaker their patented Triple Power Bomb through the announce table.

World's Strongest arm wrestler

May 3: Mark Henry had earned his nickname of "World's Strongest Man" by winning several strongman competitions, including Olympic-level weightlifting. However, Sheamus believed that he was even stronger than Henry and set out to prove it. Four days earlier, Sheamus had cheated to win a tug of war with Henry. On this *SmackDown* edition, they had an arm-wrestling contest, which Henry easily won. Sheamus took immediate revenge by kicking Henry.

May 3: Mark Henry and Sheamus demonstrate their power during a titanic Arm Wrestling Match.

Truck pull

May 10: One week after the arm-wrestling contest against Sheamus, Mark Henry wanted to demonstrate his incredible strength by setting a world record in pulling semi-trucks. Connected to two semi-trailers weighing a total of 110,000 lbs (49, 895 kg) with a harness, Henry pulled with all of his might. He struggled at first, but, with a colossal effort, Henry pulled the two trucks across the finish line. Adrenaline rushing, Henry yelled out, "That's what I do!" in celebration.

Smart choices

May 24: Damien Sandow was not shy about letting the world know he possessed a superior intellect. Claiming to be disgusted by recent brainless strength challenges he had seen on *SmackDown*, he extended an "Intellectual Challenge" to Matt Striker and Sheamus. This was to untie a "Gordian Knot," an impossibly complicated knot in a piece of rope. Before either could figure it out, Sandow produced a pair of bolt cutters and cut the knot open. Sheamus reacted by hurling Striker through the ring ropes and onto Sandow to illustrate Newton's law of gravity.

Paul Heyman was known as a Superstar maker. After all, it was thanks to him that both Brock Lesnar and CM Punk had become household names. On this edition, Paul Heyman showed off his newest "Paul Heyman Guy"—third generation Superstar Curtis Axel, who had injured Triple H in a match on *RAW* four days earlier. Axel boasted that he was more talented than his father or grandfather and, with Paul Heyman's help, he would become the most dominant competitor in all of WWE.

Always united

May 31: In this edition, the three members of The Shield—Dean Ambrose, Roman Reigns, and Seth Rollins—competed one-on-one against Superstars they had attacked over the past week. In the first match, Seth Rollins lost after Kane's friend, Daniel Bryan, shoved Rollins off the top rope and Kane chokeslammed him—though The Shield made Kane pay after the match. Next, Roman Reigns defeated Daniel Bryan by disqualification when Kane, trying to help Bryan get the victory, interfered in the match and hit Reigns. Finally, Randy Orton beat Dean Ambrose by disqualification when the full Shield attacked him during the match.

May 31: Daniel Bryan struggles to pull Roman Reigns down to the mat.

"Y2J" and the "Paul Heyman Guy"

June 7: Chris Jericho was a sports entertainment veteran and wasn't impressed by an ambitious upstart like "New Paul Heyman Guy" Curtis Axel. Jericho couldn't stand Paul Heyman either, and wanted to take out his stable of Superstars one by one. Jericho was on top, until Heyman distracted him by playing the entrance music for CM Punk, another "Paul Heyman Guy" and Jericho's chief rival. While "Y2J" was distracted, Axel rolled him up for the pin. Furious, Jericho floored Axel after the match and stared daggers at Heyman.

May 24: Damien Sandow shows off his superior intelligence by challenging other Superstars to untie his complicated knot.

June 28: Damien Sandow feels the impact of Sheamus' beer barrel during their Dublin Street Fight.

Dublin Street fight

June 28: Still annoyed by Damien Sandow's "intellectual challenges" weeks before, Sheamus challenged the self-proclaimed genius to a no-rules Dublin Street Fight. Sandow and Sheamus used chairs, kendo sticks, steel steps, even barstools against each other. It all proved too much for Sandow, who slumped onto one of the chairs, before receiving a Brogue Kick from Sheamus and losing the match.

INTRODUCING...

The Wyatt Family

July 12: Perhaps no group of Superstars was more intimidating than The Wyatt Family. Bray Wyatt, Erick Rowan, and Luke Harper came to WWE hiding their faces behind sheep masks and darkened lanterns. They grew in strength, at times adding Randy Orton, Daniel Bryan, and Braun Strowman to their ranks. Before The Wyatt family disbanded, its patriarch, Bray Wyatt, won the WWE Championship.

The Wyatt Family surveys the WWE Universe, planning one day to rule WWE.

July 12: Divas Champion AJ Lee has harsh words for her challenger Kaitlyn at their contract signing.

Diva contract signing

July 12: Divas Champion AJ Lee was set to defend her title against the number one contender Kaitlyn at the upcoming *Money in the Bank* event. General Manager Teddy Long called a contract signing to formalize the match. Once the contract was signed, however, AJ slapped Kaitlyn, who then attacked AJ and her bodyguard Big E, spearing AJ and slapping Big E.

2013

July 19: Mr. McMahon (center) turns a deaf ear to pleas from current and former General Managers of *RAW* and *SmackDown* Brad Maddox, Theodore Long, and Booker T.

General Manager chaos

July 19: *SmackDown* General Manager Theodore Long was up for a job evaluation from Mr. McMahon, worried that he would be replaced. Several others believed that Long would be replaced too, and set out to apply for his job, including former *SmackDown* General Manager Booker T and newly hired *RAW* General Manager Brad Maddox. Booker, Maddox, and Long all pled their case to Mr. McMahon, hoping to be chosen. All three candidates were shocked and disappointed when Mr. McMahon announced that Vicki Guerrero would be *SmackDown*'s new GM.

After eight years away, former WWE Champion Rob Van Dam made a long-awaited return to *SmackDown* with a match against Darren Young. RVD showed off his amazing arsenal of moves. Despite having his Prime Time Players tag team partner and mentor Titus O'Neil to distract Van Dam, Young was no match for the returning veteran, and Rob Van Dam won with a Five Star Frog Splash dive from the top rope.

Briefcase swimming

July 26: Damien Sandow had recently won the Money in the Bank briefcase, guaranteeing him a future WWE Championship opportunity whenever he wanted it. One thing Sandow didn't anticipate was Cody Rhodes stealing the briefcase. Even worse, Cody Rhodes then took the briefcase to the Gulf of Mexico. Sandow pleaded with Rhodes not to throw the briefcase into the water, but Rhodes tossed it regardless. Sandow dove in, but was unable to retrieve it. Days later, Rhodes sent deep-sea divers to look for the briefcase and, on the following edition of *RAW*, returned it to Sandow.

Elsewhere in WWE

July 28: The program *Total Divas* captured the lives outside the ring of the WWE's most popular female Superstars. Still going strong after more than five years on the air, the show has spawned two spinoffs, *Total Bellas* and *Miz and Mrs*.

Triple Threat number one contender

August 2: World Heavyweight Champion Alberto Del Rio knew he would have to defend his championship at the upcoming *SummerSlam*. What he didn't know was who his opponent would be—that was determined on this episode. Del Rio would face the winner of a Triple Threat Match. Christian defeated Rob Van Dam and Randy Orton to become Del Rio's championship opponent. He was immediately attacked from behind by Del Rio.

July 26: Cody Rhodes threatens to throw Damien Sandow's Money in the Bank briefcase into the Gulf of Mexico.

The Devil's favorites

August 9: As preparation for facing evil Bray Wyatt and his Wyatt Family in a Ring of Fire Match at *SummerSlam*, Kane, "The Devil's Favorite Demon," took on all three members of team 3MB—Drew McIntyre, Heath Slater, and Jinder Mahal. Kane made quick work of these wannabe rock stars. Following the match, Bray Wyatt appeared on the TitanTron big screen, speaking to Kane in ominous tones about their impending match.

Cage Match

August 23: At *SummerSlam* the Sunday prior, Randy Orton had won the WWE Championship. As he was celebrating in the ring on this edition of *SmackDown*, Daniel Bryan challenged him to a match. Orton refused, and *SmackDown* General Manager Vickie Guerrero was livid that Bryan had ruined Orton's moment. Wade Barrett volunteered to teach Bryan a lesson and faced him in a Steel Cage Match that night. Bryan defeated Barrett, but was hit from behind by Randy Orton right after his victory.

Best for business

September 6: As the Chief Operating Officer (COO) of WWE, Triple H often had to make unpopular decisions. One of them was firing Cody Rhodes four days earlier on *RAW*. Although he invited Superstars to express their opinions, he only pretended to be open to their views. He proceeded to punish anyone who disagreed with him by placing them in difficult matches; those who agreed with him were rewarded with nights off from competing, easier matches, or even championship opportunities.

September 6: WWE Chief of Operations Triple H and *SmackDown* GM Vicki Guerrero give the WWE Superstars a stark warning—you're either with us or against us.

Face to face

September 13: After weeks of attacks on each other, WWE Champion Randy Orton and Daniel Bryan came face to face on The Cutting Edge talk show segment. Edge reminded the WWE Universe that Orton and Bryan would be competing for the WWE Championship at the next pay-per-view, *Night of Champions*. Bryan accused Orton of being a sellout for joining the Authority stable. Orton hit Bryan, who responded by locking him in his agonizing signature Yes Lock submission hold. It took a group of referees to get Bryan off Orton.

September 13: Daniel Bryan gets Randy Orton in his Yes Lock. Submission soon follows.

Eleven on three

September 20: On the most recent edition of *RAW*, ten Superstars prevented The Shield from injuring Daniel Bryan. That night, The Shield were allowed their revenge as the three members faced Bryan and the other ten Superstars one at a time. The Shield ploughed through Darren Young, Titus O'Neil, Dolph Ziggler, Kofi Kingston, and Rob Van Dam before Triple H persuaded Vickie Guerrero to change the match to a three on three. The Shield then faced Daniel Bryan and The Usos—who ended the night victorious.

September 20: The Shield inflict pain on Dolph Ziggler, one of their 10 opponents that evening.

2013

October 25: Ryback destroys CM Punk impersonator CM Skunk.

CM Skunk!

October 25: In July, Paul Heyman turned on one of his once-favorite "Paul Heyman Guys," CM Punk, and hired Ryback as a new "Paul Heyman Guy." Ryback had his eyes set on destroying CM Punk in a future match. In anticipation of that collision, Paul Heyman arranged a warmup for Ryback on *SmackDown* introducing him to an impersonator named CM Skunk. Ryback annihilated CM Skunk, as a threatening warning to CM Punk.

The champ is here... again

November 1: For the first time in many months, John Cena returned to *SmackDown*. And his return was with a purpose. Five nights earlier, Cena had defeated Alberto Del Rio for the World Heavyweight Championship at *Hell in a Cell*. Cena had come to *SmackDown* to celebrate his victory and declare a new era in WWE with him as champion. Cesaro, Damien Sandow, and Jack Swagger disagreed and were about to attack him. Cena got help from Goldust and Cody Rhodes, and the three of them drove Sandow, Cesaro, and Swagger from the ring.

October 11: Goldust mocks Wyatt Family member Erick Rowan prior to their match that evening.

Feuding families

October 11: The Wyatt Family had been undefeated in competition for several months. That was until they battled another legendary family—Goldust and his brother Cody Rhodes. Luke Harper and Erick Rowan, representing The Wyatt Family, attacked the Rhodes with great ferocity. However, Goldust used his vast in-ring experience to work well with his brother, and Cody stole victory from The Wyatts by pinning Harper, handing The Wyatt Family their first ever WWE loss.

Violent recruitment

November 8: Bray Wyatt was looking to grow his Wyatt Family stable and wanted to add the most talented Superstar in WWE. There was only one choice: Daniel Bryan. Wyatt knew that Bryan wouldn't respond favorably if he just asked him to join. So Wyatt led physical attacks on Bryan for several weeks, breaking his spirit and manipulating him into joining. This edition of *SmackDown* saw the first of these beatdowns. Bryan eventually joined The Wyatts on the December 30, 2013, episode of *RAW*.

Cheating on a strength test

November 15: World Heavyweight Champion John Cena's opponent at the upcoming *Survivor Series* Alberto Del Rio wanted to prove he was as strong as Cena, so he challenged him to an arm-wrestling contest. Cena accepted, but it was a trap. As Cena pushed Del Rio's arm down, Del Rio punched and kicked Cena, sending him to the mat. Del Rio continued the assault, pummeling Cena with a steel chair, as if trying to break his arm before their big match.

December 13: Randy Orton seeks the approval of his Authority faction mentor Triple H.

November 15: John Cena and Alberto Del Rio lock up in an arm-wrestling contest.

Thanksgiving showdown

November 29: The day after the Thanksgiving holiday, the WWE Superstars were fighting among themselves. What had started as a match between the Rhodes Brothers and The Shield ballooned into a 12-man Thanksgiving Showdown thanks to interference by The Wyatt Family, CM Punk, The Usos, and Rey Mysterio. Punk, Mysterio, the Rhodes Brothers, and The Usos won the match, defeating the combined forces of The Wyatt Family and The Shield.

Unifying championships

December 6: At the upcoming *TLC: Tables, Ladders, and Chairs* pay-per-view, history would be made as WWE Champion Randy Orton would face World Heavyweight Champion John Cena, with both titles on the line. The winner would unify the titles becoming the WWE World Heavyweight Champion. WWE COO Triple H spoke at length about this historic match on this *SmackDown* edition. The two championships had existed for more than a combined 150 years; unifying them would mark the end of an era and the beginning of a new one.

Pleading forgiveness

December 13: WWE Champion Randy Orton had, until four days earlier, been called The Face of WWE by Triple H and Stephanie McMahon, a.k.a. The Authority. But after Orton accidentally caused Stephanie to be injured, he had fallen from favor. In this episode, Orton apologized to The Authority, bringing Triple H to the ring. Orton asked "The Game" if The Authority still believed him or if they'd sided with John Cena, choosing to replace him with Cena as the face of WWE. Triple H laughed, dismissing Orton's question and telling Orton not to worry about it, before leaving him alone in the ring.

Unified

December 20: Five days earlier at *TLC: Tables, Ladders, and Chairs*, Randy Orton made history by winning the WWE and World Heavyweight Championships, unifying them into one WWE World Heavyweight Championship. Not only did he win the titles, but he also found himself embraced by The Authority once again as The Face of WWE. Randy Orton closed out 2013 on top of the world and wouldn't let anyone bring him down during his championship celebration on *SmackDown*—especially John Cena and Daniel Bryan, who both demanded matches for the title (which Orton refused).

December 20: Randy Orton holds up the two titles of the unified WWE World Heavyweight Championship.

January 18, 2013: Big E Langston, Dolph Ziggler, and Big Show confront Alberto Del Rio and Sheamus during Del Rio's championship-celebrating "Fiesta Del Rio."

2014

UNDERDOGS AND up-and-comers were the themes of 2014 as hungry new Superstars who had made a name in NXT, such as Paige, Emma, and Bo Dallas, debuted on *SmackDown* and pursued the top Superstars and championships. Legends such as Batista, Sting, and the New Age Outlaws had one last run before saying goodbye. Daniel Bryan overcame all the obstacles put in front of him by The Authority's scheming to reach the top of WWE, rolling his "Yes Movement" out to the WWE Universe and becoming WWE World Heavyweight Champion.

"Let's just cut to the chase. Brock Lesnar, I'm challenging you to a FIGHT!"

Big Show (January 10, 2014)

Big challenge

January 10: Four days earlier, Brock Lesnar had broken Mark Henry's arm and Big Show had attacked Lesnar to help his friend. On *SmackDown*, Big Show was the guest on the Miz TV talk show and challenged Lesnar to a match. Lesnar's advocate, Paul Heyman, accepted the challenge, adding that if Big Show wanted to fight Lesnar earlier than the *Royal Rumble* pay-per-view, Lesnar was not hard to find.

January 10: Brock Lesnar's advocate Paul Heyman responds to Big Show's challenge for a match against Lesnar.

Old Doggs, new tricks

January 17: WWE veterans the New Age Outlaws—"Road Dogg" Jesse James and Billy Gunn—had returned to WWE and risen through the tag team ranks in recent weeks, earning a non-title match against the WWE Tag Team Champions, the Rhodes Brothers on *SmackDown*. The more experienced Outlaws got the victory when Gunn pinned Cody Rhodes.

10-man melee

January 24: Bad blood between The Shield and The Usos, and the New Age Outlaws and the Rhodes Brothers had reached fever pitch. On this episode, the four teams, along with Big E, squared off in a 10-Man Tag Team Match. The Shield and the New Age Outlaws were on one side, while the Rhodes Brothers, Big E, and The Usos were on the other. However, the match soon became a free-for-all brawl, with all ten Superstars attacking each other.

January 24: WWE tag team legends the New Age Outlaws reunite to face the Rhodes Brothers.

January 31: Former partners Titus O'Neil and Darren Young go one on one.

Prime-time split

January 31: Darren Young and Titus O'Neil had been tag team partners the Prime Time Players for just over a year. And while they'd had a lot of success, in recent weeks they had lost matches and were growing frustrated with each other. After losing to Curtis Axel and Ryback on this episode of *SmackDown*, Titus O'Neil snapped and attacked Darren Young with a flurry of kicks, breaking up the team.

Yes! Yes! No!

February 7: Daniel Bryan had recently joined and left The Wyatt Family and was now looking for a chance at the WWE Championship. He found support in the WWE Universe, but opposition from former tag team partner Kane, and Triple H and Stephanie McMahon, collectively known as "The Authority." On this episode, Kane interrupted Bryan's "Yes!" chant and forced him to compete against Cesaro, as punishment for disrespecting The Authority. Bryan won, but Kane then attacked him.

Elsewhere in WWE

February 24: Altering the landscape of sports entertainment forever, the WWE Network launched, offering the WWE Universe an abundance of WWE content, streaming for only $9.99. Every pay-per-view event aired live, brand-new shows like NXT aired weekly, and specials covering the careers of WWE legends and Superstars became a mainstay. It was a revolutionary advance in bringing the world of WWE into the homes of the brand's vast fanbase.

Dance off

February 21: As Fandango's dance partner, Summer Rae felt that she had proved she was the WWE's best hoofer. She was confident of winning a dance-off against NXT Superstar Emma, who was making her *SmackDown* debut. Summer Rae, dressed to the nines, was out to impress, even doing the splits; Emma, in T-shirt and sweatpants, was just having fun, and the WWE Universe made her an easy winner. To cap her victory, Emma ejected both Summer Rae and Fandango from the ring.

February 21: Emma shows off her fun moves in a dance-off with Summer Rae.

Pre- and postshows

February 28: The launch of WWE's own network meant that shows like *SmackDown* acquired their own live preshows and postshows. The first of these shows premiered before and after this *SmackDown* episode and included interviews with Superstars such as AJ Lee, who was set to defend her Divas Championship against Cameron. On the postshow, Daniel Bryan was interviewed immediately after he and The Usos had defeated Kane and the New Age Outlaws in the show's main event.

2014

WrestleMania plans

March 7: After winning the Royal Rumble Match, Batista had plans to win the WWE World Heavyweight Championship at *WrestleMania*. While Batista was reminding the WWE Universe of these plans on this edition of *SmackDown*, Daniel Bryan, who didn't have a match set for *WrestleMania*, interrupted him. Bryan wanted to face Triple H and be included in the main event against Batista and Randy Orton for the title. Batista was dismissive, but Bryan warned him not to be, leading the WWE Universe in his signature "Yes!" chant.

In tribute to André

March 21: WWE had announced that the first-ever André the Giant Memorial Battle Royal would take place at *WrestleMania 30*. To promote this exciting match, The Miz hosted Big Show on his Miz TV talk show. Big Show, as the heir apparent to André the Giant, promised to win the Battle Royal. Several Superstars disagreed and charged the ring, attacking Big Show and taking him down a peg before the big Battle Royal.

Superstar-crossed lovers

March 28: For weeks, Emma and Santino Marella had been flirting and accompanying each other to the ring for matches. Tonight they went on a date. The outing went from awkward to uncomfortable when Santino mistook looking into Emma's eyes for a staring contest. Finally, Santino started feeling sick and spat wine all over Emma.

March 7: Batista makes a statement by attacking Daniel Bryan from behind.

Elsewhere in WWE

April 6: No one believed that Brock Lesnar would end Undertaker's undefeated streak at *WrestleMania*, but on April 6, at *WrestleMania 30*, he did just that. The WWE Universe watched in stunned silence as Lesnar pinned Undertaker, breaking the streak and going down in history as "the one" in 21-1.

March 21: Superstars attack Big Show in the lead-up to *WrestleMania*'s André the Giant Battle Royal.

"I am a fan! I'm just like every one of these people. And if I were you, Batista, I'd be embarrassed that a fan took you down."

Daniel Bryan (April 11, 2014)

April 11: Daniel Bryan and veteran Hulk Hogan celebrate Bryan's championship at *WrestleMania 30*.

Yes-a-mania

April 11: At *WrestleMania 30*, five days earlier, Daniel Bryan had finally achieved his goal, defeating Triple H, Batista, and Randy Orton to become the new WWE World Heavyweight Champion. WWE Hall of Famer Hulk Hogan celebrated Bryan's victory in the ring with him in this *SmackDown* episode. The leader of Hulkamania called Bryan the leader of Yes-a-mania, declaring the future was bright for the young champion.

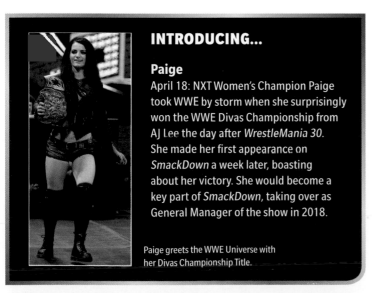

INTRODUCING...

Paige
April 18: NXT Women's Champion Paige took WWE by storm when she surprisingly won the WWE Divas Championship from AJ Lee the day after *WrestleMania 30*. She made her first appearance on *SmackDown* a week later, boasting about her victory. She would become a key part of *SmackDown*, taking over as General Manager of the show in 2018.

Paige greets the WWE Universe with her Divas Championship Title.

Ultimate goodbye

April 18: On April 5, The Ultimate Warrior was inducted into the WWE Hall of Fame. He then appeared at *WrestleMania 30* and the April 7 edition of *RAW*. Tragically and unexpectedly, The Ultimate Warrior then passed away. On this edition of *SmackDown*, WWE Superstars and the WWE Universe paid tribute to the Warrior and his legacy.

The Shield strikes back

April 25: *SmackDown* General Manager Vickie Guerrero ordered The Shield to face 11 Superstars in an 11-on-3 Handicap Match. However, The Shield spent the bulk of this episode backstage— hunting down and eliminating six of their proposed opponents. In the end, they survived the Handicap Match by defeating the remaining five: Ryback, Bad New Barrett, Alberto Del Rio, Titus O'Neil, and Damien Sandow.

April 25: Ryback feels the full force of The Shield's three-pronged attack.

May 2: Hornswoggle and El Torito face off, backed up by their respective teammates, Team 3B and Los Matadores.

Mascots war

May 2: The team 3MB—Heath Slater, Jinder Mahal, and Drew McIntyre—fancied themselves rock stars. Hornswoggle wanted to join their rock'n'roll group, and was welcomed as a sort of mascot. This proved valuable when 3MB faced off against Los Matadores and their mascot, El Torito. Hornswoggle and El Torito brawled while their teammates looked on, commencing a longstanding, entertaining rivalry.

Evolving The Shield

May 9: In the early 2000s, Evolution—Triple H, Batista, and Randy Orton—was the most dominant faction in WWE. Fast-forward a decade and The Shield had taken that title. When Evolution reformed earlier in 2014, they set their sights on defeating The Shield, determined to recapture past glories. On this episode, Batista faced an already-injured Seth Rollins, and dominated him in the match, sending a strong message to The Shield that Evolution was back and in charge.

Haunting Cena

May 23: Bray Wyatt and The Wyatt Family had attacked John Cena on *RAW* earlier in the week. Bray Wyatt, sitting in his rocking chair, boasted that The Wyatt Family destroyed the Cenation. Later that night, Wyatt promised, they would finish Cena. In the main event, The Wyatt Family attacked The Usos to prematurely end their match. Cena came to The Usos' rescue and found himself staring at Bray Wyatt who laughed manically, threatening Cena with another Wyatt Family attack in the future.

Destroying The Shield

June 6: Four days earlier on *RAW*, Seth Rollins turned on his Shield brethren Roman Reigns and Dean Ambrose and hit them with a steel chair, destroying The Shield. Tonight, Rollins and his new mentor Triple H explained his heinous actions to the WWE Universe. Rollins was watching out for himself. It was time Seth Rollins aligned with Triple H and The Authority to reach the top of the WWE mountain—alone.

June 6: Triple H proudly presents his new protegé, Seth Rollins, to the WWE Universe.

June 20: The seven competitors in the upcoming Money in the Bank Ladder Match face each other.

A sneak preview

June 20: Every year in the Money in the Bank Ladder Match, several Superstars battle each other for a chance at a WWE World Heavyweight Championship whenever they want it. In a sneak preview of this year's Money in the Bank Match, the seven Superstars competed in a 4-on-3 Handicap Match. Roman Reigns, John Cena, and Sheamus defeated Alberto Del Rio, Cesaro, Randy Orton, and Bray Wyatt.

Hypocrisy

July 18: As Chris Jericho was about to face Luke Harper in a one-on-one match in this episode of *SmackDown*, Harper's master in The Wyatt Family, Bray Wyatt, took time to address Jericho. Wyatt reminded Jericho that when he first arrived in WWE in 1999, Jericho promised to save the WWE from all that ailed it. Wyatt was disgusted at Jericho's apparent hypocrisy in becoming part of the WWE machine. Wyatt said Jericho needed "saving" and Luke Harper would do so tonight. The prophesy was wrong, however, as Jericho defeated Harper.

No disqualification

July 25: Dean Ambrose and Cesaro had been getting under each other's skin in the weeks following The Shield's dissolution. On this edition of *SmackDown,* they took out their aggression on each other in a No Disqualification Match. Both superstars made use of a variety of weapons and utilized various objects, including Cesaro planting Ambrose on some chairs with a suplex. In the end, Dean Ambrose overcame Cesaro to pick up the win.

The Architect attacks

August 8: After breaking up The Shield, "The Architect" Seth Rollins was set to face his former Shield teammate Dean Ambrose at *SummerSlam*. Ambrose was obsessed with getting revenge on Rollins, while Rollins wanted to prove his superiority to Ambrose. As a warmup match, Ambrose faced Randy Orton in the main event of tonight's SmackDown. Before the end of the match, however, Seth Rollins charged the ring and viciously attacked Ambrose, giving him his signature move, the Stomp.

July 25: Dean Ambrose attacks Cesaro with the ring bell in their No Disqualification Match.

Elsewhere in WWE

On the August 11 edition of *RAW*, the WWE Universe celebrated WWE Hall of Famer Hulk Hogan's birthday with a massive birthday party. Many of Hogan's Superstar friends appeared on the show to wish him a happy birthday. And though Brock Lesnar tried to crash the party, John Cena protected the Hulkster and joined in the celebrations.

You better "Bo-lieve" it!

August 22: Former NXT Champion Bo Dallas had come to WWE to help inspire the Superstars and the WWE Universe with motivational pep talks. On this episode of *SmackDown*, Dallas spoke to Jack Swagger who'd lost his match at *SummerSlam* earlier in the week and lost again immediately before Dallas' appearance. Dallas reminded Swagger that he was a loser but could become a winner again if he would only "Bo-lieve!"

August 22: Bo Dallas punishes Jack Swagger for not "Bo-lieving" enough in himself.

AJ's BFF

August 29: AJ Lee and Paige had a brief but storied history as they'd exchanged surprise victories over the Divas Championship in recent months. Despite the apparent animosity between the two, they acted like they were best friends. In a demonstration of friendship, AJ Lee brought Paige a box of chocolates after her match. Paige took one of the chocolates and spit it out at Lee who simply laughed and ate a chocolate herself.

August 29: Frenemies AJ Lee and Paige share a box of chocolates.

Rusev responds

September 5: Four days earlier on *RAW*, Mark Henry challenged Rusev to a match at *Night of Champions*. Tonight, Rusev and his manager Lana answered his challenge. "The Ravishing Russian" Lana and "The Bulgarian Brute" Rusev flew a giant Russian flag in the ring. They accepted Henry's challenge, warning that Rusev would not only crush Henry but all of America in their match.

September 5: Rusev and Lana carry the Russian flag proudly as they accept Mark Henry's challenge for a match.

Blinding Arm Wrestling Match

September 12: In anticipation of their match at *Night of Champions*, Rusev and Mark Henry battled each other in an arm-wrestling match. Although he was the World's Strongest Man, Mark Henry couldn't defeat Rusev because Rusev's manager Lana cheated, throwing chalk in Henry's eyes.

Refereeing error

September 26: Early in the night, 15 Superstars competed in a Battle Royal; later in the evening, the winner was set to face the Intercontinental Champion, Dolph Ziggler. Cesaro won the Battle Royal but was unable to capture the title. Ziggler pinned Cesaro, and the referee didn't see that Cesaro had grabbed the ring rope, which should have required Ziggler to release the hold. This error cost Cesaro his opportunity at championship gold.

"Fifteen years. Feels like just yesterday I was saying 'Layeth the Smacketh Down!'"

The Rock (October 10, 2014)

15 years young

October 10: This special show celebrated *SmackDown*'s 15th anniversary. The Miz's Miz TV talk show featured special guests John Cena and Dean Ambrose, who were set to face each other 11 days later at *Hell in a Cell* in a No Holds Barred Match. The winner would face Seth Rollins inside the cell later that night. Cena and Ambrose put their differences aside to attack The Miz, whom they both despised.

Highlights from the show's 15-year history were shown all night long. Former *SmackDown* General Managers Stephanie McMahon, John Laurinaitis, and Theodore Long reminisced about the show during their tenures, leading to a 15-Man Tag Team Match of Team Teddy vs. Team Johnny. In the main event, Team Teddy (Sheamus, Mark Henry, The Usos, Los Matadores with El Torito, and Jack Swagger) defeated Team Johnny (Goldust, Stardust, Heath Slater, Titus O'Neil, Hornswoggle, Damien Sandow, and Cesaro).

October 31: Cesaro staggers around with a pumpkin on his head after losing his match against Dean Ambrose.

October 10: John Cena waves his mocking "You Can't See Me" gesture over a fallen Miz.

Smacky Halloween

October 31: Halloween night is for fun and games and spooks and frights. Halloween night on *SmackDown* is no different. The Superstars showed off their best Halloween costumes in a Battle Royal and competed in frightening matches, and Cesaro ended up with a pumpkin on his head.

2014

November 7: Dolph Ziggler and Kane battle in their Steel Cage Match.

Cage warfare

November 7: It's not often that there are two Steel Cage Matches in one WWE show, but that was the case in this edition of *SmackDown*. In the first Cage Match, The Usos squared off against Goldust and Stardust for the WWE Tag Team Championship. Goldust and Startdust won the bout, retaining the titles. Intercontinental Champion Dolph Ziggler defeated Kane in the second, non-title, Cage Match.

Elsewhere in WWE

For two decades, Sting was known as the face of WWE's chief sports entertainment rival WCW. So it was a surprise when he showed up at *Survivor Series* and interfered in the main event, resulting in Triple H and Stephanie McMahon of The Authority losing their jobs. Sting would go on to compete in his first *WrestleMania* match, against Triple H.

Surviving

November 21: At *Survivor Series*, John Cena, who was tired of The Authority's abuses of power, was due to lead a team of five Superstars against five Superstars from Team Authority. If Team Authority lost, Triple H and Stephanie would be fired from WWE. To try to prevent a defeat, Triple H led a preemptive assault on members of Team Cena during this *SmackDown* episode.

November 21: Triple H hits Big Show with a chair to soften him up before their *Survivor Series* match.

It's a New Day, yes it is

November 28: For weeks on WWE programming, Kofi Kingston, Xavier Woods, and Big E had teased their new team The New Day through a series of vignettes. The big night of The New Day's debut had arrived. The positivity-centric trio competed for the first time as a team on *SmackDown* and gave a hint of what would come in the future by quickly defeating Curtis Axel, Titus O'Neil, and Heath Slater.

November 28: The New Day celebrates victory following their debut as a team.

Super SmackDown Live

December 16: *SmackDown*'s 800th episode promised to be so big it was called *Super SmackDown Live*. Airing live on Tuesday night, rather than in its usual time slot on Thursday night, the show started off with a bang as Roman Reigns returned to *SmackDown* after three months away. Roman put an exclamation point on his return by handily defeating Fandango.

Nikki Bella defended the Divas Championship against Naomi. Fired up about the event, Naomi got a good luck kiss from her husband Jimmy Uso before the match. During the match itself, The Miz and Jimmy Uso both came to ringside to cheer Naomi. Uso, livid that The Miz would cheer for his wife, hit Miz. Naomi was distracted by the chaos outside the ring, allowing Nikki to roll her up for a pin and retain the Divas Championship.

After The Authority faction was fired at *Survivor Series*, Seth Rollins felt WWE had devolved into chaos. Dolph Ziggler strongly disagreed and accused Rollins of having hidden behind The Authority for too long. The two rivals decided to settle their differences in the ring in the main event of *Super SmackDown Live*. Despite constant interference from Rollins' bodyguards J&J Security—leading the official to ban them from the ring— Dolph Ziggler was able to hit Rollins with his Zig-Zag signature move for the win.

December 16: Roman Reigns makes his *SmackDown* comeback; Dolph Ziggler overcomes the odds to defeat Seth Rollins with his Zig-Zag finisher.

"Hulkamania is running *SmackDown* tonight!"

Hulk Hogan (December 26)

Hulk rules

December 26: Hulk Hogan returned to *SmackDown* as an acting General Manager. Seth Rollins confronted and insulted Hogan at the top of the show. Dolph Ziggler came to the ring to defend Hogan. Hogan responded by creating a main event Tag Team Match for later that night—Ziggler and Roman Reigns vs. Seth Rollins and Big Show, which Reigns/Ziggler won.

Smarting after losing their WWE Tag Team Championships at *Survivor Series*, Goldust and Stardust began looking for cosmic help to further their championship efforts. The bizarre duo hovered around a crystal ball looking for answers. Goldust said that he saw great promise in their future, but stormed off after the ball gave him an electric shock. Stardust just laughed and continued to stare into the prophetic orb!

December 26: Acting *SmackDown* General Manager Hulk Hogan looks on as Seth Rollins and Dolph Ziggler have a heated exchange.

2015

THIS WAS A revolutionary year in WWE history. A trending hashtag on Twitter, #GiveDivasAChance, led to a Women's Evolution, with female Superstars taking more of a center stage. The rise of former NXT Superstars like Kevin Owens and The Ascension continued to shake things up. Owens won the United States Championship, while The Ascension tag team made a big impression on *SmackDown* and throughout WWE. The unexpected returns of The Authority faction and of legends like The Dudley Boyz shocked and thrilled the WWE Universe, adding explosive elements to *SmackDown*'s volatile mixture. On a sad note, WWE lost two of its all-time greats: Dusty Rhodes and Roddy Piper.

INTRODUCING...

The Ascension
January 2: With their fearsome haircuts and face paint featuring ancient Egyptian symbols, Konnor and Vicktor, the tag team known as The Ascension, came to *SmackDown* to dominate what they saw as a "cosmic wasteland." They had been the longest-reigning Tag Team Champions in NXT, and though they have yet to rise to that level in WWE, they were a force to be reckoned with.

The Ascension hoped to terrorize their opponents before a match even started.

Striking a pose
January 2: With The Authority still banished from WWE because of its defeat at *Survivor Series* in November (it was reinstated the following week), *SmackDown* needed leadership. WWE legends Edge and Christian hosted the show, making the matches and doing their trademark "five second pose," which, they claimed, was "for the benefit of those with flash photography."

January 2: Relishing their role as *SmackDown* hosts, Edge and Christian open the show.

Returns and revenge
January 15: Shortly after winning the WWE World Heavyweight Championship at *WrestleMania 30*, Daniel Bryan had to vacate the title due to a neck injury. After eight months, this WWE Universe favorite returned to *SmackDown* to confront The Authority, who had also returned, after being banned from WWE at *Survivor Series*. The Authority—Triple H, J&J Security, and Big Show—looked on threateningly as Bryan faced Authority Director of Operations Kane. When Bryan won by a disqualification after interference by J&J Security, The Authority ganged up on Bryan. Fortunately, Dean Ambrose and Roman Reigns came to Bryan's aid. Triple H then challenged Bryan, Ambrose, and Reigns to a Six-Man Tag Team Match against The Authority's Seth Rollins, Kane, and Big Show—which Bryan won by pinning Kane.

Casket celebration
January 29: Two weeks after they tried to spoil Daniel Bryan's return to the ring, The Authority once again placed him in a match against Kane. This time, however, it was a Casket Match, in which the winner has to shove his opponent into a casket. After escaping Kane's devastating Tombstone Piledriver, Bryan kicked Kane into the casket and closed the lid. Celebrating, Bryan stood on the casket leading the WWE Universe in his signature chant, a massive "Yes!"

March 5: Stardust attacks Daniel Bryan, one of his six opponents at the upcoming Intercontinental Championship Ladder Match at *WrestleMania 31*.

Dating games

February 5: Natalya and Tyson Kidd hoped to smooth things over with their mutual rivals Naomi and Jimmy Uso, so they went on a double date. Kidd showed up late with his tag team partner Cesaro. Things got heated when Cesaro and Kidd tried to eat Jimmy Uso's food. The two couples started yelling at each other, Kidd threw the table over, and Cesaro punched out Uso. Natalya screamed at Naomi and Jimmy that it was all their fault as she left the restaurant.

Turmoil time

February 12: Although they were to be opponents at the next pay-per-view event, *Fastlane*, Roman Reigns and Daniel Bryan were put together as a tag team for one night only to compete in a Tag Team Turmoil Match. Two teams would compete against each other, the winner then facing another team, until just one team remained. After more than an hour, in the course of which they had defeated The Miz and Mizdow, The Usos, Los Matadores, Slater Gator, The Ascension, and Kane and Big Show, Daniel Bryan and Roman Reigns won the match.

Who's got the title?

March 5: At *WrestleMania 31*, Bad News Barrett, Daniel Bryan, Dolph Ziggler, Stardust, Luke Harper, R-Truth, and Dean Ambrose were set to compete for the Intercontinental Title. They stole the title from Barrett, aggravating him beyond words. On this episode, the Superstars briefly stole the title from each other. Ziggler had it first and R-Truth left with it, despite Barrett still being the champion.

Warmup warning

March 12: At *WrestleMania 31*, Paige and AJ Lee were set to have a Tag Team Match against The Bella Twins. To prepare, they had a warm-up contest against Summer Rae and Cameron. Paige and AJ Lee had no problems quickly disposing of Summer Rae and Cameron, sending a message to The Bella Twins.

February 12: Daniel Bryan fires off a vicious dropkick on Jey Uso.

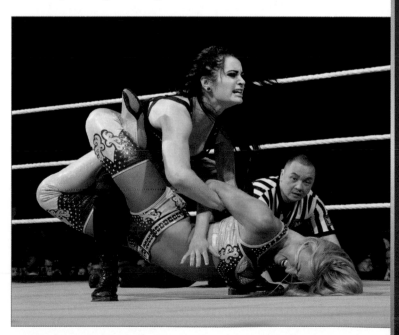

March 12: Paige punishes Summer Rae with a painful PTO submission hold.

2015

March 19: Daniel Bryan tries to power out from Dolph Ziggler in their Gauntlet Match.

Running the gauntlet

March 19: Gauntlet Matches are tough. A Superstar has to defeat all the other Superstars in the series to win. A 7-Superstar Gauntlet Match featuring the competitors for the Intercontinental Championship took place on *SmackDown*, with Dolph Ziggler eventually defeating Daniel Bryan to stand tall as the winner.

Eight-Man Tag

March 26: On the final *SmackDown* before *WrestleMania 31*, the top Superstars in WWE squared off in an Eight-Man Tag Team Match that saw the team of John Cena, Mark Henry, Daniel Bryan, and Roman Reigns defeat Seth Rollins, Big Show, Kane, and Bray Wyatt, hyping up the WWE Universe for the biggest show of the year.

Elsewhere in WWE

March 29: The main event of *WrestleMania 31* was Brock Lesnar defending the WWE Championship against Roman Reigns. Toward the end of the match, however, Seth Rollins cashed in his Money in the Bank contract to win the WWE Championship.

A viperous contender

April 2: Four days after *WrestleMania 31*, Randy Orton interrupted Seth Rollins' championship celebration, demanding to be the number one contender for Rollins' WWE Championship. Since Rollins was aligned with The Authority, Orton had to defeat another Authority member, Big Show. Orton managed to overcome Big Show, but was then attacked by The Authority's J&J Security. When Seth Rollins joined in, Orton looked to be in big trouble—until Ryback came to help him. Despite The Authority's scheming, Orton thus became the number one title contender.

The Miz's mirror image

April 9: For months, Damien Sandow had acted as The Miz's lookalike stunt double. Calling himself "Mizdow," he imitated every move The Miz made in and out of the ring. To increase the tension, Mizdow was growing in popularity, even outshining The Miz. The last straw came at *WrestleMania 31* when Mizdow eliminated Miz from the André the Giant Memorial Battle Royal. The Miz demanded an apology from Mizdow for the elimination on his talk show segment "Miz TV." Mizdow apologized instead for waiting so long to split from Miz, and smacked his former mentor in the jaw.

"You see, Jerry, you only like to call yourself a king. I, on the other hand, have earned that accolade."

Wade Barrett (May 7, 2015)

Of kings and contracts

May 7: Wade Barrett had won the King of the Ring tournament a week earlier on *RAW*. On *SmackDown*, Barrett confronted Jerry "The King" Lawler and tried to force Lawler to bend the knee, but Dolph Ziggler raced to Lawler's rescue, pulling Barrett off him.

At *Payback*, four WWE Superstars, Seth Rollins, Roman Reigns, Randy Orton, and Dean Ambrose were due to compete in a Fatal 4-Way Match for Rollins' WWE Championship. On *SmackDown*, The Authority's Director of Operations, Kane, hosted the four Superstars for a contract signing. It soon became a brawl, with Rollins dominant as the show closed.

May 7: King of the Ring Barrett seeks to prove he's more regal than Jerry "The King" Lawler.

May 7: Rollins' bodyguards, J&J Security, pound on Ambrose, while Rollins goes after Orton as a signing turns violent.

2015

INTRODUCING...

Kevin Owens

May 28: He called himself the "Prize Fighter," declaring that he would only ever compete for the big titles in WWE. Nonetheless, NXT Champion Kevin Owens garnered a lot of attention by debuting on *SmackDown* while still being NXT Champion. Owens became a dominant force in WWE and an integral part of *SmackDown*, becoming United States and Universal Champion.

NXT Champion Kevin Owens puts *SmackDown* Superstars on notice—he's here to win titles.

Owens' open challenge

June 4: For the first time in WWE history, the NXT Championship was defended on a WWE television show when Kevin Owens dared a Superstar to try to take the title from him. Owens' challenge was answered by Zack Ryder on *SmackDown*. Owens easily pinned Ryder using his signature Pop-Up Powerbomb move and promised he'd be NXT Champion forever.

June 4: Kevin Owens slams Zack Ryder with his Pop-up Powerbomb.

Farewell to The Dream

June 18: "The American Dream" Dusty Rhodes was a WWE legend. A former World Heavyweight Champion and WWE Hall of Famer, Rhodes continued to build his legacy by teaching the rookies in NXT the ins and outs of sports entertainment. One week after Rhodes sadly passed away, on June 11, all of WWE paid tribute to him on *SmackDown*, saying a final goodbye.

Elsewhere in WWE

June 23: WWE first stepped into the competition reality show realm in 2002 with *Tough Enough*, in which contestants undergo training and the prize for the winner is a WWE contract. After a five-year hiatus, *Tough Enough* returned. This newest incarnation of the series concluded with Bronson Matthews winning a one-year NXT contract.

June 25: Flanked by fellow Authority members Joey Mercury and Kane, WWE Champion Rollins triumphs over Ambrose.

Outnumbered

June 25: Ever since the dissolution of The Shield faction, former Shield teammates Seth Rollins and Dean Ambrose fought every chance they got. As they faced each other once again on *SmackDown*, Seth Rollins had a secret weapon—his new teammates in The Authority. Despite Dean Ambrose's best efforts, he couldn't overcome Rollins and friends, succumbing to The Authority's combined attack.

The Revolution's here!

July 16: The WWE Universe wanted the female Superstars of WWE to be given a new opportunity to shine. They got the hashtag #GiveDivasAChance trending, and WWE took note and instigated the "Women's Revolution," which would later be redubbed the "Women's Evolution." One of the major players, Sasha Banks, appeared for the first time on this episode of *SmackDown*, alongside her Team BAD colleagues Tamina and Naomi.

Clashes between The Shield and The Wyatt Family had passed into WWE legend. The two factions had always hated each other, so it came as no surprise when the leader of The Wyatt Family, Bray Wyatt, threatened former Shield member Roman Reigns on screen and then attacked Reigns during his match against Sheamus. The two would face each other three days later at the *Battleground* pay-per-view, when Wyatt made good on his threat, defeating Reigns with help from Luke Harper.

July 23: Nikki Bella solidifies her position in the Women's Revolution by hitting Naomi with a Rack Attack maneuver.

Total Divas Destruction

July 23: Since the debut of the Women's Revolution earlier in July, Team BAD (Sasha Banks, Tamina, and Naomi) had issues with Team Bellas (The Bella Twins and Alicia Fox). Team Bellas bragged about their reality show and in-ring skill, and Team BAD didn't like that. When the two teams faced each other in the ring, Nikki Bella pinned Naomi, while the members of both teams brawled outside the ring.

Grieving for Piper

August 6: Less than two months after mourning the loss of Dusty Rhodes, the WWE Universe grieved over the passing of another WWE Legend and Hall of Famer, "Rowdy" Roddy Piper. Piper was a fixture of sports entertainment for more than three decades, creating many memorable moments, including being in the main event of the first *WrestleMania*. As pipers played a lament, *SmackDown* paid tribute to one of WWE's greatest Superstars with a montage of some of his most memorable moments.

July 16: Bray Wyatt attacks Roman Reigns, hoping to soften him up before their *Battleground* clash.

2015

Summertime stealing

August 20: Dolph Ziggler had been out with a jaw injury for several months. When he returned to *SmackDown*, he was accompanied by Rusev's apparently former girlfriend and manager Lana. Rusev interrupted Ziggler and Lana's celebratory kiss, demanding Lana return to him. She refused, and Ziggler warned Rusev that after their upcoming match at *SummerSlam*, Ziggler would have stolen both the show and Rusev's girlfriend.

Of Boyz and monsters

August 27: One of the most decorated tag teams in WWE history, The Dudley Boyz, returned to *SmackDown* after more than ten years away. Former Tag Team Champions in WWE, WCW, and ECW, The Dudley Boyz were determined to once again capture the gold. Their quest began with a victory over Konnor and Viktor, a.k.a. The Ascension.

Over the last couple of years, members of The Wyatt family had come and gone, but on this edition, Bray Wyatt brought with him perhaps the most imposing Wyatt Family member of all—a giant named Braun Strowman. Wearing a black sheep mask, Strowman sent an intimidating signal to the WWE Universe and Superstars that The Wyatt Family was not to be messed with when he attacked Roman Reigns at the end of the show.

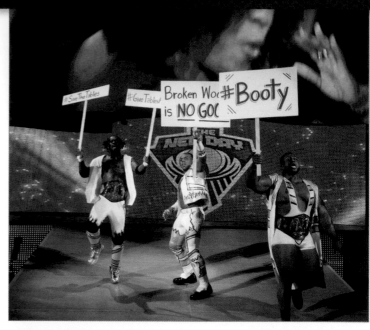

September 3: "A table is a terrible thing to waste"—The New Day appeal to the WWE Universe.

Save the tables

September 3: Throughout their long career, The Dudley Boyz were famous for slamming, dropping, or hurling opponents through tables. The WWE Tag Team Champions The New Day, who knew The Dudley Boyz were gunning for them, started a campaign to "Save the Tables," hoping to stop The Dudley Boyz from using tables anymore. On *SmackDown*, they shared leaflets, chanted the slogan, and picketed in the ring.

August 27: The Dudley Boyz team up to give The Ascension's Konnor their Whassup move.

Champ vs. champ

September 10: Intercontinental Champion Ryback hated Seth Rollins, who was both United States and WWE World Heavyweight Champion. He thought Rollins was a cowardly weasel, and wanted to get his hands on him where Rollins couldn't escape. The two champions faced off in a non-title Lumberjack Match, where other Superstars surround the ring to make sure the action stays in-ring. Ryback's plan backfired, however, as Rollins' Authority teammates, who were Lumberjacks, attacked him, giving Rollins the win.

"I did start the women's revolution, and I deserve a little bit of recognition!"

Paige (September 24, 2015)

Woman in revolt

September 24: When the Women's Revolution began two months earlier, former Divas Champion Paige had joined forces with Charlotte Flair and Becky Lynch to form Team PCB. However, Paige had grown jealous of her teammates and abandoned them during a match three days earlier on *RAW*. On this *SmackDown* episode, Paige declared Team PCB officially over. When Natalya came to the ring, trying to make peace, Paige slapped Natalya in the face.

September 24: Becky Lynch looks on as her PCB teammate Paige dissolves the team.

Cosmic cards

October 8: Like his brother Goldust, Stardust was known for being eccentric. On this episode, he revealed his latest quirk—using playing cards to tell fortunes and read the future. No one but him understood his card readings. One thing was for sure, however: Stardust was trying to scare the other WWE Superstars, especially Wade Barrett and Neville, whose dire fates he foretold.

October 22: Summer Rae finds new love with Tyler Breeze.

Unlucky in Love

October 22: For a few weeks, Dolph Ziggler was in a relationship with Lana. But when Lana's secret engagement to Rusev was revealed, Lana left Ziggler. Summer Rae, who was supposedly dating Rusev, left him and hooked up with Ziggler. However, after a few weeks of dating, Summer Rae dumped Ziggler and joined Tyler Breeze—all during this edition's Miz TV segment.

2015

Face the Fear

October 29: It was a spooky night on a special Halloween edition of *SmackDown*. Bo Dallas, calling himself "Boo Dallas" went around backstage trying to scare everyone by jumping up behind them yelling "Boo." But the most frightening part of the night was the main event—a Six-Man Tag Team Match between the "New Faces of Fear," The Wyatt Family, against Dean Ambrose, Cesaro, and Ryback. On this night, appropriately, the sinister Wyatt Family was victorious.

Championship tournament

November 12: Due to a severe knee injury, WWE World Heavyweight Champion Seth Rollins was forced to vacate the title. A tournament to crown the new champion commenced on *RAW* three days earlier and continued on *SmackDown* with three first-round matches that saw Neville, Kalisto, and Alberto Del Rio advance to the second round.

November 12: Neville crashes atop Wade Barrett to win their WWE Championship Tournament Match.

The brothers of destruction

November 19: As The Wyatt Family led a large group of sheep mask-clad druids to the ring and boasted about their destructive power, Undertaker and Kane appeared on the big screen, warning them to stay away from powers they didn't understand. As Undertaker uttered the words "And they shall all rest in peace," there was an explosion and all the Wyatt druids fell to the floor. The WWE Universe took up the chant "Rest in peace," while The Wyatt family looked on defiantly.

Giving thanks, WWE-style, and a new contender

November 26: On a Thanksgiving night episode of *SmackDown*, new WWE Champion Sheamus set out to get under Roman Reigns' skin by mocking Reigns' brief—just minutes-long—championship reign at *Survivor Series* the previous Sunday. Reigns raced to attack Sheamus for the insults, but the wily Irishman ran away to safety.

Dean Ambrose had come up short in the finals for the WWE World Heavyweight Championship tournament at *Survivor Series* earlier in the week, but he bounced back quickly, setting his sights on a new title: the Intercontinental Championship held by Kevin Owens. Ambrose defeated Dolph Ziggler and Tyler Breeze in a Triple Threat Match to become the number one contender for the Intercontinental Title.

November 26: Dean Ambrose flies in the face of Tyler Breeze to become the number one contender.

Roman and the League of Nations

December 3: Before he could get his hands on WWE Champion Sheamus and his title on an upcoming *RAW*, Reigns had to face all four members of Sheamus' stable, the League of Nations in a 4-on-1 Handicap Match. Despite the odds, Reigns was able to punish the four League of Nations members, Sheamus, Rusev, Wade Barrett, and Alberto Del Rio, so severely outside the ring that none of them were able to make it back to the ring before the referee counted to ten.

Elsewhere in WWE

December 14: At *Survivor Series*, Roman Reigns had won his first WWE World Heavyweight Championship, but Sheamus immediately cashed in his Money in the Bank opportunity to steal the title. Three weeks later, on the December 14 edition of RAW, Reigns won the championship back to become a two-time champion in a three-week period.

Holiday wishes

December 22: It was three days before Christmas and the WWE Superstars on *SmackDown* were in a festive mood. Roman Reigns delivered holiday wishes to the WWE Universe. Santino Marella and Stardust argued over the proper way to decorate a Christmas tree, and Superstars like The New Day showed off their holiday outfits. This special live episode was capped off by Dean Ambrose successfully defending his Intercontinental Championship against both Dolph Ziggler and Kevin Owens.

Happy Bo year

December 31: Bo Dallas' favorite activity was giving motivational, albeit condescending and insulting, speeches to the WWE Universe and Superstars. Dallas spent 2015's last episode of *SmackDown* giving teasing New Year's "re-Bo-lutions" to his fellow Superstars, such as advising Curtis Axel to wear deodorant every day in 2016, which were not received well.

December 31: Bo Dallas has an unwelcome New Year's "re-Bo-lution" for Curtis Axel.

December 22: Holiday wishes from Santa's three favorite unicorns, The New Day.

2016

THIS EXCITING YEAR for *SmackDown* began with a change of name for the blue brand. For the first time in its history, the show was broadcast live every week, and so was retitled *SmackDown Live*. Furthermore, WWE split its roster of Superstars between *SmackDown* and *RAW* so that each brand had its very own Superstars, championships, and events led by a Commissioner and General Manager. Shane McMahon was the Commissioner for *SmackDown,* and he hired Daniel Bryan as General Manager, before Daniel gave the post up to return to the ring. Emphasizing that an exciting new era was dawning for the blue brand, the *SmackDown* Women's and Tag Team Championships were introduced.

Big moves

January 7: *SmackDown* had been broadcast on the SyFy channel since October 1, 2010. However, for the first episode of the show in 2016, the blue brand made a big move to the USA Network. In the evening's main event, Intercontinental Champion Dean Ambrose faced Kevin Owens. The two rivals battled outside the ring, pummeling each other until both were counted out, resulting in a no-contest draw.

Alberto wins

January 14: Alberto Del Rio was a former WWE Champion, and while he had aspirations of one day regaining that prestigious title, he had no problem winning other championships in the meantime. On this episode, Del Rio managed to steal the United States Championship from Kalisto, with a little help. Del Rio's partner in the League of Nations faction, King Barrett, assisted Del Rio by pulling him out of the way of a high-flying kick from Kalisto. This allowed Del Rio to place Kalisto in a painful submission hold, forcing him to submit.

January 14: Alberto Del Rio leaps at Kalisto in a dramatic aerial assault.

January 21: The League of Nations celebrates victory over Roman Reigns in 4-on-1 Handicap Match.

A swath of destruction

January 21: Earlier in the week on *RAW*, Mr. McMahon informed WWE World Heavyweight Champion Roman Reigns that he would be defending his title in the annual 30-Man Royal Rumble Match and that Reigns would enter the Rumble at number one. To prepare for the multi-Superstar Rumble, Reigns entered a 4-on-1 Match against the League of Nations—Alberto Del Rio, King Barrett, Rusev, and Sheamus. Reigns won by disqualification when all four League of Nations members attacked him at once. However, Reigns then had to contend with the entire Wyatt Family!

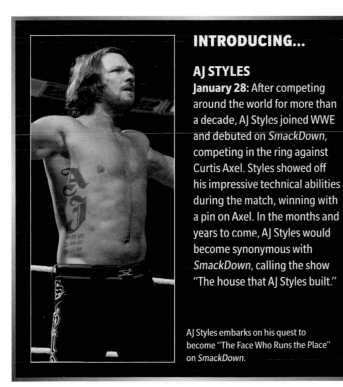

INTRODUCING...

AJ STYLES

January 28: After competing around the world for more than a decade, AJ Styles joined WWE and debuted on *SmackDown*, competing in the ring against Curtis Axel. Styles showed off his impressive technical abilities during the match, winning with a pin on Axel. In the months and years to come, AJ Styles would become synonymous with *SmackDown*, calling the show "The house that AJ Styles built."

AJ Styles embarks on his quest to become "The Face Who Runs the Place" on *SmackDown*.

The best and the phenomenal

February 11: Both AJ Styles and Chris Jericho were known around the world for being amazing in-ring competitors. Both had won championships in Japan and Mexico. On this episode, Styles and Jericho competed against each other for only the second time in their illustrious careers. Styles had won their first encounter two weeks earlier on *RAW*, so Jericho was determined to defeat Styles this time. It was a back-and-forth contest, but in the end, Jericho used his signature Codebreaker move to win the match.

The Beast is back

February 18: From 2002, "The Beast" Brock Lesnar was a fixture on *SmackDown*. Signed from *RAW* by the General Manager at the time, Stephanie McMahon, Lesnar became the show's marquee attraction until he left WWE in 2004. A dozen years later, and nearly four years after rejoining WWE, Lesnar made his return to *SmackDown*. He put an exclamation point on this rare appearance by attacking his upcoming opponent at *WrestleMania*, Dean Ambrose, as well as Ambrose's former SHIELD teammate Roman Reigns, to end the show.

February 18: Brock Lesnar slams Roman Reigns with his F-5 maneuver.

The champ with a warning

February 25: WWE COO and WWE Champion Triple H was set to defend WWE's most prestigious title against Roman Reigns in six weeks' time at *WrestleMania*. Ever-confident, 14-time World Champion Triple H had harsh words for Reigns as they both prepared for *WrestleMania*. Triple H warned Reigns that it might feel good to challenge authority like Triple H, but in the end it would be fruitless. Triple H added that he was bigger than any single authority figure or WWE Champion, and Roman Reigns didn't have a chance against him.

Diva destruction

March 3: On this edition, Sasha Banks and Becky Lynch battled each other to decide who would become the number one contender for the WWE Divas Championship, held by Charlotte Flair. As the match was building to its peak, Flair, who had been watching the match ringside, couldn't resist the urge to attack both her rivals, ending the match in a draw. Later that night, Flair learned that her intervention had given a championship match to both Banks and Lynch, and at *WrestleMania*, Charlotte Flair would have to defend her title against both women.

2016

Face off

March 24: Charlotte Flair, Sasha Banks, and Becky Lynch were set to compete against each other at *WrestleMania* where the Divas Championship would be retired and a new WWE Women's Champion would be crowned. The three female Superstars knew each other very well. They'd all trained together in NXT. They'd competed against each other one on one all over the world. But in less than a week, they'd fight in a Triple Threat Match. They each appeared on *SmackDown* to make a statement and warn their opponents about what they were going to experience at *WrestleMania*.

March 25: Brock Lesnar takes The Wyatt Family's Erick Rowan to Suplex City.

Best enemies

March 25: Brock Lesnar returned to *SmackDown* with a challenge for his *WrestleMania* opponent Dean Ambrose: Lesnar wanted to fight Ambrose that night, not wait a week until *WrestleMania*. Instead of Ambrose answering the call, however, The Wyatt Family came to the ring and surrounded Lesnar. Just as The Wyatt Family moved to attack Lesnar, Ambrose raced to the ring, saving Lesnar from the attack. But Ambrose then turned on Lesnar, beating him with a kendo stick until Lesnar managed to break the kendo stick over his knee and slam Ambrose to the mat.

April 7: The Social Outcasts play rock-paper-scissors to determine who faces Apollo Crews.

Social outcasts

April 7: The Social Outcasts were a faction of Superstars made up of Heath Slater, Bo Dallas, Adam Rose, and Curtis Axel. The Supers had all struggled to win their matches and believed their luck would change if they joined forces. Their team was asked to pick a member to compete against Apollo Crews, who was making his *SmackDown* debut. After a fierce game of rock-paper-scissors, Axel won the chance. However, Crews defeated Axel in a few short minutes.

A first time for everything

April 14: This episode of *SmackDown* was "A Night of Firsts." Several Superstars competed against each other in the ring for the first time, while others made their first apearance on the show. Superstars such as Sami Zayn and Chris Jericho became opponents (as did AJ Styles and Alberto Del Rio). Debuting Superstars Big Cass and Enzo Amore showed what they could do on the microphone by entertaining the WWE Universe with their unique brand of trash-talking.

April 14: Chris Jericho hits Sami Zayn with a perfect dropkick in their first-ever match.

Clubbing

April 21: Years earlier, AJ Styles, Luke Gallows, and Karl Anderson were members of a Club of Superstars in Japan. Upon joining WWE, they reformed The Club, helping each other win matches. On this episode, AJ Styles was competing in a match against The Miz. Believing he was sure to lose, The Miz tried to escape to the locker room. Gallows and Anderson stood in his way and forced him back into the ring, where he duly lost to Styles.

April 21: AJ Styles springs high off the rope to hit The Miz with his Phenomenal Forearm.

Reigns meets The Club

April 28: WWE World Heavyweight Champion Roman Reigns and Intercontinental Champion The Miz were in the main event in a non-title Champion vs. Champion Match. Reigns defeated The Miz but didn't have time to celebrate his victory because The Club—AJ Styles, Luke Gallows, and Karl Anderson—attacked him. Reigns' cousins The Usos raced to the ring to even the odds, causing The Club to run away from the fight.

Breezango is born

May 12: In this episode, Fandango and Goldust were competing in a Tag Team Match against R-Truth and Tyler Breeze. The two teams were supposed to be rivals but suddenly, in the middle of the match, Breeze and Fandango turned on their partners and attacked Goldust and R-Truth. As the duo stood over their fallen partners, they celebrated their surprise attack and formed a new tag team they named Breezango.

Caged in

May 19: Dean Ambrose had an extreme dislike for Chris Jericho. The two had agreed to fight each other in an Asylum Match inside a cage with weapons at the next *Extreme Rules*. To promote the match, the asylum cage hung above the ring on *SmackDown*. Jericho stood in the ring for an interview where he repeatedly berated Ambrose. Jericho called for the cage to be lowered, covering the ring and locking him inside. Without warning, and seemingly from out of nowhere, Ambrose appeared in the cage and beat Jericho with the weapons inside.

May 19: Chris Jericho invites an unimpressed Dean Ambrose to "drink in" Jericho's greatness.

Trash talk and tongue lashings

May 26: Since their arrival in WWE six weeks earlier, the tag team of Enzo Amore and Big Cass had annoyed a lot of WWE Superstars with their braggadocio attitudes, ending their trash-talking with their catchphrase "You can't teach that." They annoyed no one more, perhaps, than The Dudley Boyz. The Dudleyz were the most-decorated tag team in WWE history and had grown tired of the rookies' arrogance. On this edition, The Dudley Boyz gave Enzo and Cass a tongue lashing, only to get one back from the snide Superstars.

2016

Club Day

June 2: Angry about losing the Tag Team Championship to The Club three days earlier on *RAW*, The New Day challenged any member of The Club to face any member of The New Day. AJ Styles accepted the challenge, facing Kofi Kingston in a match. As Styles and Kingston battled in the ring, their teammates fought each other outside. Kingston was briefly distracted by this brawl, allowing Styles to get a pinfall victory.

June 2: The New Day's Kofi Kingston flies down on The Club's AJ Styles in their match.

A tribute to the greatest

June 9: A special video tribute was aired to celebrate the boxing legend Muhammad Ali, who had passed away six days earlier. Considered by many to be the greatest boxer who ever lived, Ali was a big fan of WWE and sports entertainment. In fact, Ali confirmed that his flamboyant style had been inspired by watching WWE Hall of Famer Gorgeous George on television. Ali did not confine his appreciation of WWE to watching—he also served as a special guest referee in the main event match at the first-ever *WrestleMania* on March 31, 1985.

Highlight Reel confrontation

June 16: In three days, six WWE Superstars were set to compete in the annual Money in the Bank Ladder Match, where the winner would get a WWE Championship Match whenever they wanted it. Six Superstars—Sami Zayn, Dean Ambrose, Chris Jericho, Kevin Owens, Cesaro, and Alberto Del Rio—confronted each other in the ring as part of Chris Jericho's Highlight Reel talk show segment. This led to an immediate 3-on-3 Match, in which Dean Ambrose, Cesaro, and Sami Zayn defeated Jericho, Owens, and Del Rio.

June 30: The New Day mocks The Wyatt Family's attempts to spook them.

New Day haunts

June 30: Following a very quick match in which Wyatt Family members Braun Strowman and Erick Rowan dominated their unidentified opponents, The New Day appeared on the big screen. They were sporting Wyatt Family-style sheep masks, though with The New Day's trademark unicorn horns on them. Kofi Kingston and Big E proceeded to mock The Wyatt Family, asking them if what they were most afraid of was soap. Bray Wyatt noticed that The New Day member Xavier Woods appeared to be nervous about mocking the Wyatts and warned the rest that they should follow Woods example and be afraid of The Wyatt Family.

Elsewhere in WWE

July 13: An all-new event unlike any other in WWE history kicked off with the first round of the Cruiserweight Classic Tournament. Thirty-two Superstars, each weighing less than 205 lbs to qualify as "Cruiserweights" and representing 17 countries from around the world, competed in the tournament, which was broadcast exclusively on WWE Network. The winner of the tournament, TJ Perkins, was declared the new WWE Cruiserweight Champion. Following the tournament, a new WWE television show was born, featuring only cruiserweights called *205 Live*. The show aired live on WWE Network straight after *SmackDown* ended its weekly broadcast.

Remaking Darren Young

July 14: Darren Young and Bob Backlund guested on a Miz TV talk show segment. At this point in his career, Young was on a losing streak in WWE and was looking for a mentor to help him get back to winning ways. He found the perfect one in the two-time former WWE Champion and WWE Hall of Famer Backlund. Backlund's upbeat personality helped to motivate Young. With the slogan "Make Darren Young Great Again," Young and Backlund declared their intentions to strive for greatness and win championships—especially The Miz's own Intercontinental Title.

SmackDown Live

July 19: For the 16-and-a-half years of its existence, *SmackDown* had always aired a few days after it had been taped. However, a new *SmackDown* era was born this month when the show began airing live every week and was renamed *SmackDown Live*. This first edition featured the WWE draft, where WWE divided its roster of Superstars between *RAW* and *SmackDown*. Superstars were permitted to appear on only one of the two shows. Daniel Bryan began his tenure as the blue brand's General Manager, working with Commissioner Shane McMahon to make Dean Ambrose *SmackDown*'s first pick in the draft.

There were epic matches as well, with John Cena defeating Luke Gallows, Darren Young and Zack Ryder beating The Miz and Rusev, Bray Wyatt over Xavier Woods, Charlotte and Dana Brooke besting Sasha Banks in a Handicap Match, Jericho pinning Cesaro, and WWE World Heavyweight Champion Ambrose defeating Seth Rollins to retain the championship.

July 19: John Cena pins Luke Gallows, cheered on by Enzo Amore and Big Cass, his teammates at the upcoming *Battleground* pay-per-view; Sasha Banks takes Charlotte Flair down during her Handicap Match with Flair and Dana Brooke, temporarily defying the two-against-one odds.

Six to one

July 26: Six *SmackDown* Superstars—Dolph Ziggler, John Cena, Bray Wyatt, Baron Corbin, Apollo Crews, and AJ Styles—entered the ring for a Six-Pack Challenge Match, where all six Superstars compete at once with the first Superstar to get a pin or submission wins the match, for the chance to become number one contender for the WWE World Heavyweight Championship. It was a hard-fought battle among the six competitors, but Dolph Ziggler went on to win and challenge for the prestigious title at the upcoming *SummerSlam* pay-per-view.

July 26: Superstars stalk each other before their Six-Pack Challenge Match to decide the number one contender for the WWE Championship.

American Alpha arrives

August 2: Former NXT Tag Team Champions American Alpha—Jason Jordan and Chad Gable—made their WWE and *SmackDown* debut on this episode. The duo were both successful amateur wrestlers, and Gable had even competed in the 2012 Olympics. The duo showed off their in-ring talents by defeating Aiden English and Simon Gotch, a.k.a. The Vaudevillains.

August 2: The Vaudevillains feel the wrath of American Alpha in their first match on *SmackDown*.

2016

Elsewhere in WWE

August 2: Following the August 2 episode of *SmackDown Live*, a new live postshow began airing on WWE Network titled *Talking Smack*. Featuring commentator Renee Young and *SmackDown* General Manager Daniel Bryan teaming up to interview *SmackDown* Superstars about that night's show, *Talking Smack* lived up to its name. Superstars smack-talked their opponents and sometimes Young and Bryan as well.

August 16: AJ Styles pays dearly for daring to attack John Cena from behind.

Slater gets his contract, and Cena beats back Styles

August 16: Heath Slater was the only WWE Superstar not drafted to either *RAW* or *SmackDown*. He was devastated, exclaiming, "I've got kids," to convey his concern about how he was going to feed his family. Desperate to be signed by one of the shows, Slater showed up on *SmackDown* hoping to get in Commissioner Shane McMahon and General Manager Daniel Bryan's good graces so they'd give him a contract. They offered Slater a deal: If he could defeat Randy Orton in a match, he would get a contract. Fortune smiled on Slater, who won the match—and apparently a *SmackDown* contract—when Orton was disqualified for throwing Slater through a table. Later in the evening, however, Shane McMahon revoked the contract, and Slater found himself a free agent once again.

For weeks, AJ Styles had attacked WWE Champion John Cena, threatening to take his championship at their upcoming match at *SummerSlam* and boasting about how he loved to "Beat up John Cena." At the end of this episode, just after Cena had won a match against Alberto Del Rio, Styles slyly attacked Cena from behind, nailing him with his trademark Phenomenal Forearm move. As he tried to continue the assault, the infuriated Cena countered, slamming Styles through the announce table.

Blue is the color

August 23: Because WWE Tag Team Champions The Prime Time Players and WWE Women's Champion Charlotte Flair had both been drafted by *RAW*, *SmackDown* was left without a Tag Team or Women's Champion. On *SmackDown*, Shane McMahon and Daniel Bryan unveiled all-new Tag Team and Women's Championships that *SmackDown* Superstars would compete for in the weeks to come. The titles featured the show's brand color, blue, and were immediately coveted by the Superstars in both the Women's and Tag Team divisions.

Gore for more

August 30: To discover the new *SmackDown* Tag Team Champions, Daniel Bryan and Shane McMahon set up an eight-team tournament to be held over several weeks. This episode hosted the first round. Heath Slater teamed with long-time sports entertainment veteran Rhyno to face the returning Headbangers, who last competed in WWE 16 years earlier. Slater and Rhyno beat The Headbangers after Rhyno hit Headbanger Thrasher with his signature Gore spear tackle. Slater and Rhyno went on to win the championships four weeks later at *Backlash*.

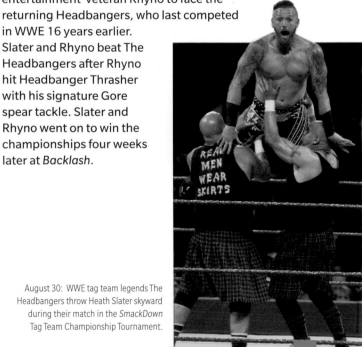

August 30: WWE tag team legends The Headbangers throw Heath Slater skyward during their match in the *SmackDown* Tag Team Championship Tournament.

Hometown hero?
September 27: In Cleveland, Ohio, local boy The Miz was celebrating *SmackDown* coming to his hometown. He set up an elaborate homecoming celebration in the ring, complete with self-portraits, and his parents sitting ringside. Dolph Ziggler interrupted the party, challenging The Miz to one more Intercontinental Championship Match at the impending *No Mercy* event. The Miz at first declined, but when Ziggler said he would retire from WWE if he didn't win, The Miz accepted.

Ambrose's trophy gift
September 6: In five days, at *Backlash*, WWE World Heavyweight Champion Dean Ambrose was set to defend his title against AJ Styles. On this *SmackDown* episode, the two Superstars had a face-to-face interview. In recent weeks, Ambrose had mocked Styles, calling him a "Soccer Mom" because of his long hairstyle. Ambrose now presented Styles with a "Soccer Participation Trophy" saying it was the only trophy Styles would be getting from him. Styles responded by promising to take Ambrose's favorite trophy, his WWE Championship. When Ambrose talked back, Styles gave Ambrose a low blow.

Cheaters never prosper
September 13: Two nights earlier at the *Backlash* pay-per-view, The Miz retained his Intercontinental Championship when his wife, Maryse, sneakily attacked challenger Dolph Ziggler. Although they celebrated the victory as legitimate in the ring, Ziggler disagreed and confronted The Miz and Maryse about it. The Miz essentially ignored Ziggler until *SmackDown* General Manager (and The Miz's long-time rival in and out of the ring) Daniel Bryan announced that, because of his cheating ways, The Miz would be forced to again defend his Intercontinental Championship against Ziggler at an upcoming WWE event.

A sneak attack on the champ
September 20: Just over a week earlier, Becky Lynch had won a Six-Pack Elimination Match against five others to become the first-ever SmackDown Women's Champion. Alexa Bliss had won a Fatal 5-Way Match to become the number one contender for the championship. On this night, Lynch and Bliss would make their match official by signing a contract for the match to take place at *No Mercy*. Bliss insulted Lynch, calling her a loser, and hit her with the contract clipboard. She then made her escape before Lynch could avenge this sneaky attack.

September 27: The Miz patronizes Dolph Ziggler during his Miz TV talk show.

We got spirit!

October 4: Early in his WWE career, Dolph Ziggler was a member of a faction of male cheerleading Superstars who competed in the ring under the name The Spirit Squad. This team left WWE in 2006. Playing mind games with Ziggler prior to their upcoming match, The Miz brought The Spirit Squad back to WWE, and Ziggler's former teammates attacked him, seemingly jealous that he'd had success in WWE after the Squad broke up.

Ambrose lends a hand

October 11: WWE World Heavyweight Champion AJ Styles announced that he would defend his title. Dean Ambrose, believing Styles would defend against him, came out to the ring, but Styles said that it wasn't Ambrose's turn for a title match. Instead, Styles introduced James Ellsworth, a relatively puny wannabe Superstar who'd never won a WWE match. General Manager Daniel Bryan claimed he was a "big fan" of Ellsworth and sanctioned the match. He also made Dean Ambrose the special guest ref. As Styles was about to pin Ellsworth, Ambrose attacked Styles, eventually enabling the dazed Ellsworth to get his first WWE win—by pinning the WWE Champion, no less!

October 11: James Ellsworth pins WWE Champion AJ Styles as Styles' rival, special referee Dean Ambrose, gives the three count.

Elsewhere in WWE

October 17: Former World Heavyweight Champion Goldberg had left WWE after defeating Brock Lesnar at *WrestleMania XX* in 2004. After 12 years away, Goldberg wanted to return to WWE to show his son how he used to compete. Upon hearing of Goldberg's desire to return, his vanquished foe, Brock Lesnar, challenged Goldberg to a match at *Survivor Series*. Goldberg returned on the October 17 edition of RAW, striding to the ring just as he used to, in a fiery display of pyrotechnics and accepted Lesnar's challenge.

If you can't beat them...

November 1: The notorious Wyatt Family had made a habit of attacking Randy Orton, trying to beat him into submitting to The Wyatt Family's crazed leader Bray Wyatt's influence. This time, Wyatt tried a different tactic, helping Orton win a match against Kane. Following the match, Wyatt whispered to Orton, who agreed to join The Wyatt Family.

November 1: The Wyatt Family, including its newest member, Randy Orton, pose victorious over a beaten Kane.

900 episodes come with a warning

November 15: The 900th episode of *SmackDown* featured an appearance by Undertaker. The legendary Superstar had come to *SmackDown* to confront the show's team for an upcoming 5-on-5 Survivor Series Match against five *RAW* Superstars at the *Survivor Series* pay-per-view. On Edge's Cutting Edge talk show segment, Undertaker warned the members of Team *SmackDown*—WWE Champion AJ Styles, Dean Ambrose, Bray Wyatt, Randy Orton, and Shane McMahon—that if they failed to defend *SmackDown*'s honor at *Survivor Series*, he would be back to take revenge on the team.

November 15: Undertaker warns *SmackDown* Commissioner Shane McMahon of grave consequences if Team SmackDown loses at *Survivor Series*.

SmackDown's newest Superstar

November 22: Despite defeating AJ Styles and helping Dean Ambrose win (and lose) matches, James Ellsworth wasn't a full-time *SmackDown* Superstar. However, he was offered a contract with the blue brand if he could defeat AJ Styles in a Ladder Match where the contract would hang above the ring. If Ellsworth could get the contract before Styles, he'd be hired to *SmackDown*. The odds were against him, but with a little help from Dean Ambrose, who attacked Styles, Ellsworth climbed the ladder and retrieved the contract to become a genuine *SmackDown* Superstar.

November 22: James Ellsworth and Dean Ambrose celebrate Ellsworth's surprise win over AJ Styles.

Two number one contenders

December 13: This episode of *SmackDown Live* featured the crowning of two new number one contenders for two different *SmackDown* Championships. First, The Hype Bros defeated American Alpha, The Vaudevillains, The Ascension, Breezango, and Heath Slater and Rhyno in a Battle Royal to become number one contenders for the Tag Team Championship. In the main event, Dolph Ziggler won a Fatal 4-Way Elimination Match against Dean Ambrose, The Miz, and Luke Harper to become the number one contender for AJ Styles' WWE Championship.

December 13: Rhyno, Heath Slater, and Aiden English, among the rest of the tag team division, battle to become number one contenders for the SmackDown Tag Team Championship.

La Luchadora

December 20: *SmackDown* Women's Champion Alexa Bliss didn't want to compete on this night because of an injury she said she had picked up in a previous match. She hoped General Manager Daniel Bryan would excuse her from competing, but she was disappointed—Bryan required her to compete against a masked woman named La Luchadora. La Luchadora quickly put Bliss in a submission hold and won the match. She then unmasked, to reveal she was actually Superstar Becky Lynch.

December 20: Alexa Bliss turns her back on her mysterious opponent La Luchadora.

Three championships on the line

December 27: In the final *SmackDown* of 2016, three Championships were up for grabs. American Alpha won the *SmackDown* Tag Team Championship by defeating former Champions The Wyatt Family as well as The Usos and Heath Slater and Rhyno in a Fatal 4-Way Match. Alexa Bliss retained the Women's Championship by beating Becky Lynch, after an unidentified female Superstar disguised as Lynch's own alter ego, La Luchadora, attacked Lynch. And AJ Styles was still WWE Champion after winning a Triple Threat Match against Dolph Ziggler and Baron Corbin.

November 22, 2016: SmackDown Women's Champion Becky Lynch screams defiance as she defends her title against Natalya.

2017

THIS WAS A YEAR of firsts for *SmackDown*. It was the first full year the show was broadcast live; it was the first time a women's Money in the Bank Ladder Match was held, as well as the first one-on-one intergender match between a male and female Superstar. Jinder Mahal won and lost his first WWE Championship. The first-ever tag team rap battle in *SmackDown* history took place between The New Day and The Usos. And by the end of 2017, Dolph Ziggler became the first United States Champion to forfeit his title.

January 10: Natalya refuses to let up in her attack on Nikki Bella.

January 3: Dean Ambrose pins The Miz to win the Intercontinental Championship.

Ambrose goes intercontinental

January 3: The Miz was used to getting help from his wife, Maryse, to protect his Intercontinental Championship. Whether attacking opponents or distracting the referee so The Miz could cheat, Maryse had proved a great asset. But on this night, when The Miz was battling Dean Ambrose, the referee had had enough. After Maryse once again tried to interfere on her husband's behalf, the referee ejected her from ringside, allowing Ambrose to hit The Miz with his Dirty Deeds move and claim the title.

Total Divas destruction

January 10: Natalya was jealous of Nikki Bella's fame and had recently attacked Nikki backstage several times. They were set to have a match on this episode, giving Nikki a chance to get revenge. However, Natalya once again attacked Nikki backstage before the match, injuring her leg. Furious, Nikki made her way to the ring and charged at Natalya. As officials tried to step in, Natalya threw Nikki out of the ring and got her in a painful Sharpshooter leglock before walking off. The match had not even officially started.

A masked intruder

January 17: Becky Lynch was battling SmackDown Women's Champion Alexa Bliss in a steel cage so no one could interfere. However, somehow a female Superstar disguised as Lynch's alter ego, La Luchadora, got into the cage and attacked Lynch. After Bliss won the match and retained the title, thanks to La Luchadora's help, the mysterious masked Superstar removed her mask to reveal her identity: it was former WWE Women's Champion Mickie James.

Family woes

January 24: Randy Orton had joined The Wyatt Family several weeks earlier, but long-time member Luke Harper was angry. He didn't believe Randy Orton was sincere about joining and deeply resented being bumped from being Bray Wyatt's tag team partner in favor of Orton. Orton and Harper competed in a match with the stipulation that, if Harper lost, he'd be out of the family. Orton won the match, and Bray Wyatt slammed Harper with the Sister Abigail move, officially kicking him out of The Wyatt Family.

February 7: Contracts are signed for Becky Lynch vs. Mickie James and Alexa Bliss vs. Naomi.

A double signing and a family affair

February 7: At the *Elimination Chamber* pay-per-view, there were going to be two high-profile women's division matches. The contracts for these two matches were signed simultaneously on *SmackDown*. The first of these was Becky Lynch vs. Mickie James as a result of James' costing Lynch her a chance at the *SmackDown* Women's Championship. The other was Naomi getting a shot at the title held by Alexa Bliss. After each contract was signed, the four women brawled with each other. James and Bliss escaped the ring and ran away.

For more than a decade, John Cena and Randy Orton had partaken in a legendary on-again/off-again rivalry in WWE. They'd competed against each other for championships and personal pride on *RAW* and countless pay-per-views. Surprisingly, they'd never faced each other on *SmackDown*. This match was designed by Bray Wyatt to have the newest member of The Wyatt Family—Randy Orton—soften up Cena before Wyatt faced him at the *Elimination Chamber* pay-per-view for the WWE Championship. Former Wyatt Family member Luke Harper attacked Orton, giving Cena a chance to pin Orton and win the match.

First title defense

February 14: Two days earlier, Bray Wyatt had won the WWE Championship from John Cena. In his first title defense, Wyatt battled Cena and AJ Styles. Wyatt defeated both men and held onto the title. Wyatt's acolyte, Randy Orton, who'd won the Royal Rumble Match a month earlier and was entitled to challenge Wyatt for the championship at *WrestleMania,* then came to the ring and declared he would not face Bray Wyatt.

Women's Championship challenges

February 21: Just over a week earlier, Naomi won the *SmackDown* Women's Championship from Alexa Bliss. However, she also suffered a serious knee injury and, after consulting with her doctors, had to surrender the championship to *SmackDown* General Manager Daniel Bryan and Commissioner Shane McMahon. Naomi swore she'd return and regain the title. In the meantime, a new champion was crowned that night when Alexa Bliss defeated Becky Lynch in a match for the gold.

February 14: New champion Bray Wyatt celebrates the news that Wyatt Family member Randy Orton will not challenge him for the title at *WrestleMania*.

February 28: Randy Orton looks on in triumph as the Wyatt Compound goes up in flames.

"If you can't beat them, join them. And then after you join them, when the time is right, screw them."

Randy Orton (February 28, 2016)

Liar, liar, house on fire

February 28: Wyatt Family member Randy Orton had declared that he wouldn't face the leader of the faction, WWE Champion Bray Wyatt, at *WrestleMania* despite having won the Royal Rumble Match and earning the opportunity. However, this was all a lie. Orton had infiltrated The Wyatt Family to learn Bray's secrets. He showed up at the Wyatt Compound in the woods, and set fire to it. Wyatt broke down when he saw his family home going up in flames. Adding insult to injury, Orton then revealed that he would take on Wyatt for the championship at *WrestleMania* after all.

From two to one

March 7: Because Randy Orton had previously announced that he wouldn't use his Royal Rumble Match win to face Bray Wyatt for the WWE Championship at *WrestleMania,* a new number one contender was named in AJ Styles. Once Orton changed his mind and decided to have his earned match, there were suddenly two number one contenders to Wyatt's title. Orton and Styles were forced to have a match against each other with the winner getting the Championship Match at *WrestleMania.* Orton won the match and would go on to face his former Wyatt Family leader.

A phenomenal attack

March 14: AJ Styles, the so-called "Phenomenal One," felt that *SmackDown* General Manager Daniel Bryan and Commissioner Shane McMahon treated him unfairly. The latest example was revoking his number one contendership to the WWE Championship a week earlier. He confronted Bryan about it, but Bryan was dismissive. When McMahon arrived at the arena, Styles brutally attacked the Commissioner backstage.

Total parody

April 4: The romantic relationship between John Cena and Nikki Bella was no secret. In fact, it was the focus of the reality series *Total Bellas*. Married couple The Miz and Maryse hated Cena and Nikki, so they performed parodies of the *Total Bellas* show and the Cena/Bella relationship on *SmackDown*. The Miz portrayed John Cena as a robotic, controlling jerk, and Maryse acted like a dim-witted version of Nikki Bella.

April 4: The Miz and Maryse mockingly imitate John Cena and Nikki Bella.

Elsewhere in WWE

April 3: Three days after being inducted into the WWE Hall of Fame over *WrestleMania* weekend, former WWE Champion and Olympic gold medallist Kurt Angle was hired by Commissioner Stephanie McMahon to be the new General Manager of *RAW*. He was tasked with making matches between Superstars and enforcing the rules.

April 4: Claiming the number 10 for his own, Tye Dillinger makes his *SmackDown* debut.

SmackDown gets the "Perfect 10"

April 4: Every year, the first *SmackDown* after *WrestleMania* includes the introduction of new Superstars alongside other surprises. This year, the incredibly popular NXT Superstar Tye Dillinger became part of the blue brand where he'd have the chance to win championships and show off his impressive in-ring talent. The WWE Universe would quickly learn why he called himself "The Perfect Ten."

INTRODUCING...

Shinsuke Nakamura

April 4: Shinsuke Nakamura was a world-renowned Superstar, having won championships in Japan and become a dominant champion in NXT. Two days after *WrestleMania 33*, Nakamura joined *SmackDown*. The popular Superstar thrilled the WWE Universe with a spectacular entrance and hard-hitting in-ring moves called "Strong Style." Nakamura would become a fixture on *SmackDown* winning the Royal Rumble Match and United States Championship within his first year on the show.

Nakamura's knowledge of mixed martial arts has stood him in good stead in his WWE career.

Superstar shakeup

April 11: One week after *WrestleMania*, *SmackDown* and *RAW* underwent a "Superstar Shakeup" where Superstars were traded between the shows. Some Superstars who'd appeared only on *SmackDown* were now seen on *RAW* and vice versa. Perhaps the biggest name to jump to *SmackDown* was United States Champion Kevin Owens who declared *SmackDown* was now "The Kevin Owens Show."

SmackDown with Flair

April 18: As part of the Superstar Shakeup, former *RAW* Women's Champion Charlotte Flair was traded to *SmackDown*. In her first match since returning to the blue brand, Charlotte Flair gave a preview of how dominant she would be on the show by defeating *SmackDown* Women's Champion Naomi in a non-title match.

April 18: Charlotte Flair shows Naomi why the WWE Universe calls her "The Queen."

May 2: Kevin Owens tries to put Chris Jericho to sleep in their United States Championship Match.

2017

The face of America

May 2: Kevin Owens and Chris Jericho had been best friends, but that friendship had fallen apart, resulting in a match between the two at *WrestleMania 33,* where Owens won the United States Championship from Jericho. A couple of weeks later, Jericho took the title back by beating Owens. On *SmackDown,* Kevin Owens once again defeated Jericho to win back the United States Championship. He then declared himself "The Face of America."

Mahal brings the fireworks

May 23: Jinder Mahal had surprised the WWE Universe by winning a No. 1 Contenders' Match on the April 18 episode of *SmackDown.* At the *Backlash* pay-per-view on May 21, Mahal then defeated Randy Orton to win the WWE Championship. The first WWE Champion of Indian descent, Mahal proudly trumpeted his historic championship win in the ring on this episode. His lavish Punjabi celebration featured a troupe of dancers, a drummer, and pyrotechnics, as well as the Singh Brothers, Sunil and Samir, who joined Mahal in the ring.

The fashion files

June 6: The tag team Breezango (Tyler Breeze and Fandango) were calling themselves the Fashion Police and conducting investigations into "crimes of fashion" committed by their fellow Superstars. On *SmackDown,* they performed one of these investigations in a segment titled The Fashion Files with The New Day. The New Day wanted to hire Breezango to investigate their rivals The Usos and gather some intelligence on them, which Breezango promised to do.

Robbing the bank

June 20: At the *Money in the Bank* pay-per-view two days earlier, history was made when the very first Women's Money in the Bank Match in WWE history was held. The winner, Carmella, cheated by allowing her quasi-boyfriend James Ellsworth to grab the briefcase hanging above the ring containing a contract for a Women's Championship Match for her. On *SmackDown,* General Manager Daniel Bryan announced that he felt the win was invalid because a man had grabbed the briefcase, and he stripped Carmella of the win and briefcase.

May 23: New WWE Champion Jinder Mahal declares himself to be the "Modern-day Maharaja" as the Singh brothers look on.

Carmella gets a second chance

June 27: One week after stripping Carmella of her Money in the Bank briefcase, General Manager Daniel Bryan declared a do-over, giving the women of *SmackDown* another chance to make history in a Money in the Bank Ladder Match. James Ellsworth, who'd helped Carmella grab the original Money in the Bank briefcase, was banned from the arena while Natalya, Charlotte Flair, Carmella, Becky Lynch, and Tamina competed in the match. Even though she didn't have Ellsworth to help her, the result was the same as the previous match: Carmella once again grabbing the Money in the Bank briefcase.

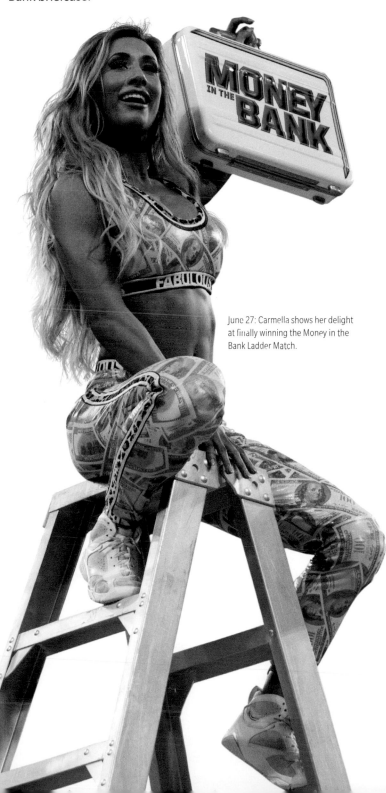

June 27: Carmella shows her delight at finally winning the Money in the Bank Ladder Match.

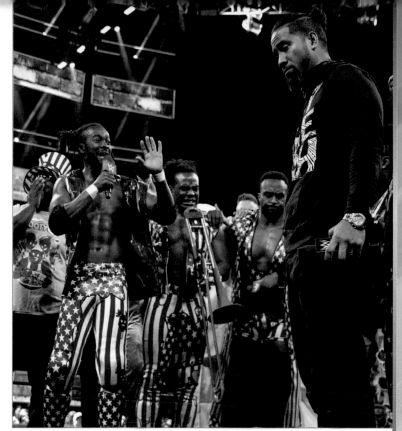

July 4: The New Day and The Usos roast each other during their rap battle.

Rap battle

July 4: Growing issues between The New Day and The Usos took a personal turn when the two tag teams faced each other in a rap battle. The members of both teams improvised raps, insulting the other team in vicious personal attacks. The judge of the rap battle was popular hip-hop artist Wale. After a particularly stinging barb from Xavier Woods, The Usos tried attacking The New Day. Wale disqualified The Usos for getting physical and declared The New Day the winners of the rap battle.

Punjabi prison

July 18: Five days before he would defend the WWE Championship against Randy Orton in a Punjabi Prison Match at *Backlash*, Jinder Mahal stood inside the massive structure to give Orton a warning. The Punjabi Prison was two cages, one surrounding the ring and another surrounding the inner cage, made of bamboo. Mahal reminded Orton that this type of match was extremely dangerous as the bamboo is prone to splinters, piercing the bodies of the competitors inside. There was no way, Mahal warned, that Orton would defeat him (and he would prove to be right).

Sneaky moves

July 25: United States Champion Kevin Owens, his former best friend Chris Jericho, and *SmackDown* Superstar AJ Styles had been competing against each other over the United States Championship in recent weeks at WWE live events and pay-per-views. But on *SmackDown*, the three Superstars competed for the title in a Triple Threat Match. After hitting his opponent with his signature move, the Pop-Up Powerbomb, Kevin Owens pinned Jericho. However, AJ Styles moved Owens off Jericho and pinned him himself, winning the United States Championship.

2017

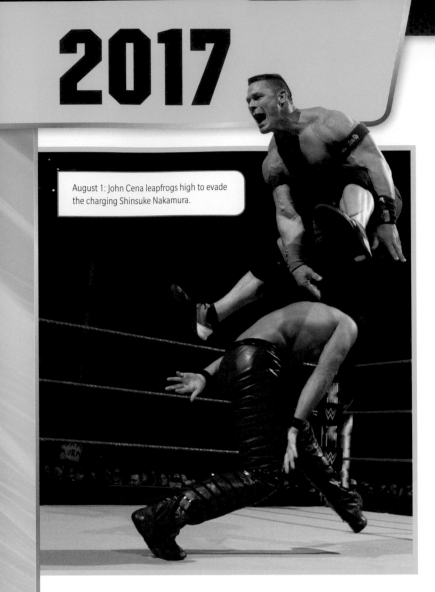

August 1: John Cena leapfrogs high to evade the charging Shinsuke Nakamura.

Cena and Shinsuke

August 1: For the first time ever, 16-time World Champion John Cena competed in a match against the self-proclaimed "King of Strong Style" Shinsuke Nakamura. This was no ordinary match, either. It was to become the number one contender for the WWE Championship held by Jinder Mahal at *SummerSlam*. The two titans fought hard, matching each other move for move, but Nakamura escaped Cena's Attitude Adjustment move and responded with a fierce knee to Cena's face. Nakamura got the pin and the win. After the match, the two Superstars shook hands in a show of mutual respect.

Unsuccessful cash-in

August 15: Two months after winning the men's Money in the Bank briefcase, which gave him a championship match whenever he wanted it, Baron Corbin thought he'd picked the prime time to cash in his briefcase and win the WWE Championship on *SmackDown*. John Cena was about to defeat Champion Jinder Mahal in a non-title contest when Corbin raced to the ring and attacked Cena with the briefcase. Corbin cashed in, planning to pin the semiconscious Jinder, but Cena returned to the ring, momentarily distracting Corbin. It was long enough for Mahal to surprise Corbin with a pin, thus keeping the championship. Corbin, furious at failing to win the title after his Money in the Bank cash-in, swore vengeance against Cena.

The New Alpha, and a Glorious debut

August 22: Chad Gable's American Alpha tag team partner Jason Jordan had moved to *RAW,* breaking up the team. However, General Manager Daniel Bryan had a surprise for Gable: a new tag team partner. This wasn't just any tag team partner. It was WWE veteran Shelton Benjamin, who had returned to WWE after eight years. Gable was extremely excited about the possibilities that awaited the new team. Benjamin, a former Tag Team, Intercontinental, and United States Champion, was a little wary of Gable's enthusiasm but was willing to give the team a try.

Three days earlier, Bobby Roode lost the NXT Championship to Drew McIntyre. However, without having to defend the title in NXT, Roode was free to join *RAW* or *SmackDown*. Roode chose *SmackDown* and had his debut that night. The WWE Universe exploded in cheers as Roode's entrance theme resounded through the arena. Roode showed off his skill by quickly defeating Aiden English in his first match on *SmackDown*.

August 22: On his *SmackDown* debut, Bobby Roode makes short work of Aiden English.

Big entrances

September 5: Dolph Ziggler felt that the WWE Universe didn't respect him. He mocked them for liking Superstars with big flashy entrances on *SmackDown*. To further insult the WWE Universe and his fellow Superstars, Ziggler impersonated the over-the-top entrances of several WWE Superstars and legends, including Shawn Michaels, Bayley, and Randy "Macho Man" Savage. He declared that, moving forward, he would not use theme music or any other extravagances to announce his own entrance.

September 12: Jey and Jimmy Uso fall victim to the crushing weight of Big E's big splash.

New tag team champs, and a dangerous rebellion

September 12: The New Day were already the longest-reigning Tag Team Champions in WWE history, but they hoped to build on their legacy by becoming *SmackDown* Tag Team Champions for a second time. They fought current champions The Usos in a Las Vegas Street Fight, where there are no rules and weapons can be used. Big E slammed Jimmy Uso from the top rope, and Kofi Kingston dove on him for the pin, getting The New Day their desired titles.

Kevin Owens was out of control. In the weeks prior, he had verbally attacked *SmackDown* Commissioner Shane McMahon because he felt McMahon had been undermining his efforts to become WWE Champion. Shane attacked Owens, but Owens took the blows rather than fighting back. Owens announced that he was going to sue WWE for Shane's assault. Shane's father, WWE Chairman Vince McMahon, confronted Owens in the ring on *SmackDown*, hoping to prevent a lawsuit. Mr. McMahon rebuked Owens for his lack of courage in his clash against Shane. Mr. McMahon told Owens he'd have to fight Shane in a Hell in a Cell Match, enraging Owens. Owens slammed Mr. McMahon with a vicious headbutt and leaped on him from the top rope.

Rusev Day!

September 26: Superstar Rusev was given a special honor in the ring as he received the key to his hometown of Plovdiv, Bulgaria. With the Bulgarian flag unfurled behind him in the ring, and his friend Aiden English singing the Bulgarian national anthem, Rusev declared that it was the first-ever "Rusev Day!"

September 26: Rusev displays the key to his hometown, and Aiden English announces "Rusev Day."

October 10: Newly reunited best friends Sami Zayn and Kevin Owens celebrate their friendship.

Best friends forever

October 10: Kevin Owens and Sami Zayn had been friends and enemies nearly their entire lives. Growing up together in Quebec, Canada, the two trained for in-ring competition and traveled around the world together. When they arrived in WWE, their friendship fell apart in a rivalry over the NXT Championship. However, two days before this edition of *SmackDown*, at the *Hell in a Cell* pay-per-view, Zayn saved Owens from being severely injured by Shane McMahon. After Owens thanked Zayn for saving him, Zayn explained that Owens would always be his brother and renewed their friendship. They each promised to work together to take down Shane McMahon.

A champion's challenge

October 24: The upcoming *Survivor Series* pay-per-view was going to feature 5-on-5 Elimination Matches between teams from *SmackDown* against teams from *RAW*. WWE Champion Jinder Mahal wanted to up the stakes by challenging *RAW*'s WWE Universal Champion Brock Lesnar to a non-title Champion vs. Champion Match at the event. Mahal was confident he could prove he was a superior Champion and *SmackDown* was the superior WWE brand by defeating Lesnar. A week later on *RAW*, Lesnar accepted the challenge.

It's goodbye Ellsworth and hello to a new champion

November 7: Ever since he'd allied with Carmella months earlier, James Ellsworth had helped her win matches by attacking other female *SmackDown* Superstars on her behalf. The ladies of *SmackDown* had had enough and ordered Ellsworth into the ring to face Becky Lynch. Ellsworth was so confident he'd beat Lynch that he agreed to put his career on the line if he lost. Lynch had no trouble defeating Ellsworth, who disappeared from WWE after the match.

WWE Champion Jinder Mahal was preparing to face WWE Universal Champion Brock Lesnar at *Survivor Series* and was required to defend the title against AJ Styles on *SmackDown*. Mahal claimed Styles was just an appetizer, preparing him for the main course of Lesnar. However, Styles defeated Mahal, winning the WWE Championship and replacing Mahal in the match against Lesnar at *Survivor Series*. With this episode of *SmackDown Live* taking place in Manchester, England, this was the first time the WWE Championship had been won outside of North America.

November 7: Becky Lynch hits James Ellsworth with a big kick, knocking him right out of WWE.

A Flair family celebration and a *RAW* invasion!

November 14: Charlotte Flair defeated Natalya to become the new SmackDown Women's Champion in a match that displayed both Superstars' incredible in-ring skill as they matched each other move for move and hold for hold. Following the match, Charlotte dedicated her victory to her father, 16-time World Champion and two-time WWE Hall of Famer Ric Flair, who had recently gone through life-threatening health challenges. As Charlotte walked up the entrance ramp, she was moved to tears as her dad joined her on the arena floor and celebrated her victory with her.

On the October 23 episode of *RAW*, Shane McMahon led the *SmackDown* Superstars in an invasion of *RAW*, trying to hurt them before the show vs. show matches at *Survivor Series*. On this episode of *SmackDown*, *RAW* Superstars, led by their General Manager Kurt Angle, invaded *SmackDown*. The *RAW* Superstars attacked the entire *SmackDown* roster, ending their invasion with The SHIELD—Roman Reigns, Seth Rollins, and Dean Ambrose—giving their trademark triple powerbomb to Shane McMahon and promising more attacks the following Sunday at *Survivor Series*.

The Riott Squad and The Bludgeon Brothers debut

November 21: NXT Superstars Ruby Riott, Liv Morgan, and Sarah Logan showed up backstage at *SmackDown* and immediately made their presence known by attacking Naomi and injuring Becky Lynch. Calling themselves The Riott Squad, the trio also interrupted a match between Charlotte Flair and Natalya by attacking them, too. The Riott Squad put the entire *SmackDown* Women's Division on notice: they meant business.

For years, Luke Harper and Erick Rowan had been members of The Wyatt Family. But months after breaking free from Bray Wyatt's control, the two sadistic Superstars joined forces again to form a tag team named The Bludgeon Brothers. Wearing the sheep masks they'd made famous in The Wyatt Family, and carrying massive mallets to the ring, The Bludgeon Brothers debuted their new team on *SmackDown*, destroying The Hype Bros—Zack Ryder and Mojo Rawley—in their first match under their new name.

Ziggler Walks

December 19: Having criticized the WWE Universe for disrespecting him and abandoning any sort of flamboyant entrance, Dolph Ziggler was seemingly distancing himself from WWE. He felt no one deserved to watch him compete because of this perceived disrespect. Ziggler had won the United States Championship at *Clash of Champions* two days before, but now he walked silently to the ring. Before the *SmackDown* crowd, Ziggler forfeited the US Title, throwing it to the ground and walking out of the arena and away from WWE. The WWE Universe was left to wonder whether they'd seen the last of Dolph Ziggler.

November 21: Former members of The Wyatt Family, Luke Harper and Erick Rowan, appear as The Bludgeon Brothers.

2018

THE WWE UNIVERSE has learned to expect the unexpected on *SmackDown*. That was never more true than in 2018. This year, the WWE Universe rejoiced when General Manager Daniel Bryan announced he'd been medically cleared to return to in-ring competition, years after his enforced retirement due to injury; Carmella shockingly cashed in her Money in the Bank Championship contract to win the *SmackDown* Women's Championship; AJ Styles was reunited with his teammates in The Club; and Shinsuke Nakamura earned the WWE Universe's ire when he showed his true colors by turning against AJ, formerly his friend.

Hurting AJ

January 2: After injuring Shane McMahon and his father, Mr. McMahon, Sami Zayn and Kevin Owens set their sights on WWE World Heavyweight Champion AJ Styles. After several weeks of being attacked by them backstage, Styles was eager to get his hands on Owens and Zayn. *SmackDown* General Manager Daniel Bryan granted the request, but in an unexpected way. Bryan announced that Styles would have a Handicap Match against Owens and Zayn at *Royal Rumble*. Owens and Zayn were excited at the prospect, while Styles felt that Bryan was obviously stacking the deck against him.

Elsewhere in WWE

January 16: WWE has always been at the forefront of technology. The latest example was WWE *Mixed Match Challenge*, a weekly tournament featuring mixed-gender tag teams. The show was aired live on Facebook Watch, the social network's broadcasting platform from *SmackDown* arenas, after the show itself had gone off air. The Mixed Match Challenge tournament involved 12 tag teams. The Miz and Asuka won, defeating Bobby Roode and Charlotte Flair.

A Roode Champion

January 16: After Dolph Ziggler's forfeited the United States Championship back in December, a tournament was held to crown a replacement champion. Bobby Roode, Baron Corbin, Zack Ryder, Mojo Rawley, Tye Dillinger, Jinder Mahal, Xavier Woods, and Aiden English all competed for the title. In the tournament finals, held during this episode of *SmackDown Live*, Bobby Roode beat Jinder Mahal, Corbin, and Rawley, to win the tournament and claim the United States Championship.

January 16: Flanked by Daniel Bryan and Shane McMahon, Bobby Roode celebrates his victory in the eight-man United States Championship Tournament.

January 30: AJ Styles soars toward Kevin Owens, while his partner Shinsuke Nakamura looks on.

Future opponents, present partners

January 30: AJ Styles had escaped the *Royal Rumble* still WWE World Heavyweight Champion. Meanwhile, Shinsuke Nakamura won the Royal Rumble Match, earning a championship opportunity against Styles at *WrestleMania 34*. Two nights after *Royal Rumble*, on *SmackDown*, Styles and Nakamura teamed up in a Tag Team Match against Kevin Owens and Sami Zayn, who both felt that they, not Nakamura, should be facing Styles at *WrestleMania*. During the match, Zayn grew frustrated with Owens and walked away, giving Styles and Nakamura the advantage over Owens.

"Riddle me this: who even wants to see you two as tag team champions? Who? Who? Nobody!"

Xavier Woods (February 13, 2018)

Pancake power

February13: The New Day—Kofi Kingston, Big E, and Xavier Woods—had always been about the power of positivity, but recently they'd discovered something else that gave them power: pancakes. Big E set out to break the world pancake-eating record on this *SmackDown Live* episode. Just as he started, Shelton Benjamin and Chad Gable interrupted, mocking The New Day and saying, "Nobody likes pancakes." That insult immediately led to a match between The New Day and Benjamin and Gable, which The New Day dominated. They gained their win when Kingston flew off the top rope, plowing Gable off of Big E's shoulders. To celebrate, the trio ate—what else?— pancakes!

February 13: The New Day's Big E attempts the world pancake-eating record, encouraged by teammate Xavier Woods.

A fastlane to *WrestleMania 34*

February 27: John Cena returned to *SmackDown,* announcing that he didn't yet have a match for *WrestleMania 34* but wanted to earn one. General Manager Daniel Bryan responded by giving Cena a non-title match against WWE Heavyweight Champion AJ Styles. If Cena could win, he'd be added to the multi-Superstar WWE Championship Match at the upcoming *Fastlane* pay-per-view on March 11. Cena accepted and, after a bruising encounter inside and outside the ring, slammed Styles to the mat for the vital pinfall.

The underdog growls

March 6: Ruby Riott desperately wanted the SmackDown Women's Championship. She and her Riott Squad teammates, Sarah Logan and Liv Morgan, repeatedly attacked champion Charlotte Flair, until Flair agreed to put the title on the line at *Fastlane*. During this episode, Riott warned Charlotte not to underestimate her. Riott believed that the WWE Universe, and Charlotte herself, thought that Riott had no chance of winning the title, but Riott was determined to prove otherwise.

Elsewhere in WWE

March 11: At *Fastlane*, AJ Styles retained his WWE Championship and secured his place at *WrestleMania* by winning a Six-Pack Challenge against John Cena, Kevin Owens, Sami Zayn, Dolph Ziggler, and Baron Corbin. Randy Orton became United States Champion, defeating Bobby Roode and, although Riott battled hard, Charlotte Flair retained her title.

2018

Shane gets a beating, and it's Empress vs. Queen

March 13: *SmackDown* Commissioner Shane McMahon hated Kevin Owens and Sami Zayn. They'd injured his father, WWE Chairman Vince McMahon, battled Shane in matches, and defied his authority at every turn. In response, Shane had suspended them, placed them in matches against multiple opponents, and even physically attacked them backstage. Realizing that this was conduct unbecoming of the *SmackDown* Commissioner, Shane announced that he was taking an indefinite leave of absence from the show. Wanting to get one more attack in before he left, however, Zayn and Owens charged the ring and beat down Shane, until WWE officials pulled them away.

The *Royal Rumble* in January had featured the first 30-Woman Royal Rumble Match. The winner could choose which WWE Women's Championship she would compete for at *WrestleMania 34*. The match was won by Asuka, "The Empress of Tomorrow." It was assumed that Asuka would challenge *RAW* Women's Champion Alexa Bliss, because Asuka was on the *RAW* roster. However, Asuka declared that she wanted a greater challenge: a contest against SmackDown Women's Champion, Charlotte "The Queen" Flair. (The following month, at *WrestleMania*, "The Queen" would defeat Asuka by submission.)

Bryan's back

March 20: On February 8, 2016, Daniel Bryan stood in the center of the ring in his hometown of Seattle, Washington, on *RAW* and announced that, because of serious injuries he'd sustained in the ring, he was forced to retire. Just over two years later, on this episode of *SmackDown*, Daniel Bryan once again stood in the middle of the ring and announced that he had been medically cleared to return to action and was coming out of retirement. The WWE Universe exploded in cheers and also yelled Bryan's signature "Yes!" chant, in celebration of the return of one of their favorites.

March 20: Daniel Bryan leads the WWE Universe in a "Yes!" chant to celebrate his return to the ring.

March 13: Kevin Owens tries to save his best friend Sami Zayn from *SmackDown* Commissioner Shane McMahon.

Blocking The New Day's road

March 27: The New Day were on the road to *WrestleMania* to fight *SmackDown* Tag Team Champions The Usos. However, in recent weeks, a new tag team, The Bludgeon Brothers, had made themselves roadblocks for The New Day and a threat to The Usos by attacking both teams. During this episode, The New Day were pitted against The Bludgeon Brothers. During the match, The Bludgeon Brothers tried to use their massive mallets on The New Day, only to be stopped by The Usos. After the match, awarded to The Bludgeon Brothers by disqualification, all three teams fought each other in a chaotic brawl.

March 27: The New Day protects Kofi Kingston from further attacks by The Bludgeon Brothers.

Paige is GM, Carmella's in the money

April 10: One night earlier on *RAW*, former WWE Women's Champion Paige tearfully announced that she had to retire from competition. Tonight on *SmackDown*, Commissioner Shane McMahon announced that, filling the vacancy left by Daniel Bryan, who was returning to in-ring action, the new General Manager would be—Paige! She immediately set the crowd cheering with her first match: Daniel Bryan vs. WWE Champion AJ Styles.

For ten months, Carmella had carried her Money in the Bank briefcase, with its contract for a championship match whenever she wanted, waiting for the opportune moment to strike. That moment came on this first *SmackDown* after *WrestleMania 34*. Charlotte Flair had successfully defended her Women's Title against Asuka at *WrestleMania* and was celebrating her victory in the ring when she was suddenly attacked by debuting tag team The IIconics. Carmella saw her chance, cashed in her Money in the Bank contract, and pinned Charlotte to win the SmackDown Women's Championship.

April 10: Shane McMahon congratulates Paige, *SmackDown*'s new General Manager.

INTRODUCING...

The IIconics

April 10: Billie Kay and Peyton Royce, together known as The IIconics, came to *SmackDown* from NXT. The Australian duo were the best of friends, but had no love for any of the other female Superstars on *SmackDown*. In their debut, they attacked Charlotte Flair, costing her the SmackDown Women's Championship. In the weeks that followed, they made a habit of making fun of their opponents, backing up their insults with in-ring skills that brought them many wins.

The IIconics show little respect for other female Superstars.

Shaking things up again

April 17: One week after *WrestleMania 34*, the annual Superstar Shakeup, where Superstars are traded between *RAW* and *SmackDown,* took place on each show. Several *RAW* Superstars joined the blue brand. Perhaps the biggest names to jump to *SmackDown* were Samoa Joe and the United States Champion Jeff Hardy.

April 17: Samoa Joe shows off his dominance against Sin Cara in his first *SmackDown* match.

Club reunion

April 24: Nearly two years earlier, at the original Superstar Draft, the members of The Club—Gallows and Anderson, and AJ Styles—were drafted to different shows, with Gallows and Anderson to *RAW* and Styles to *SmackDown*. However, during the Superstar Shakeup a week earlier, Gallows and Anderson were traded to *SmackDown* and reformed The Club with AJ Styles. Their first match following their reunion was a Six-Man Tag Team Match against Rusev, Aiden English, and Shinsuke Nakamura. Despite the reunion, The Club lost when Nakamura pinned Luke Gallows.

Styles and Nakamura go to war

May 15: At *WrestleMania 34*, Shinsuke Nakamura and WWE Champion AJ Styles had an intense match that saw Styles come out on top, only to be attacked by a vengeful Nakamura. Subsequent matches, at *Greatest Royal Rumble* and *Backlash,* had ended in hard-fought draws. On this *SmackDown Live* episode, Styles and Nakamura went to war again, this time with the winner choosing the stipulation for their match at *Money in the Bank*. Nakamura pinned Styles to win and declared that their next contest would be a Last Man Standing Match.

May 15: Shinsuke Nakamura escalates his rivalry with AJ Styles with a sharp kick.

May 29: Daniel Bryan nails Big Cass with a missile dropkick from the top rope.

Triple threat qualifier

May 29: Several matches were held that would allow Superstars on both shows to qualify for the upcoming Money in the Bank Match the following month. Originally, that night's qualifier was scheduled to be Daniel Bryan against Samoa Joe, but Big Cass persuaded *SmackDown* General Manager Paige to insert him into the match as well. Cass was determined to get his hands on Daniel Bryan, whom Cass felt had disrespected him. Because Bryan and Cass were focused on battling each other, Samoa Joe took advantage and locked Bryan in a submission hold, knocking him out, and winning the match.

Rusev number one

June 19: To determine who would be the number one contender for the WWE Championship, *SmackDown* General Manager Paige announced a Gauntlet Match, in which two Superstars battle. The winner then faces another Superstar, and the winner of that match faces another Superstar, and so on. The Superstars involved in this match were Big E, Rusev, Daniel Bryan, The Miz, and Samoa Joe. In the final round, The Miz battled Rusev, and "The Bulgarian Brute" was victorious, becoming the number one contender for AJ Styles' WWE Championship.

Feel the glow

June 26: The popular television series *GLOW* tells the story of a fictional all-female sports entertainment company called "*GLOW*: The Gorgeous Ladies of Wrestling." Just as the show's second season was about to premiere, the stars of *GLOW* paid a visit to *SmackDown* and met Lana and Naomi backstage. They encouraged Lana and Naomi, who had been at odds, to set aside their differences and work together to dominate *SmackDown*'s women's division.

From outta nowhere

July 17: Two days earlier, Shinsuke Nakamura had defeated Jeff Hardy for the United States Championship by giving him a low blow. On this episode, Hardy got a rematch against Nakamura. Just as it looked like Hardy was going to win, Randy Orton appeared, seemingly out of nowhere, and brutally attacked Hardy. Orton threw Hardy into the ring steps and even ripped out Hardy's ear gauges and stretched his earlobes. Nakamura looked on in surprised pleasure, while the WWE Universe—and even Hardy himself—were left to wonder what provoked Orton's attack.

Becky's back

July 24: Becky Lynch was the first-ever SmackDown Women's Champion, but had lost the title in the winter of 2016. However, she always fought hard, and the WWE Universe got right behind her, wanting her to regain the championship. *SmackDown* General Manager Paige told Becky that if she could defeat the current champion Carmella in a non-title match, she would become the number one contender and get a match for the SmackDown Women's Championship at *SummerSlam*. Highly motivated, Becky Lynch made quick work of Carmella, forcing her to tap out to Lynch's painful Disarm-Her submission hold for the win.

July 24: Becky Lynch forces *SmackDown Live* Women's Champion Carmella to tap out to her Disarm-Her submission hold in a non-title matchup.

> "I wasn't born to be a champion. No, I fought to be a champion. And I will fight mind, body, and soul."
>
> **Becky Lynch (July 31, 2018)**

Joe makes it personal

July 31: After Renee Young had opened the show with an interview with Becky Lynch, *SmackDown* General Manager Paige named Samoa Joe the number one contender for the WWE Championship. He was set to face AJ Styles at *SummerSlam* one month later. Styles and Joe had known each other for nearly 20 years, competing all over the world. They had been friends and even roommates. But with the WWE Championship in the balance, Samoa Joe started playing mind games with Styles, dumping their friendship and insulting him and his family. What was originally a match between two talented Superstars suddenly became very, very personal.

July 17: Randy Orton brutalizes Jeff Hardy, stretching his ear lobes in an unprovoked attack.

2018

Special edition

August 21: General Manager Paige called this episode a "Special Edition." Airing two days after *SummerSlam*, it featured many incredible moments: Daniel Bryan and The Miz got into a confrontation that saw Bryan's wife, Brie Bella, attack The Miz and his wife, Maryse, for insulting Bryan; Becky Lynch had harsh words for former best friend Charlotte Flair, leading Flair and Lynch to pound each other; Rusev and Lana defeated Andrade "Cien" Almas and Zelina Vega, when Almas tapped out to Rusev's Accolade submission move; Jeff Hardy got revenge on Randy Orton for his brutal attack a month earlier by putting him through a table; Samoa Joe knocked out WWE Champion AJ Styles by attacking him from behind; and The New Day won their fifth WWE Tag Team Championship by defeating The Bludgeon Brothers.

Day of royalty

August 28: This episode began with The New Day celebrating their fifth WWE Tag Team Championship. They were surprised when WWE Hall of Famer "King" Booker T joined them in the ring. Booker T was known to refer to himself as the "five-time, five-time, five-time, five-time, five-time WCW Champion," and welcomed The New Day into the five-time champions club. As self-proclaimed "King," Booker T knighted The New Day, giving them new names: "Lord Xavier the Wise," "Sir Kofi the Brave," and "Big E" (because he already had "Big" in his name).

Story time with Samoa Joe

September 12: Taking things to a new level of personal, Samoa Joe told a rhyming bedtime story that cast himself as a noble hero destined to defeat WWE Champion AJ Styles. The story ended with Samoa Joe promising to replace AJ Styles as the husband and father in his family.

Becky's coronation

September 18: After defeating Charlotte Flair two nights earlier at *SummerSlam*, new SmackDown Women's Champion Becky Lynch held a "championship coronation" in the ring. Lynch invited Flair to the ring so she could gloat in front of the former champion. Lynch told Flair to raise her hand, put the title around her waist, and start referring to her as the new "Queen" (Charlotte Flair's nickname). Flair refused and the pair started brawling. However, Becky stood tall at the end of the show, having beaten Flair down.

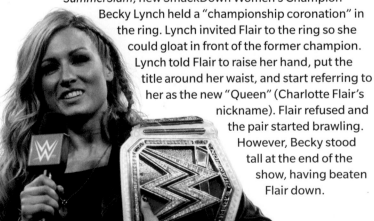

September 18: Becky Lynch holds up her SmackDown Women's Championship.

"You want your show back? I'll fight you for it—right now!"

R-Truth (September 25, 2018)

September 25: Daniel Bryan is the first guest on the premier edition of the Truth TV talk show, hosted by R-Truth and Carmella.

Truth TV

September 25: The second season of WWE's new series broadcast on Facebook, Mixed Match Challenge, well underway, one of the teams involved in the Mixed Match Tournament—R-Truth and Carmella—took over The Miz's talk show segment Miz TV and renamed it Truth TV. R-Truth and Carmella danced, talked trash about their opponents in the Mixed Match Challenge tournament, interviewed Daniel Bryan, and mocked The Miz. An irate Miz burst from the locker room, demanding R-Truth and Carmella stop insulting him and give him back his show. R-Truth challenged Miz to fight him for it. Miz begrudgingly accepted the challenge and defeated R-Truth to reclaim the talk show.

Qualifying for the cup

October 9: One month after this episode of *SmackDown Live*, WWE was set to hold a special event called *Crown Jewel*. That event would feature an eight-Superstar tournament called "WWE World Cup." Four Superstars from *RAW* and four from *SmackDown* would compete in the tournament. On this night, Jeff Hardy defeated Samoa Joe, and Randy Orton bested Big Show, both qualifying for the WWE World Cup Tournament.

October 9: Samoa Joe unsuccessfully tries to make Jeff Hardy submit to a painful hold in the WWE World Cup Tournament qualifying match.

SmackDown 1,000

October 16: Celebrating the first 1,000 episodes of *SmackDown*, this special edition opened with a montage of some of the show's very best moments. Things started to get crazy when Vince, Stephanie, and Shane McMahon joined R-Truth and Carmella on Truth TV, with a McMahon family dance break. AJ Styles and Daniel Bryan, set to be opponents at November's *Crown Jewel* event, then teamed up, only to lose to The Usos in a Tag Team Match. Past *SmackDown* General Managers John Laurinaitis, Teddy Long, and Vickie Guerrero joined Paige in making a Tag Team Championship Match that saw The Bar defeat The New Day to win the Tag Team Championship (thanks to help from Big Show, who attacked The New Day's Kofi Kingston).

Evolution—one of the most dominant factions in WWE history—reunited, with Batista reminding Triple H that "The Game" had never beaten him. The Miz qualified for the WWE World Cup Tournament by pinning Rusev, who then attacked his former friend, Aiden English. WWE Hall of Famer Edge returned to interview SmackDown Women's Champion Becky Lynch and Charlotte Flair on his Cutting Edge talk show. The Rock and John Cena shared special memories of *SmackDown* on social media. Rey Mysterio returned to full-time competition in WWE after more than four years away and defeated Shinsuke Nakamura in a Crown Jewel WWE World Cup qualifying match. This momentous episode concluded with a rare appearance by Undertaker, who warned D-Generation X that they would "Rest in Peace" at *Crown Jewel*.

October 16: Just some of the glittering array of Superstars to feature on *SmackDown's* 1,000th episode (clockwise from left): Evolution—Ric Flair, Randy Orton, Triple H, and Batista; Undertaker; Shinsuke Nakamura and Rey Mysterio.

November 20: Dressed as pilgrims, The New Day celebrate Thanksgiving in style with the WWE Universe.

The big one

October 30: In the weeks prior to their WWE Championship match at *Crown Jewel*, champion AJ Styles and challenger Daniel Bryan had frequently clashed. Their confrontations reached boiling point on this edition: The two Superstars didn't want to wait until *Crown Jewel* and engaged in a classic contest. Both men showed off impressive in-ring skills, and the match could've gone either way. In the end, AJ Styles scored the pin, retaining the WWE Championship. Styles and Bryan shook hands in a show of mutual respect, only to both be attacked by Samoa Joe, who then took Bryan's challenger spot against Styles at *Crown Jewel*.

Elsewhere in WWE...

November 2: In the main event of the international event *Crown Jewel*, Brock Lesnar and Braun Strowman competed against each other for the WWE Universal Championship, which had been vacated by Roman Reigns due to illness. Before the match began, *RAW* Acting General Manager Baron Corbin hit Strowman with the Universal Championship Title, knocking him to the ground. Lesnar capitalized, hitting Strowman five times with his trademark F-5 move to win the championship for a second time.

Championship Chaos

November 13: Following a confrontation earlier in the evening, AJ Styles and Daniel Bryan faced each other in this week's main event for Styles' WWE Championship. When the referee was looking away, Bryan used a low blow to defeat Styles and become new WWE Champion.

Positively Thankful

November 20: For this year's Thanksgiving episode, R-Truth dressed up as legendary WWE turkey the Gobbledy Gooker, and The New Day dressed as pilgrims to compete in a Thanksgiving Feast Fight Match against The Bar and Big Show. All six competitors used traditional Thanksgiving food (set up on a ringside table) as weapons—Big E even used a turkey to hit Cesaro and get the pin. Following the match, The New Day covered Cesaro in Thanksgiving fare, with all the trimmings.

2019

For 20 years, *SmackDown* has been the preeminent show in sports entertainment. In the fall of 2019, *SmackDown* will return to its network television roots, leaving cable network USA for mainstream broadcast network FOX. The show will continue to air live every week on Friday nights, showcasing stunning sports entertainment action and a roster of the greatest Superstars in the world. The best is yet to come. Stay tuned!

GLOSSARY

3-D A.K.A THE DUDLEY DEATH DROP: One of The Dudley Boyz grabs an opponent and throws him toward the other Dudley, who catches him and slams down on top of him.

450 SPLASH: Justin Gabriel finisher, where he somersaults off the top rope and lands on his prone opponent's chest.

619: Named after Rey Mysterio's area code, this signature move involves draping an opponent over the middle rope; Mysterio then administers a kick while swinging around and holding onto the top and middle ropes.

ACCOLADE: Rusev submission move, in which he sits astride his opponent, who is facedown on the mat, siezes his head and pulls upward; also known as the Camel Clutch.

ANACONDA VICE: CM Punk floors his opponent and, lying across him, locks his head and arm and pulls upward.

ANGLE SLAM: Kurt Angle lifts his already stunned opponent onto his shoulders and slams him either head or back first onto the canvas.

ANKLE LOCK: An agonizing submission move associated with Kurt Angle. With his opponent facedown on the mat, he seizes their leg and puts pressure on their ankle.

ATTITUDE ADJUSTMENT: Cena finishing move in which he lifts his weakened opponent onto his shoulders and slams him onto the mat.

BATISTA BOMB: Batista lifts his opponent onto his shoulders and slams him into the canvas.

BOOM DROP: A spectacular Kofi Kingston move, in which he springs into the air and lands both his legs onto his prone opponent.

BROGUE KICK: Sheamus finisher, in which he runs at his opponent and delivers a flying kick with his right foot.

CELTIC CROSS: Finlay finisher, in which he hoists his opponent onto his shoulders then propels himself backward, using their body to break his fall.

CLOTHESLINE FROM HELL: JBL signature move, in which he springs off the ropes to hit his opponent across the upper chest with his arm, flattening him.

COBRA: Santino Morella finisher, in which he forms his right arm into the shape of a striking snake and jabs his opponent in the head.

CON-CHAIR-TO: Edge and Christian finisher, in which the tag team simultaneously smack their opponent with steel chairs.

CROSS ARM BREAKER: Alberto Del Rio doubles up his opponent, hooks their left arm with his right arm, then swings his left leg over their doubled-up body. He then pulls them both to the mat, still gripping his opponent's arm.

CROSS RHODES: Cody Rhodes finisher, in which he seizes his opponent from behind, spins him around, and slams him into the mat.

DDT: A Superstar gets his or her opponent in a headlock and then drives their face down into the mat by falling down or falling backward.

DIAMOND CUTTER: Diamond Dallas Page's finishing move, in which he applies a three-quarter facelock before falling backward as he pulls his opponent to the mat.

DIRTY DEEDS: Dean Ambrose seizes his opponent in a headlock and drives him into the canvas.

DOOMSDAY DEVICE: A tandem move made famous by the Legion of Doom tag team. One of the team hoists his dazed opponent onto his shoulders in a sitting position; the other team member leaps off the ring post, hitting the opponent and sending him crashing backward to the mat.

DRAGON SLEEPER: For this submission move, a Superstar attacks his opponent from behind, seizing him and bending him backward.

EDGECUTION: Edge seizes his opponent and pulls him to the mat.

F-5: Brock Lesnar doubles up his opponent with a blow to the stomach, lifts them up into the air, his left arm behind their head, and hurls them facedown onto the mat.

FAMEASSER: Mr. Ass doubles up his opponent, then leaps into the air, clamping him between his thighs, and slamming him into the canvas.

FROG SPLASH: A favorite finisher of Eddie Guerrero's, in which he jumps off the top rope, landing flat on his prone opponent.

FUTURE SHOCK: Drew McIntyre doubles up his opponent, hooks both their arms and kicks out at their legs hauling them forward to the mat.

GLAM SLAM: Beth Phoenix gets behind her opponent and picks her up holding her arms; as she lets her fall, she seizes her around the thighs, slamming her down onto the mat.

GO TO SLEEP (GTS): CM Punk lifts his opponent onto his shoulders and then hurls him down; Punk strikes him on the chin with his knee as he falls.

GORE: Rhyno crashes into his already stunned opponent, winding him.

HELL'S GATE: Undertaker submission finisher, in which, on his back, "The Deadman" traps his opponent between his forearm and shinbones in a triangle choke.

HURRICANRANA: Rey Mysterio leaps into the air, seizes his opponent between his legs, and hurls them to the mat.

KILLSWITCH: Christian seizes his helpless opponent's arms, spins him around so that his head is positioned against Christian's back, and then drops to the mat, slamming him into the canvas.

LAST RIDE: Undertaker raises his opponent onto his shoulders and lifts him upward, before slamming him to the canvas.

LIONSAULT: Chris Jericho backflips off the top rope onto his opponent.

MONEY SHOT: Val Venis leaps off the turnbuckle onto the prone body of his opponent.

MOONSAULT: A Superstar backflips from the top rope onto the (usually) prone body of his or her opponent.

OLD SCHOOL: Undertaker seizes his opponent's hand and climbs onto the top rope. He walks along the rope leading his opponent and then jumps off with his full weight descending on their shoulder and arm.

PEDIGREE: Triple H traps his already unsteady opponent between his legs, hooks his arms, and slams him down on the canvas.

PEOPLE'S ELBOW: The Rock's finisher move, in which he slams his opponent to the mat and, when they are prone, pulls off his elbow guard, swings his arms, and drops down, smashing his elbow into their body.

PHENOMENAL FOREARM: AJ Styles springs from the top rope and delivers a forearm smash to his opponent.

PLAYMAKER: MVP delivers a blow to the stomach, locks his leg around his opponent's head and brings him crashing down onto the canvas.

POP-UP BOWERBOMB: Ken Owens lifts up his opponent so his legs are astride, resting on each of Owens' shoulders; he then slams his opponent down onto the mat.

RINGS OF SATURN: Perry Saturn forces his opponent to submit by downward pressure on his shoulder joint.

RKO: Randy Orton hurls his opponent against a ring post. As he staggers back across the ring, Orton grabs him and slams him into the mat.

ROCK BOTTOM: The Rock grabs his opponent by the upper body or neck, lifts him up, and slams him to the mat.

SAMOAN DROP: A finisher employed by several Superstars, including Rikishi, which involves him hoisting his opponent onto his shoulders and falling backward so that his opponent's back slams into the mat.

SCISSORS KICK: Booker T springs off the ropes, jumps into the air, and traps his opponent between his legs as he falls to the mat.

SNAPSHOT: A double-team move associated with MNM, in which they both lift their opponent into the air and slam him facedown to the mat.

SPEAR: Finishing move in which a Superstar runs at his opponent, often using the ropes as a springboard, and smashes into him with his shoulder.

SPINEBUSTER: Batista grabs his opponent around the waist and slams him down onto the canvas.

SPRINGBOARD BULLDOG: Billy Kidman seizes his opponent, springs off the top rope, and slams him to the mat.

STARSHIP PAIN: John Morrison spins off the top rope landing on his prone opponent.

STINK FACE: A humiliating move introduced by Rikishi, where the Superstar rubs his buttocks on the face of an opponent.

THE STOMP: Seth Rollins runs toward his already weakened opponent, who is on hands and knees, and stomps down on him, ramming him into the canvas.

STONE COLD STUNNER: Stone Cold Austin finisher, in which he boots his opponent in the stomach, turns away to reach back and grab him, then bounces their chin off his shoulder.

SWANTON BOMB: Jeff Hardy climbs the ropes, flips himself over as he jumps through the air, and lands on his opponent back first.

SWEET CHIN MUSIC: Shawn Michaels runs from one corner of the ring toward his opponent in another and delivers a kick to their chin.

TAZZMISSION: Taz grabs his opponent from behind, with one arm around his opponent's neck and the other around his arm, before dragging him onto the mat and increasing pressure with a scissor hold.

TEXAS CLOVERLEAF: Sheamus' agonizing submission move, which compresses his opponent's legs, while putting immense strain on his spine and abdomen.

TOMBSTONE PILEDRIVER: Undertaker finisher, in which he lifts his opponent into the air, turns him upside down, and then falls to his knees, forcing his opponent onto the canvas.

TORTURE RACK: Ezekiel Jackson lifts his opponent, faceup, onto his shoulders and pulls him down onto the canvas.

TROUBLE IN PARADISE: Kofi Kingston spins and delivers a flying kick to his opponent's head.

TWIST OF FATE: Hardy brothers' finisher, in which one Hardy locks his opponent in a front facelock, pivots 180 degrees, and catches his opponent in a three-quarter facelock with his free arm while he falls onto his back, forcing the opponent facedown onto the mat.

WALLS OF JERICHO: Chris Jericho submission finisher, in which he sits astride his opponent, putting great strain on their back.

WASTELAND: Wade Barrett hoist his opponent onto his shoulders and slams him back first onto the mat.

WEST COAST POP: Rey Mysterio leaps off the top rope, wraps his legs around his opponent, and rolls them for the pin.

WHASSUP: Dudley Boyz double-team finisher; one of the Boyz positions his opponent on his back with his legs in the air and apart; the other leaps off the top rope to deliver a low blow.

X-FACTOR: X Pac finisher, in which he grabs his opponent, jumps in the air, and slams him into the mat. Also employed by other Superstars, including Brie Bella.

YES LOCK: Daniel Bryan signature submission move, in which he lies on his opponent's back, hauls his arm backward and applies a crossface move, simultaneously targeting elbow, shoulders, neck, and nose.

ZIG-ZAG: Dolph Ziggler finisher, in which he leaps on his opponent from behind, grabs his head, and slams him to the mat.

August 24, 1999. The Rock strikes a pose for the WWE Universe before his unsuccessful challenge for Triple H's championship.

INDEX

Senior Editor Alastair Dougall
Project Editor Pamela Afram
Senior Designer Nathan Martin
Project Art Editor Ray Bryant
Designer Anna Pond
Senior Pre-Production Producer Marc Staples
Producer Louise Daly
Managing Editor Paula Regan
Managing Art Editor Jo Connor
Art Director Lisa Lanzarini
Publisher Julie Ferris
Publishing Director Simon Beecroft

Global Publishing Manager Steve Pantaleo
Vice President, Consumer Products Sylvia Lee
Executive Vice President, Consumer Products Casey Collins
Vice President—Photography Bradley Smith
Photo department Josh Tottenham, Frank Vitucci,
Georgiana Dallas, Jamie Nelson, Melissa Halladay, Mike Moran
Senior Vice President, Assistant General Counsel—Intellectual Property
Lauren Dienes-Middlen
Senior Vice President, Creative Services Stan Stanski
Creative Director John Jones
Project Manager Sara Vazquez

Dorling Kindersley would also like to thank Helen Peters for the index;
Jennette ElNagger for proofreading; Helen Murray for editorial assistance.

First published in Great Britain in 2019
by Dorling Kindersley Limited.
80 Strand, London, WC2R 0RL
A Penguin Random House Company

Page design copyright ©2019 Dorling Kindersley Limited
DK, a Division of Penguin Random House LLC
19 20 21 22 23 10 9 8 7 6 5 4 3 2 1
001–312825–May/19

A CIP catalogue record for this book is available from the British Library.

ISBN: 978-0-2413-6377-5

Printed and bound in China

A WORLD OF IDEAS:
SEE ALL THERE IS TO KNOW

www.dk.com
www.wwe.com